Human Rights Discourse on Dams, Displacement and Resettlement

Human Rights Discourse on Dams, Displacement and Resettlement

By

Namita Gupta

Cambridge
Scholars
Publishing

Human Rights Discourse on Dams, Displacement and Resettlement

By Namita Gupta

This book first published 2023

Cambridge Scholars Publishing

Lady Stephenson Library, Newcastle upon Tyne, NE6 2PA, UK

British Library Cataloguing in Publication Data
A catalogue record for this book is available from the British Library

ISBN (10): 1-5275-1003-4
ISBN (13): 978-1-5275-1003-6

Dedicated to my daughter Ananya who inspired me to start working on the book during the Covid-19 pandemic

TABLE OF CONTENTS

PREFACE

Since the 1990s, development-induced displacement has emerged as a major human rights concern. At the heart of this debate lies the issues of equity, governance, justice and power. The reason for the same is the mounting number of those displaced due to multiple development projects. A large number of examples are available throughout the world where dam-induced displacement and resettlement has been mismanaged and has led to enormous social and environmental costs. The devastating impacts of such projects on the life and livelihood of those resettled led to resentment and a proliferation of public actions, campaigns, protests and resistance. Such mass mobilization against the development projects brought issues of participation, legitimacy, accountability and transparency to the fore, and into the policy domain, questioning the authority of planners and policy-makers at different levels. The developing impasse necessitated fresh insights into the life-worlds of affected people, and a review of assumptions, questions and options in social engineering, a challenge that was taken up in sociological and anthropological research.

The recent conflicts and social movements on the subject have led to the academic debates and policy discussions on the issue per se. This scrutiny by the various stakeholders has led to the major agencies funding development projects and as well as national authorities to re-examine the process as well as the purpose of development. It has now been accepted that any developmental activity can be meaningful only when the dispossessed and displaced people are taken care of and adequately rehabilitated. With this newly found attention of the academicians and policy makers, the issue of displacement has also gauged interest of media and urban elites recently. There have been increasing calls for attention to social and political aspects of displacement, particularly by social scientists. Researchers have analyzed a range of complexities in particular situations of displacement and resettlement, such as lack of effective participation of project affected communities, socio-economic consequences on the displaced and missing attention on the specific needs of women, indigenous peoples, encroachers and squatters, and other such groups. Academic scholarship on this important issue, however, has been both sporadic and inconsistent.

This book is an endeavour to provide a comprehensive outlook on the human rights issues involved in the development induced displacement and resettlement. This book is organized into four sections. The first section of the book has been titled 'Development Induced Displacement and Resettlement: Risks and Rights'. The introductory chapter provides a brief conceptual understanding of the term displacement and deliberate upon some serious human rights issues involved in dam induced displacements. Keeping Cernea's impoverishment risks as a reference point, it discusses at length the consequences of these displacements on indigenous communities and women, who undoubtedly are amongst the most vulnerable and marginalized of all affected. The ecological consequences of these projects have also been discussed briefly. The second chapter provides a critique of neoliberal model of development which relied heavily on capital investment and advancement of technology for economic growth by harnessing existing natural and human resources. The dams have been considered to be the most desirable option by policy makers, ignoring the irreversible long-term social and environmental costs of such projects. By comparing the radical and reformist approach to development, this chapter emphasizes on the need to have a development model that is economically viable, socially equitable, and environmentally sustainable. The third chapter starts with providing conceptual and theoretical understanding of resettlement and rehabilitation. As a well-articulated resettlement plan helps in mitigating the adverse impacts of displacement and in creating better development prospects for project affected people, this chapter deliberates upon various essential components of a resettlement action plan in detail.

The second section of the book has been titled 'Dams, Displacement and Resettlement: International Perspective'. The first chapter of this section discusses the existing international framework for the resettlement of the displaced. Tracing the origin of the human rights discourse of forced displacement in the international human rights law, the chapter endeavours to critically analyze the resettlement principles framed by various international agencies such as World Bank, Asian Development Bank, Organization for Economic Cooperation and Development and International Finance Corporation. It further suggests the adoption of these international policy standards for involuntary resettlement in the legal and regulatory frameworks at the national level. The second chapter of this section shares the resettlement experiences of some most controversial hydroelectric projects across the world. Starting with the Aswan High Dam in Egypt, followed by the Three Gorges Dam in China, and the Ilisu Dam in Turkey and Belo Monte in Brazil, it highlights that though these big dams may have been successful in achieving the predetermined goals (electricity, flood control, irrigation, navigation), these have led to severe socio-economic hardships to the displaced communities and have also played havoc to the ecosystem.

The third section 'Displacement and Resettlement in India: Legacies, Challenges and Solutions' specifically deals with the dam induced displacement issues in India. The first chapter of this section while tracing the origin of the land acquisition laws in the colonial era comprehensively discusses the various existing laws and policies for the resettlement of the displaced in India. While critically analysing these laws in context of certain social justice issues such as: What constitutes public purpose? Who is entitled to the compensation? What will be the mode of compensation? It asserts that though new legislations and policy initiatives attempt to introduce a right based approach in the process of acquisition of land; growth-centric and market-centric paradigm of development still dominates. The second chapter of this section discusses two of the most prominent hydropower projects in India. The resettlement policies and its implementation in the case of the Bhakra Dam Project has been analyzed as the project with one of the largest investment schemes in newly independent India and has faced least resistance from displaced people. The second case study is of the Sardar Sarovar Project, as the project faced lots of resistance from displaced people as well as from civil society organizations, both at the national and global level. The third chapter 'Social Resistance against Dams and Displacement in India and Role of Civil Society Organizations', while tracing the earliest resistances against dams in India, elaborates various tactics and strategies such as: Protests and Agitations, Publications, Lobbying at the international and national level, Mobilization at International Conferences and Workshops and Litigations, adopted by the civil society organizations and individual activists to uphold the rights to equality and justice for the displaced persons. The last chapter of this section discusses how large dam projects have been a subject of litigation in the courts of India. Through various case laws, it specifically elaborates judicial stances on some most contentious human rights issues such as: defining public purpose; issue of compensation and resettlement of the displaced; ecological concerns and the rights of the tribal communities.

The last section of this book looks for answers to the most pertinent question of human rights discourse on dams induced displacement and resettlement i.e., is there a way forward? In our quest to develop and economic growth, state agencies have already caused irreparable damages to the ecosystems as well the life of the people affected due to these projects. While this quest does not seem that it will end in the coming years, there is a need to introspect on some fundamental questions: What sort of development should we be aiming at? How can we ensure that this development involves the equitable distribution of benefits and burdens, opportunities and risks? How can we ensure that human rights are observed? How can we ensure that the ecosystems' limited ability to cope is taken into account? It further calls for collective learning and decision making to enable diverse stakeholders to work together to address issues at the earliest stages of planning and to find common ground without compromising individual values.

Though sincere efforts have been made to provide a critical analysis of the environmental, social and economic impacts of the development projects, I admit my scholastic limitations to discuss the issues in great depth. There is already a plethora of literature available on the issues concerning dam induced displacement as well as on the politics of development. I have tried to cite a large number of literatures covered on the issue concerned. There is a huge need for, and variety of, social science research on development discourse as well as on the human rights issues of those displaced during the process, not only from the scholastic perspective but also from the view point of subaltern groups, including those who got displaced by the projects as well as from the perspective of women and indigenous communities. It further calls for a serious deliberation on the human rights aspects of development induced displacement.

SECTION I:

DEVELOPMENT INDUCED DISPLACEMENT AND RESETTLEMENT: RISKS AND RIGHTS

CHAPTER 1

INTRODUCTION

The last two decades have witnessed an enormous increase in the number of internally displaced people across the world but more so in the countries of South Asia. Though various factors may lead to internal displacement including wars and natural calamities, there are serious human rights issues involved in these displacements. While people crossing their national borders are called refugees and are protected by a large number of international conventions; people displaced internally are considered the responsibility of the concerned state and hence, the issue stays out of the purview of international humanitarian law. Out of all the factors responsible for internal displacements, the development induced displacement has affected the largest proportion of the population. The displacement caused due to development projects is quite different from other forms of displacement. Displacement due to wars and natural calamities is temporary and people always have an option to come back to their native places, once the situation returns back to normal. On the other hand, the development induced displacement does not only take away their right to property but also leads to displacement which is permanent in nature. Secondly, displacement due to natural calamities and political, social or religious upheavals are generally sudden in nature, to some extent unanticipated and hence, the kick start of the resettlement process may take some time; however, displacement due to development activities is always well articulated and hence, the planning for rehabilitation needs to be made in advance and much before the occurrence of actual displacement. Besides these fundamental differences, each category of displacement may further be distinguished on their legal and administrative status as quantum and process of assistance vary on the basis of the nature of displacement.

Broadly, all development projects can be categorized into three types: industrial, which includes thermal power, mining and port projects; urban infrastructural, which includes highway, school and hospital projects, among others; and irrigation and hydroelectric power projects. The first two categories require land, though the displacement caused is much lesser in comparison to the displacement caused by dams and other irrigation projects

(Mishra 2014). While no reliable figures exist to indicate the scale of global resettlements, the Internal Displacement Monitoring Centre's estimates of global resettlements suggests about 20 million people annually (Cernea and Maldonado 2018). According to another estimate, the total number of persons displaced due to large dams is pegged at 40 million (Negi and Ganguly 2011).

One of the reasons for the lack of consensus on the magnitude of dam induced displacement is the difference in the opinion on what constitutes displacement. The term displacement has two subcategories—direct and indirect. In direct displacement, people are directly displaced from their habitations due to commissioning of some development projects. This occurs not only from the inundation of reservoirs but from the installation of project facilities and associated infrastructure. They are dis-placed in a real sense. On the other hand, indirect displacement emanates, first of all, from a process whereby the functioning of a project continuously pushes up the consumption of the natural resources of an area, leading native inhabitants being deprived of their traditional means of sustenance. This leads to such people moving from the project site to other places for their livelihood (Das 2005). Cernea (2006) also discussed this expansion of the concept of displacement in terms of 'restriction of access'. This redefinition was introduced first in the resettlement policy of the World Bank in 2002 was later on replicated and introduced in the policies of other multilateral donors such as the Asian Development Bank, the Inter-American Development Bank, and the African Development Bank, for their programs. According to this definition, the imposition of 'restricted access' to certain resources in protected areas is a form of involuntary population displacement. Besides this, it broadens the definition of 'displacement' beyond its usual acceptance as geographic relocation, to also include occupational and economic dislocation not necessarily accompanied by the physical (geographic) relocation of the local users (Cernea 2006:25).

'Development caused displacement has negative socio-economic consequences in countries characterized by a land-based economy and low employment flexibility, together with strongly rooted social stratification' (Terminski 2015:55). The inundation of land and alteration of riverine ecosystems affects the resources available for land and riverine based productive activities. In the case of communities dependent on land and the natural resources base, this often results in the loss of access to traditional means of livelihood, including agricultural production, fishing, livestock grazing, fuel wood gathering and collection of forest products, to name a few. Not only does this disrupt local economies, it effectively displaces people—in a wider sense—from access to a series of natural resources and environmental inputs into their livelihoods. This consequently leads to a loss of their means of production and disruption in their existing socio-cultural milieu (WCD 2000). Though, in legal terms, such movement is considered 'voluntary' and is called 'migration'; in true sense, these people have been displaced due to development projects, indirectly. Hence, internally displaced persons can be called 'exodus within the borders' and 'homeless at home'. Therefore, a vast number of displacements by these projects pose a challenge before policy makers in tackling this menace.

Consequences of Displacement

There is no denying the fact that displacement due to development projects invariably have an impoverishing experience for the displaced. A large number of ethnographic studies in the field time and again reaffirmed the adverse consequences of these projects on displaced persons. Failure to mitigate the resettlement effect often generates 'new poverty' as opposed to the old poverty of people before displacement (See Cernea 2000 and 2002; Downing 2002a and 2002b; Scudder 2005). The victims found themselves summarily removed (with insufficient compensation) to make way for projects that were imposed ostensibly in the wider 'public purpose' for a state to which they may have little prior knowledge or allegiance. These displacement inducing projects have strong structural bias, favouring the elites while millions of people pay the price without reaping the benefits (Parasuraman 1999).

The socio-economic impacts of a project are the likely consequences that a project may have on the social ordering and the economic sustenance of displaced persons. Vanclay describes social impact as changes in lifestyle, cultural and political systems, well-being, property rights, environment and aspirations (Vanclay 2003). In the Guidelines and Principles for Social Impact Assessment developed by the Inter-Organisational Committee on Guidelines and Principles for Social Impact Assessment (1994:2), social impacts are described as 'the consequences to human populations of any public or private actions that alter the ways in which people live, work, play, relate to one another, organize to meet their needs and generally cope as members of society'. While these definitions offer a basis on which to understand social impact, the social variables contemplated by these definitions remain difficult to quantify. Indeed, Sairinen's (2004: 510) assertion that 'social impacts are [...] perceived differently by different people through socially-mediated understandings of what is "normal" or "natural" or "to be expected" or even acceptable', is a reminder that assessing this form of impact can be daunting. Economic impacts are more definite in that they relate to the material and financial resources for sustaining livelihood capacities (Adeola and Viljoen 2018) such as the loss of farming land, forests, grazing lands, fishing grounds or water sources undermining or destroying livelihoods and the means of subsistence, and the sociocultural features of rural communities (Koenig 2009). Furthermore, resulting in loss of income sources and kinship networks, leading to impoverishment as well as lost identity.

Michael Cernea (1998:48-53), by going beyond economic factors, attempted to study social, psychological, cultural and health parameters of displacement. He identified eight areas of impoverishment risks after studying displacement cases all over the world. These impoverishment risks are:

Landlessness: Expropriation of land removes the main foundation upon which people's productive systems, commercial activities and livelihood are constructed. This is the principal form of de-capitalization and pauperization of the displaced people, as they lose both physical and man-made capital.

Joblessness: Loss of wage employment occurs both in urban displacement and in rural areas, and those losing jobs are landless laborers, enterprise or service workers, artisans and small businessmen. But creating new jobs is difficult and requires substantial investments. The resulting unemployment and underemployment among resettlers lingers long after physical relocation.

Homelessness: Loss of housing and shelter may only be temporary for many displaced, but for some homelessness remains a chronic condition. In a broader cultural sense, homelessness is also placeless-ness, loss of a group culture space and identity, or cultural impoverishment.

Marginalization: It occurs when families lose their economic power and slide on a downward mobility path; middle income households do not become landless, but become small landowners; small shopkeepers and craftsmen are downsized and slip below poverty thresholds.

Increased Mobility and Mortality: A serious decrease in health levels resulting from displacement causes social stress, insecurity, and psychological traumas, and outbreak of diseases. An unsafe water supply and poor sewerage system increases the vulnerability to epidemics. The weakest of the demographic segment—Infants, children and the elderly—are affected the most.

Food Insecurity: Forced uprooting increases the risk that people will fall into chronic undernourishment and food insecurity, defined as calorie-protein intake levels below the minimum necessity for normal growth and work.

Loss of Access to Common Property: Loss of access to common property assets belonging to communities that are relocated represents a major form of income and livelihood deterioration. Typically, such lost resources remain uncompensated by the government relocation schemes.

Social Disintegration: It tears apart the social fabric and the existing patterns of social organization. Production systems are dismantled, kinship groups and family systems are often scattered, local labor markets are disrupted, and people's cultural identity is put at risk. Life sustaining informal social networks of mutual help among people, local voluntary associations, self-organized service arrangements, etc., are dispersed and rendered inactive. This unravelling represents a massive loss of social capital incurred by the uprooted people, yet a loss that remains un-quantified and uncompensated.

Though Cernea provided a detailed illustration of how the oustees get trapped into the vicious circle of impoverishment due to faulty resettlement policies, various researchers have suggested the inclusion of some missing risks. While Mahapatra added educational risk (1999), Robinson suggested including other community services (2003) and Downing (2002a) considered violation of human rights to be a major risk. Rajagopal (2000) enumerated five human rights challenges that arise in relation to development-induced displacement: Right to Development and Self-Determination; Right to Participation; Right to Life and Livelihood; Rights of Vulnerable Groups; and Right to Remedy.

Whatever terminology we use to highlight the trauma of displaced people, there is no denying the fact that there is an urgent need to highlight that while development projects may create vulnerability through impoverishment; development induced displacement disproportionately affects certain groups, particularly indigenous groups and women. Similarly, the ecological impacts of large dams have been one of the less deliberated issues in the development discourse. These three often neglected dimensions of development induced displacement have been discussed below.

Impact on Indigenous and Tribal Communities

Though a growing body of literature is available on development-induced displacement and resettlement; a disproportionate share of such studies focuses on the impact of these development projects on indigenous people, who undoubtedly are amongst the most vulnerable and marginalized among all displaced (Hagen and Minter 2020). Kothari (1996) found that out of 110 projects studied, tribals consisted of around 50 percent of the displaced population. In India, 40-50 percent of those displaced by development projects were tribal people, who account for around 8 percent of the nation's one billion people (WCD 2000).

The current definition of development does not have the same outcomes for all social groups. The persuasion of this pattern leads to 'internal colonialism' of the people which are relatively isolated and culturally distant such as the scheduled tribes (Mathew 1996). On the one hand, the affected tribal people get impoverished, on the other hand, the advanced sections of society get enriched. The whole displacement process leads to the dispossession of tribals from ownership of means of production and deprivation of the products of their labor. The social effects produced by it are observed in the loss of their political autonomy, the breakup of their community and the devaluation of their culture. The political overtones of this development are articulated through the slogan of integration and assimilation which is eventually intended to destroy their identity and distinct status. This development virtually reduces them to a subhuman level of existence. In short, this paradigm of development essentially thrives on the progressive underdevelopment and destitution of displaced tribal people (Saxena 2008a). These people are not only alienated permanently from their traditionally inhabited lands but are also uprooted from their traditional cultural base and life system. Since very little attention is paid to rehabilitation, displacement results in bitter suffering and exploitation at the hands of officials, contractors, middlemen and others (Fernandes and Thukral 1989). The loss of land and traditional homes consequently leads to the loss of livelihood. They are left with no other option than to get connected to the larger market economy in place of their own forest-based subsistence economy. This dependency on the external market puts these tribal people socially in a disadvantageous position where they are engaged as menial workers of various kinds (Pattnaik 2013). The employer, conditioned by the caste mentality, often sees them as 'low caste'. Overtime, they themselves internalize a caste mentality and develop a low self-image of their own community (Debasree 2014).

The World Commission on Dams Report (2000) also highlighted that the large dams have had serious impacts on the lives, livelihoods, cultures and spiritual existence of indigenous and tribal peoples. Due to neglect and lack of capacity to secure justice because of structural inequities, cultural dissonance, discrimination and economic and political marginalisation, indigenous and tribal peoples have suffered disproportionately from the negative impacts of large dams, while often being excluded from sharing in the benefits.

Displacement from Gender Lens: The Neglected Dimension

Women are an important component of the displaced population. Though there are studies that have stressed the need to focus on women's experiences of displacement (See Colson 1971 and 1999; Parasuraman 1993; Koenig 1995; Indra 1999; Mehta and Srinivasan 2000; Scudder 2005), inadequate attention has been paid to specific problems faced by women during displacement. For example, Jobin's Dams and Diseases (1999) has discussed the gender in displacement in regard to women's fertility only, while ignoring other aspects. Elizabeth Colson (1971 and 1999), in her study of the Kariba Dam, highlighted how women were exposed to physical violence, bad marriages, loss of property rights and the deterioration of status due to displacement. Similarly, various studies pointed out adverse economic impacts of displacement on women (See Parasuraman 1993; Koenig 1995).

Displacement adversely affects women's general welfare as well as their status within the household. The incidences of intimate partner violence as well as physical abuse from other male relatives increases as the sense of self-worth of male members gets undermined by displacement. Furthermore, women are psychologically, economically and socially disadvantaged due to two major reasons. Firstly, women's strong emotional bond with their homes leads to more stress due to physical removal. Women enjoy a sense of security in their native lands. As most of these displacements take place in the area where villages are small, sparsely populated and scattered, displacement creates a sense of uncertainty and insecurity among the women (Berreman 1963). Secondly, most of the resettlement policies are gender blind, and they totally ignore that job opportunities have to be created for women as well. This further widens the gender disparities among the displaced persons either by imposing a disproportionate share of social costs on women or through an inequitable allocation of the benefits generated. Extensive research has documented gender inequalities in access to, and control of, economic and natural resources (WCD 2000). In Asia and Africa, for example, women may have used rights over land and forests, but are rarely allowed to own and/or inherit the land they use (Mehta and Srinivasan 1999).

The situation further worsens for tribal women. Tribal women fare worse than men do because their dependence on informal economy is greater. Three other aspects basic to the life of tribal women in particular, ensure their greater deterioration. Firstly, the natural resources from which land acquisition alienates them are the very foundation of tribal women's economy, culture, social systems and political structures. The woman had some control over them as long as they were community assets. Since they have less exposure to the external world than men, they end up in low paid unskilled jobs. Thus, the woman is denied economic independence. In land-based resettlement, land is allotted to an individual, almost invariably a man, considered the head of the family. It is then transferred to his son. Land is a symbol of social power. With no rights over land, the woman ceases to be economically productive and also stops being a decision maker in the family. This power is transferred to the man and from him to his son (Fernandes 2001).

Examining the relationship between gender and development, Bina Agarwal argues that gender should be used as a 'lens' and cautions about treating women merely as an 'additive category' or as a 'special focus or target group' (Agarwal 1994). When considering women and involuntary displacement, a similar approach is required. Involuntary displacement needs to be examined through the experiential lens of the women affected (Bisht 2009). There is no denying the fact that there are studies that narrate instances where dams have served as opportunities for reducing gender disparities, primarily among women in households or communities that receive access to project services. However, such success stories are few and rare. Although many countries and funding agencies have adopted specific gender policies in recent years aimed at mainstreaming gender issues in their development interventions, actual project planning and implementation continue to overlook gender aspects. An assessment by the World Bank of its own funded projects noted that the experiences studied 'were largely oblivious of the gender aspect of resettlement' (OED 1998:60). After the Asian Development Bank approved a gender policy in 1998, a review of its dam projects observed that the impacts on gender at the project preparation and implementation stages were often not considered (ADB 2003). Where planning is insensitive to gender, project impacts can at best be neutral, and at worst aggravate existing gender disparities to the extent of radically affecting the pre-project gender balance. Scudder (2005: 59) rightly said that 'Looking to the future, women will continue to suffer until they are incorporated within the options assessments and decision-making processes to the extent that the necessary economic, social and political opportunities are also made available to them'.

Impact on Ecosystems

The ecology-economics interface subordinates the environment to the primacy of economic growth. Nature is repudiated for the generation of wealth, goods, and services. The ecological degradation resulting from this distorted priority has emerged as a pervasive consequence of the pattern of development (Kothari 1996). The large dams were declared as part of a flawed paradigm that causes an increasing disconnection between the necessary environmental health of river basins and the current needs of people and governments for the provision of water, energy, and food (Scudder 2005). It further led to inequitable development and environmental degradation. Though the major ecological impacts of dams are known well, most of these are not fully understood nor, in most dam projects, fully assessed. Few studies are conducted to determine the ecological, economic and cultural importance of rivers before they are dammed. Similar is the case of long term environmental and social consequences of areas after the construction of a dam. River basins are renowned as the cradles of civilization and cultural heritage. Ancient and modern communities alike have depended on rivers for livelihoods, commerce, habitats and the sustaining ecological functions they provide. Throughout history, alterations to rivers—natural or human generated—have affected riverine communities in one way or another.

The immediate impacts involve the physical, chemical, and geomorphological consequences of blocking a river and altering the natural distribution and timing of stream flow. Secondly, it leads to irreversible damage to the primary biological productivity of ecosystems including effects on riverine and riparian plant-life and on downstream habitats such as wetlands. Thirdly, it leads to alterations to fauna (especially fish) caused by a first-order effect (such as blocking migration) or a second-order effect (such as decrease in the availability of plankton). Besides this, modifying the ecosystem changes the biochemical cycle in the natural riverine system. Reservoirs interrupt the downstream flow of organic carbon, leading to emissions of greenhouse gases such as methane and carbon dioxide that contribute to climate change (WCD 2000:74).

The alternative uses of land interfere with all elements of the environment. They pollute and overdraw water resources, degrade quality of air and damage biodiversity. The soil in the vicinity is impaired affecting its productivity and even fertility. The incidence of reservoir induced seismicity is increased in many Dam projects (Kothari 1996). Development opens the environment for large-scale commercial exploitation which destroys its values besides generating social conflict with communities who use it for subsistence. The ecological imbalance destroys the existing symbiosis between people and their environment and threatens the survival of those dependent on it. It also leads to irreversible loss of natural genetic diversities evolved over the years. The shrinking of the resource base of an increasingly large number of people causes an imbalance in men-nature relationships. It forces people dependent on it to overexploit the reduced environmental space for survival which causes further degradation, reducing its utility for the very communities dependent on it. The deterioration in the local environment also leads to the spread of new diseases unknown to the area (Fernandes and Thukral 1989; Pandey 1998). Thus, environmental destruction and social injustice go together (Saxena 2008a). For sheer survival, impoverishment forces the communities that had till then treated forests and other natural resources as renewable, into destructive dependence on the same. Thus, it results not merely in poverty and ecological degradation but also in the weakening of the culture that ensured renewability (Fernandes 2001). What is more important is that even in cases where some of these may have been assessed, there is no comprehensive impact statement - each impact is studied on its own, in isolation. Further, there is little assessment of how the dam and its impacts interact with the rest of the environment (Dharmadhikary 2001). The ongoing struggle against the large dams across the globe challenges this dominant model of development that holds out the promise of material wealth through modernization but perpetuates an unequal distribution of resources and wreaks social and environmental havoc (Scudder 2005).

The development projects, because of their very nature, have not been able to create alternative sources of livelihood for the majority of those who were displaced (Mishra 2011). Therefore, displacement has a dual effect. On the one hand, it leads to conflict over land, and on the other, it signifies a radical shift in public policy towards a market-oriented approach. The process of displacement affects not only immediate displaced persons but even the host communities.

In brief, it can be stated that displacement is a deeply traumatic experience with multiple dimensions affecting production systems, social network, trade and market connections, and cultural bonding. In the case of tribal communities, displacement causes a loss of cultural identity which produces stress and mental disorders (Kothari 1996; Mahapatra 1999). Impoverishment remains a legacy of displacements from large dams which suggests that there are some basic flaws in the way involuntary resettlement is carried out (McDonald and Webber 2010). The WCD (2000) found that a lack of obligation as well as capacity to tackle displacement has led to the impoverishment of a large number of affected people and has consequently led to the opposition to these projects worldwide. Any developmental activity can be meaningful only when the deprived and displaced people are taken care of and adequately rehabilitated, which has not been ensured in most of the dams.

Development projects are usually undertaken with the expectation that they make significant and sustainable contributions to the society and environment through commitment to environment, social and economic benefit of society. While the direct objective with any development project might be obviously related to maximizing the benefits, there are also usually unintended consequences which such projects bring upon the society and the environment (Ashley and Hussein 2000). It is therefore very important and mandatory that the social, cultural, economic and ecological impacts of development schemes and projects must be assessed before they go ahead and thoroughly analyzed before damage is done on those impacted.

CHAPTER 2

DISPLACEMENT AND THE CRITIQUE OF NEOLIBERAL MODEL OF DEVELOPMENT

> *"The debate about dams is a debate about the very meaning, purpose and pathway of development as well as the role that the state plays."* (WCD 2000: 198)

'Development' first emerged as a subject area in the second half of the twentieth century. The most basic assumption underlying the study of development, especially in the southern part of the globe, both in theory and practice is that the term implies, narrowly, to poverty reduction and by extension, accretions over time in overall well being for the mass of people; that is, an increase in 'human development'. This was the fundamental assumption behind the emergence of development studies after the Second World War, when the concept of development first appeared on the international agenda. During the 1950s, the term development became more complicated with the emergence of large numbers of post-colonial countries (Haynes 2008).

Lewis (1954) stated that economic development is a process of capital accumulation. During this process, labor is transferred from low productivity agriculture and other traditional occupations to high productivity modern industry. The academic deliberations that dwelled upon Lewis' framework of dualism subsequently emphasised the importance of raising agricultural productivity, along with industrial growth, to maintain stable terms of trade between agriculture and industry, crucial for an unhindered capital accumulation in the industrial sector (Jorgensen 1961; Dixit 1973). However, the emphasis was always on the accumulation of capital. This emphasis on physical capital accumulation shifted to human capital accumulation from the mid-1980s with the pioneering work of Romer (1986, 1990) and the emergence of endogenous growth models. However, neither of the two schools of thought, one emphasising physical capital and the other emphasising human capital as the main constraint to development, had visualised that land could become a serious constraining factor to the process of development. The underlying assumption was that land requirement is negligible for industries and therefore can be safely ignored. At the macroeconomic level this was justified. If one looks at the physical requirement of land for building up industries, services and infrastructure like roads, townships, seaports, airports or bridges, the total requirement may not be very large compared to the total agricultural land in a less developed agrarian economy. There, however, exists a serious microeconomic problem (Sarkar 2007).

In the post-colonial era, development was perceived in terms of modernization, improved standard of living and industrial progress. The route to achieve it lay in the growth of Gross National Product which would generate wealth, raise incomes and create incentives for investment. This model of economic growth relied heavily on capital investment and advancement of technology to harness existing natural and human resources. All this required land which was usually procured through compulsory acquisition by the government. When land was acquired for the aforesaid purposes, it invariably entailed eviction of people from their traditional livelihood and surroundings.

The displacement of people subsisting on such land has therefore been considered as inevitable and unavoidable. This articulation of the development paradigm rested on certain assumptions. One was that development benefits people across society and leads to social welfare. The other assumption was that development and national progress were intertwined. As the pursuit of national progress has been the utmost priority, other aspirations and considerations should be superseded. With these assumptions, development induced displacement was considered both necessary and desirable. The sacrifice made by the displaced was presumed to be a small cost for achieving the higher national goals (Saxena 2008b).

Since the 1970s, the construction of large dams became—in the eyes of many—synonymous with development and economic progress. Viewed as symbols of modernization and humanity's ability to harness nature, dam construction accelerated dramatically. This can be substantiated by the fact that from 1970 onwards, on average two or three large dams were commissioned each day somewhere in the world. While the immediate benefits were widely believed sufficient to justify the enormous investments made (more than $2 trillion), secondary and tertiary benefits were also often cited. These included food security considerations, local employment and skills development, rural electrification, and the expansion of physical and social infrastructure such as roads and schools. The benefits were regarded as self-evident, while the construction and operational costs tended to be limited to economic and financial considerations that justified dams as a highly competitive option (WCD 2000:XXX).

Pushed by this development strategy, the construction of large dams has been justified on economic, social, and political grounds. The benefits highlighted by the government agencies were major and could not be overlooked by the general public especially in developing and less developed countries. During the late twentieth century, large dams emerged as one of the most significant and visible tools for the management of water resources. According to an estimate, 16 percent of the world's electricity is generated through dams (World Bank 2015).

In the neoliberal process, land is commodified and moved from local people to private companies and wealthy elites. Natural resources are appropriated, and alternative, indigenous, forms of production and consumption are suppressed (Renee and Minter 2020). This process leads to ever increasing levels of social inequality and instability, and is contingent on and promoted by policies of the state (Harvey 2003, 2007). As a development choice, large dams became a focal point for the interests of politicians, dominant and centralized government agencies, international financing agencies and the dam-building industry. In the early 1970s and 1980s, when dam construction was at its peak, few studies were being carried out to determine the ecological, economic and cultural importance of rivers before they were dammed. Similar has been the case of long term environmental and social consequences of areas after the construction of a dam. Involvement from civil society varied with the degree of debate and open political discourse. The dams were considered to be the most desirable option by policy makers when needs reach crisis or near-crisis propositions, ignoring the irreversible longer-term social and environmental costs of such projects. These large hydro projects provided an easy and sustainable solution available to deal with the rising demands of the expanding human population, which already has surpassed the carrying capacity of earth's ecosystem.

The ongoing struggle against the large dams across the globe challenges this dominant model of development that holds out the promise of material wealth through modernization but perpetuates an unequal distribution of resources and wreaks social and environmental havoc (Scudder 2005). The economically driven displacement of environmental costs is principally affecting the human rights of two constituencies: today's poor and future generations (Barry and Woods 2013: 390). By the beginning of the third millennium, there was an emergence of two polarized interpretations of what needs to be done to ameliorate development outcomes in developmentally under-achieving countries in the developing world i.e., radicals and reformists (Rai 2005). The *Reformist perspective* totally ignores the debate on questioning the assumptions of the dominant development paradigm and reasserts that displacement is an inevitable outcome of economic development. This school of thought believes that displacement of some people is justified in order to initiate development activities. This approach ignores the political and ethical context within which displacement occurs (Dwivedi 2002). On the other hand, the *Radical perspective* is openly critical of the current development paradigm and advocates for alternative development paradigms (Ganguly and Dutt 2012). According to this approach, large-scale development projects and consequent forced displacement has been legitimized by the State to enhance the power of the state and private capital. It is also critical of the existing neoliberal phase of development which has further led to land being regulated by market forces (Jaysawal and Saha 2018). Most debates, however, about development and how to achieve it in the developing world feature an unresolved—often implicit tension—between these two viewpoints. As far as the major question of the development project of large dams is concerned, scholars are divided.

Dam construction has led to momentous social upheavals particularly in terms of displacement. Forced displacement symbolizes a perverse and inherent incongruity in the context of development (Nayak 2013). They raise major ethical questions because they reflect an inequitable distribution of development's benefits and losses. 'Nevertheless, the involuntary displacements caused by such programmes create major impositions on some population segments. It restricts population rights by state-power intervention. This raises major issues of social justice and equity' (Cernea 2000: 3659). For those displaced, such projects represent the antithesis of real development. Understanding the discourse from the perspective of Rawls' 'general conceptions of justice', these large development projects—such as dam projects—and its impact of displacement is a utilitarian nightmare. The projects, which promote greater good for a greater number, impoverish 'oustees' and compel them to sacrifice for the 'greater good', are intolerable. Rawls' general conception of justice enables us to recognize that 'an unsuccessful resettlement scheme creates new inequalities by depriving oustees not only of income and wealth but also of social goods in two other ways: liberty and opportunity and social bases of respect' (Drydyk 1999:1-8; Rawls 1971).

However, since the 1960s, practitioners have already started questioning, in fact, criticizing the undesirable and avoidable environmental and social impacts of dams. The large dams were declared as part of a flawed paradigm that causes an increasing disconnection between the necessary environmental health of river basins and the current needs of people and governments for the provision of water, energy and food (Scudder 2005). At the same time, alternative perspectives on human rights and development are being more clearly expressed. The preamble to the Right to Development, adopted by the UN General Assembly (1986) argued that ‘development is a comprehensive process aimed at the constant improvement of the well-being of the entire population’. More vocal criticism has mounted against the prevailing globalization process asserting that this process facilitates few forgings ahead, while leading to social exclusion of already vulnerable groups. It also emphasizes an equal distribution of resources to ensure better quality of life for all. As experience accumulated and better information on the performance and consequences of dams became available, the full cost of large dams has also begun to emerge as a serious public concern. Driven by information on the impacts of dams on people, river basins and ecosystems, as well as their economic performance, opposition began to grow. Debate and controversy initially focused on specific dams and their local impacts. Gradually these locally driven conflicts evolved into a global debate about the costs and benefits of dams. Global estimates of the magnitude of impacts include some 40-80 million people displaced by dams while 60 percent of the world’s rivers have been affected by dams and diversions. The nature and magnitude of the impacts of dams on affected communities and on the environment have now become established as key issues in the debate (WCD 2000).

The displacement debate also sharply underlines the unequal power relations in society. The power structure these relations produce tends to concentrate decision making of the government in a small privileged class representing the dominant social and economic groups. The class constituting these groups has wide access to economic assets, knowledge creation avenues, creation and opportunities for advancement. It commands control over resources both economic and intellectual. Development policies and structures are a manifestation of this power. In contrast, the larger sections of poor, particularly the more vulnerable sections among them, are denied this access through a wide range of discriminatory and exclusionary practices. In such a situation, the decision making by the state whether for regulatory or developmental activities is controlled by this small privileged class. This enables decision makers to make decisions for the whole society which includes those who may be adversely affected by them. These decisions inevitably reflect the premises and logic of their costs and benefits as seen by the decision makers. The decision makers assume that the logic and assumptions influencing a particular decision are shaped by others as well. That is why development decisions involving displacement never consider possible alternatives which avoid this consequence. Rather, they tend to justify them by arguing that the adversely affected people should make this sacrifice for the larger national progress and advancement of society. This self-serving logic is pursued precisely because they are not the ones who suffer the adverse consequences of decisions. This paradigm of development, therefore, very eloquently advocates inclusive participation in decision making by which this inequality of power distribution is neutralized. Those who are adversely affected also have an equal stay in the decisions taken so that the conflicts of interests are adequately resolved without leaning in favor of any class. The alternative sought is for democratic and participatory decision making (Saxena 2008b).

There has been a generalized failure to recognize affected people and empower them to participate in the decision-making process. The World Commission on Dams in its report (2000) rightly pointed out that once a proposed dam project passed preliminary technical and economic feasibility tests and attracted interest from government or external financing agencies and political interests, the momentum behind the project often prevailed over further assessments. In any event, project planning and appraisal for large dams was confined primarily to technical parameters and the narrow application of economic cost/benefit analyses.

This discourse on development has also brought into sharp focus the iniquitous nature and impact of its activities across social groups. This is reflected in the prosperity and advancement for some, and the impoverishment and misery for others. The acquisition of land leads to its transfer from people who use it for their subsistence to more affluent sections of society who already have access to productive resources and other avenues of income. This is particularly true where the acquired land is used by corporate agencies for profit making and by housing societies for providing houses to the better off sections. This resource transfer is contrary to the ethos of a welfare state (Saxena 2008a).

In a society, characterized by wide social and economic inequalities, development like other political goals is a widely contested notion with sharply antagonistic meaning given to it. This is because development is not a neutral phenomenon with uniformly beneficial implications. Development activities have dissimilar effects on different social groups depending on how they are placed in society and what their interests are. Some may gain from them while others may lose. Therefore, the perception of what constitutes development is not the same with all social groups. Both the meaning of development and the route to achieve it are therefore viewed in different terms by different groups. Each group tends to interpret development in terms of how its interest can be served and how the distribution of benefits would affect it. This articulation of development, serves the interests of dominant social and economic groups because they are in position to benefit from it. For those who faced displacement with attendant adverse consequences, this model is the very negation of development. It causes a spiral of impoverishment, social disruption, emotional trauma and an uncertain future (Saxena 2008a).

The redefinition of development implies that its activities should benefit all irrespective of the social, economic status of any group. The costs, if any, of such development should be equally shared by all groups. Alternatively, where this parity is difficult to achieve despite sincere efforts, the losses should be compensated in a manner that balances the benefits derived by the winners so as to achieve the most equitable outcomes to the losers. This brings forth a whole range of ideas and suggestions on how this balance can be achieved, such as minimization of displacement as against its assumed inevitability, alternatives to compulsory acquisition, replacement of productive assets, and provision of stable and assured employment. The discourse, therefore, involves a reversal of the prevailing assumptions and logic of the current ideology of development and its replacement by construction of a fair and just paradigm.

Summing Up

Massive technological development hurts. This is a fact largely ignored by economic planners, technicians and political leaders. In planning drastic alterations in the environment that uproot populations or make old adjustments impossible, they count the engineering costs but not the social costs (Colson 1971). To Parasuraman (1999:265), 'displacement is inherent in the ideology and policy of development'. He therefore calls for a reconsideration of the type of development that leads to large-scale displacement and the 'need for radical changes in the dominant model of development' (Parasuraman 1999: 267).

Cernea described displacement as a development 'pathology' epitomizing 'inequitable distribution of pains and gains', which makes it 'profoundly contradictory to the goals of development' (Cernea 1997:1569-70). He has compiled an impressive global database on displacement effects to show how policies fail to protect those at risk. But he emphasizes the need for 'not only studying disruptions, but helping formulate reconstructive strategies to turn displacement into development opportunities' (Cernea 1999:29). To him, there are ways to fully avoid specific instances of involuntary displacement or at least to decrease their magnitude. Reconstruction of lives and livelihoods is seen as viable: 'It is certainly possible, under enlightened policies, to protect much more effectively than current practices do the civil rights, human dignity and economic entitlements of those subject to involuntary relocation' (Cernea 2000:13).

Damodaran and Padel (2018) asserted that in the post-reform context, the well-worn term development-induced displacement should be replaced with a new terminology of investment-induced displacement? The economics of investment-led growth need to be questioned from a holistic balancing of costs against benefits (Padel and Das 2010). Shouldn't water, food, and livelihood security be central to real development? (Padel 2012). Shouldn't we be viewing people's movements aimed at safeguarding their local resources as the cutting edge of real development? It is essential to develop other less risky and less disruptive solutions for rural communities suffering from environmental fragility while developing the economy of the regions concerned. By sharing successful adaptation experiments that do not involve forced population displacement, researchers may be able to sensitize political leaders to the existence of alternative models, helping to build their willingness and ability to adopt flexible and participatory approaches in solving environmental problems (Dubé 2016). 'The principal goal of development policy is to create sustainable improvements in the quality of life for all people. While raising per capita incomes and consumption is part of that goal, other objectives - reducing poverty, expanding access to health services, and increasing educational levels - are also important. Meeting these goals requires a comprehensive approach to development' (World Bank 1999: 13). 'Development requires the removal of major sources of unfreedom: poverty as well as tyranny, poor economic opportunities as well as systematic social deprivation, neglect of public facilities as well as intolerance or over activity of repressive states' (Sen 1999:3). The state is considered to be the major resource for developmental and welfare activities. People rely on the state as the sole provider and dispenser of social services and hence the 'welfare' state is becoming increasing relevant (Dash 2008). Therefore, development must be defined not through the prism of market-led growth, but through the metric of freedom from want, human welfare and the right to life with dignity. Equitable development and poverty reduction must take precedence over 'market freedom' (Bidwai 2012).

The World Commission on Dams (2000:2) also raised certain serious questions about the sustainability of dams by stating that, dams are a means to an end, not an end in themselves: 'What is that end? How central are the challenges that large dams set out to meet? And how well can dams meet them? The end of any dam project must lead to the substantial improvement of general welfare which is economically viable, socially equitable, and environmentally sustainable. If a large dam is the best way to achieve this goal, it deserves our support. Where other options offer better solutions, we should favour them over large dams'.

Hence, improving the development process and its outcomes must start with a clear understanding of the shared values, objectives and goals of development and their implications for institutional change. The World Commission on Dams (2000:24) grouped the core values informing its understanding on these issues under five main headings: Equity, Efficiency, Participatory decision-making, Sustainability and Accountability. Applying these values will deliver the most favourable development results.

CHAPTER 3

RESETTLEMENT AND REHABILITATION PLANNING AND MANAGEMENT: KEY COMPONENTS, ISSUES AND CHALLENGES

On average, around 10 million people are annually displaced across the globe due to development projects such as dams, highways, ports and urban infrastructure. According to an estimate, 50 million people have been displaced in India itself in the last five decades (Roy 1999). The magnitude of the affected people itself raises serious policy questions. It has been time and again substantiated by various field studies that involuntary resettlement leads the oustees into a vicious circle of impoverishment. This holds true for the resettlement process in almost all the development projects (except few success stories). This scenario itself questions the current definition of development which fulfils the interest of the elite ignoring the larger social welfare. Despite an on-going debate on the need to rethink and redesign the current development model, it is now an accepted fact that involuntary displacement associated with development projects is going to stay for the foreseeable future. It is obvious why governments across the world endorse the belief that these large projects are a prerequisite for the persuasion of larger development goals and hence, the sacrifice made by a few (through loss of land, livelihood and other) is seen as justified. The issue raised here is not that the project should not be undertaken, because it involves displacement of people, but how to carry out the development projects in such a manner that adverse socio-economic consequences of the project, on already marginalized people, can be minimized. Furthermore, resettlement must be carried out in such a manner that it does not lead to impoverishment risks.

Since the 1970s and 1980s, when the dam construction became synonymous with development, resettlement of oustees has largely remained a neglected aspect of development. The focus of the project executing agencies has always been on the technical soundness of the project. The removal of people from the project area was always considered as the end of the resettlement process. Resettlement programmes have primarily laid emphasis on the process of physical relocation rather than on the economic and social development of the displaced and other project affected communities (Cernea 1999; Cernea and McDowell 2000; Cernea and Guggenheim 1993). Dwivedi (2002) calls this the 'reformist-managerial approach' which treats development and the consequent displacement as a given, with the only concern being minimizing the negative impacts of displacement at minimum cost, rather than minimizing the displacement in the first place. Persuaded by economics, this approach legitimizes the presence of the project with solutions being developed internally to minimize costs. The goal of successful resettlement—to improve or at least restore livelihoods and living standards and to enable displaced people to share the benefits of the project—remains a goal rarely achieved. The impoverishment risks such as *landlessness, joblessness, homelessness, marginalisation, increased morbidity, food insecurity, loss of access to common property, and social disarticulation* (See Cernea 1998: 48-53) are obvious implications of such a faulty resettlement programme.

As the intellectual discourse on development induced displacement and resettlement began in the 1980s, several models on resettlement emerged. The first such model was developed in 1982 by Scudder and Colson. This model was conceptualized as a framework for the study of populations undergoing forced displacement. It used data from a number of dam resettlements and constructed a predictive model of how communities and individuals respond to resettlement. The model recognized four stages of relocation i.e., recruitment, transition, preferential development and handing over/incorporation (Scudder and Colson 1982). Scudder (1993:13) termed the period following the actual physical displacement, as a 'transitional stage' and argued that it is a difficult stage because it involves dealing with multidimensional stress that includes 'physiological, psychological and sociological' components. The stress results from peoples' exposure to a new and unfamiliar habitat, neighbours and production techniques, and people respond to these stresses by falling back on what is familiar. The theory was broadly criticized in two broad contexts. The first one was with regard to the four-stage framework which seems to be formulated to explain the similarities rather than the differences in people's reactions to involuntary relocation (de Wet 2001). Secondly, Weist (1995) noted that an emphasis on stages does not do justice to the dynamic coping strategies involved.

Cernea developed another model of resettlement, 'Impoverishment Risks and Reconstruction' (IRR), in the early 1990s. The model, while focusing on the nature and content of displacement and resettlement, introduced two key concepts: 'risks' and 'impoverishment'. This model deconstructed the multifaceted process of displacement into its principal risks. Cernea (1997, 2000) also alluded to the four functions of the IRR model: (a) predictive, (b) diagnostic, (c) problem-resolution and (d) research. The predictive function of the model is its capacity to anticipate and warn of hidden problems in new situations. The diagnostic function is one of assessing specific project conditions. The problem-resolution function guides strategic reconstruction of resettlers' livelihoods. The research function is the possibility that it offers as a 'conceptual scaffolding' for conducting fieldwork (Dwivedi 2002). Cernea viewed displacement as a *pathology of induced development*, but also recognized the indispensable nature of projects that produced great public benefits, but also led to the displacement of people. Cernea's model acknowledged the economic challenges faced by people in re-establishing themselves and emphasized for appropriate resettlement of the displaced (Ganguly and Dutt 2012). The IRR model put social losses squarely into the process of impoverishment and called for systematic efforts to counter those social losses. This model directed research beyond the narrowly economistic perspective and required consistent measures to address social loss (McDowell and Morrell 2007). The model, however, failed to highlight many crucial issues such as consent, terms of participation, dispute resolution. Hence Cernea's (1997:1577) claim that the model 'enables the resettlers to explore alternatives, to resist unjustified or inadequately prepared displacement before it occurs and to pursue their rights and entitlements when displacement is unavoidable' seems questionable (Dwivedi 2002). Mehta explicitly stated that the initial purpose of designing IRR model was not to identify impoverishment risks due to displacement but to create a tool for planners (Mehta 2009a).

The latest theoretical intervention in this domain has been made by Downing and Downing in 2009 by reframing the psycho-socio-cultural (PSC) dimension of displacement. This theory argued that involuntary displacement transforms routine culture into dissonant culture and then yields a transformed, different routine culture. As per this theory, even though people may be resettled together as a group, 'culturally what was, is no more'. Dissonant culture ultimately gets transformed into a 'new routine culture' and the relocation process passes from 'routine culture' to 'dissonant culture' and eventually to a 'new routine culture'. The time period between the dissonant culture and re-emergence of a new culture has been called the 'dissonant interval'. It further stated that this re-emergence of a new routine culture takes place in a 'block by block', 'piecemeal' manner' (Downing and Downing 2009:469). They asserted that mitigation of PSC damage is always more problematic as most of the projects do not make an effort to mitigate this risk (Bisht 2009). The theory further points out four fallacies (Downing 2002a:458) which conveniently block further discussions and actions:

(a) *The policy-planning fallacy* believes that if proper involuntary resettlement plans or policies are in place, the PSC recovery will follow.
(b) *The economic deterministic fallacy* holds that if the economic restoration or recovery is adequately financed and executed, PSC issues will work themselves out.
(c) *Blaming the victims fallacy* asserts that those who are getting displaced are at fault as they are incapable of understanding or taking advantage of economic opportunities offered to them. This fallacy is an excuse made by those responsible for resettlement when they try to assert that there is no fault at resettlement policy implementation level but it still leads to PSC impoverishment.
(d) *The someone-else-should-pay-fallacy* holds that the project designers, governments and financiers are neither legally nor economically liable for psycho-socio-cultural changes.

By focusing on the psycho-socio-cultural perspective of displacement, the model attempted to highlight the importance of, and to dispel misunderstandings about, the socio-cultural changes arising from displacement. The importance of a socio-cultural perspective on displacement had earlier been highlighted by the Asian Development Bank in its Handbook on Resettlement as early as in 1998. The document clearly mentioned the resettlement effects such as the 'loss of physical and non-physical assets, including homes, communities, productive land, income-earning assets and sources, subsistence, resources, cultural sites, social structures, networks and ties, cultural identity and mutual health mechanisms' (ADB 1998:1-126).

Despite some ideological contrasts in all these models, there is no denying the fact that the resettlement planning and management issues are crucial to any effort directed at improving the lives of people adversely affected by development projects (World Bank 2004).

The recent studies have started highlighting the fact that an adequate resettlement process is justified not only on ethical grounds, the idea that as people are sacrificing their land for the development of the nation, they must be fairly resettled; it also makes economic sense to resettle the displaced properly. The lack of adequate resettlement leads to discontentment among the people which further turns into serious protests. This completely upsets project implementation schedules, resulting in huge time and cost overruns. This cost overrun is often more than the cost of adequate resettlement. Despite the reassertion from various scholars time and again, inadequacies of resettlement planning and management persist in most projects, adding further to hardships of the people affected. Experience suggests that, though stubborn, the resettlement problems are not insurmountable. A fuller understanding of the issues involved in conducting resettlement operations is, however, essential, if projects are to stay on track, harming none and yet generating benefits for all (Mathur 2006).

Conceptual Understanding

Resettlement is a distinctive form of mobility in that why, where, and how people move are determined by authorities ahead of displacement. The degree of external planning, preparation, and investment distinguishes resettlement from reactive movements in response to disasters or conflict, or more self-directed forms of mobility in response to slow onset economic and environmental change. The World Bank describes resettlement as the process by which those adversely affected (by development projects) are assisted in their efforts to improve, or at least restore, their incomes and living standards (World Bank 2015).

Involuntary resettlement includes social and economic impacts that are permanent or temporary and are caused by: acquisition of land and other fixed assets; change in the use of land; or restrictions imposed on land due to a project operation (Mathur 2006). Resettlement is involuntary when it happens without the free and informed consent of the communities affected or when the choice gets exercised in the absence of reasonable alternatives. Resettlement is also involuntary when it occurs in the presence of an explicit or implicit threat of expropriation or exercise of eminent domain by the power of the state. Involuntary resettlement generally consists of two interrelated processes. The first one leads to the displacement of people from their native lands and consequently deconstructs their social, cultural, and economic fabric. The second one involves the resettlement of oustees at a new location and a restructuring of their livelihood and social networks. Both the processes have their own content, dynamics, logistics, and demands on people and institutions. Resettlement then refers both to the processes of physical relocation of those displaced and to their socioeconomic reestablishment as family household micro-units and as larger communities (Cernea 2005; IFC 2002).

In recent years, the policy makers have started using an alternative and more inclusive term to define these two processes. The term resettlement has a narrow connotation with emphasis only on physical relocation of displaced people, while the term rehabilitation widens the ambit by focussing on restoration of lost economic and social abilities. Whatever terminology, however, we may use to define the process, it is pertinent to understand that if resettlement is not to leave people worse off than before, it must be addressed as a process of sustainable development (Scudder 1997).

Types of Resettlements

The International Finance Corporation (IFC 2002:6) provided common types of resettlements and the issues associated with them:

***Rural Resettlement*:** The displacement of people in rural areas typically results from the acquisition of farm land, pasture, or grazing land or the obstruction of access to natural resources on which affected populations rely for livelihoods. Major challenges associated with rural resettlement include: requirements for restoring income based on land or resources; and the need to avoid compromising the social and cultural continuity of affected communities, including those host communities to which displaced populations may be resettled.

***Urban Resettlement*:** Resettlement in urban or peri-urban settings results in both physical and economic displacement affecting housing, employment, and enterprises. A major challenge associated with urban resettlement involves restoration of wage-based or enterprise-based livelihoods that are often tied to location (such as proximity to jobs, customers, and markets). Resettlement sites should be selected to maintain the proximity of affected people to established sources of employment and income and to maintain neighbourhood networks.

***Linear Resettlement*:** Linear resettlement describes projects having linear patterns of land acquisition (highways, railways, canals, and power transmission lines). In sparsely populated rural areas, a linear project such as an electric transmission line may have minimal impact on any single landholder. Compensation is characterised by a large number of small payments for the temporary loss of assets such as standing crops. If well designed, linear projects can easily avoid or minimise the demolition of permanent structures. Conversely, in a densely populated urban area, a linear project such as a road upgrading may require the demolition of structures along the project right-of-way, thereby significantly affecting large numbers of people.

***Site-specific Resettlement*:** Site-specific resettlement is associated with discrete, non-linear projects such as factories, ports, highway interchanges, hotels, commercial plantations, etc., where land acquisition encompasses a fixed area. However, site-specific resettlement associated with mining and other extractive industries such as oil and gas may require progressive land acquisition over long periods. As a result, displacement of communities may occur in phases over a number of years, even decades. The major challenge in such incremental resettlement is maintaining a consistent approach to compensation and income restoration over the life of the project.

Key Components

A successful resettlement must lead to assessable enhancements in the economic situations and social well-being of affected communities. This requires an effective resettlement and rehabilitation planning and management. A well-articulated resettlement plan helps in mitigating the adverse impacts of displacement and in creating better development prospects for project affected people. The essential components of a resettlement action plan have been discussed below.

(a) Estimation of the Affected People: The success of any resettlement plan lies in how effectively the magnitude of the problem has been calculated. The miscalculation may create multiple problems in the resettlement process at the later stage such as unnecessary delays, escalated costs, and adverse impacts on affected communities. Despite this obvious fact, this has been the single most important reason for failure of resettlement in various dam projects. For projects that the World Bank funded, a review found the actual number of people to be resettled 47 percent higher than the estimate made at the time of appraisal (World Bank 1996).

(b) Social Impact Assessment: Social Impact Assessment (SIA) is an assessment and estimation process in which the social consequences of any development project are assessed and predicted before the impacts are to be brought about by implementing the project. This assessment provides the basis for project decision-making, project programming and mitigation measures to be incorporated in the project design and execution. The SIA must include the survey of those who are going to be directly affected by the project such as those whose land, houses and other assets will be taken;

along with those who will be indirectly affected due to the project, for instance people affected due to restrictions on access to rivers and natural resources. The needs of women, elderly and indigenous people must get specific attention. 'The issues associated with adverse effects associated with resettlement in host communities including increased pressure on land, water, natural vegetation (forests, woodlands, savannas, grasslands, and wetlands), plantations and woodlots, or other common property resources, public infrastructure, and services must be addressed at the planning stage itself' (IFC 2002:12). 'While the theory of social assessment may seem to demand multidisciplinary teams of exceptionally gifted individuals working over an extended period, the reality is usually somewhat more prosaic' (Lucas 2000:98-106). This is also true of projects financed by the World Bank, known for its meticulous methods of researching and documenting the minutest project details (Scudder 2005). The needs of the resettled population were often ignored. It is therefore important that social impact assessments are treated as a distinct type of project preparation activity in much the same way as other assessments.

(c) Participation of the Stakeholders: It is an accepted fact that active participation of all the stakeholders leads to the success of the project. It becomes all the more important in the cases where resettlement is involuntary. The participation of the affected communities in the decision making must be seen as a right of the oustees as by giving up their homes and livelihoods for the sake of projects they make an important contribution to the development process as a whole. Participation also provided planners with access to the expectations, beliefs, and knowledge system of the people for whom they were planning, which made possible the prevention of design errors by checking proposal details with them (Partridge 1993:367). The free flow of information between project sponsors and stakeholders is essential to promote effective public discussion and participation and to accomplish the purposes of resettlement planning (IFC 2002). While the importance of involving the host population is increasingly recognized in a general way, yet in practice this remains one of the most neglected dimensions of relocation planning. The host populations generally look at newcomers with some suspicion to begin with that can easily turn into hostility. Hence, it is significant to involve the host population in the decision-making process in the beginning of the project to avoid any problems at the later stage. In general, participatory strategies are still aimed at avoiding conflict rather than including stakeholders and displaced communities in decision making and sharing responsibilities central to the project and people's lives (Mejia 1999).

(d) Vulnerable Groups: 'Resettlement planners must give particular attention to vulnerable groups living in the project area. These groups may include households headed by women or children, people with disabilities, the extremely poor, the elderly, and groups that suffer social and economic discrimination, including indigenous peoples and minorities' (IFC 2002: 15). The resettlement policies have generally been gender blind. Resettlement opens up a pandora's box of challenges for women at a new site, such as loss of income opportunities; loss of access to food, fodder and fuel-wood; and losing the sense of security. Women have been seldom consulted on their problems and needs while designing resettlement plans by the project authorities. Recognizing the need for the same, the Asian Development Bank has brought out a Resettlement Gender Checklist to guide resettlement planners (ADB 2003). Another group which bears the brunt of the development is the indigenous people. Development projects prove harmful to indigenous peoples, especially because they often lack legal recognition and a voice in governance issues. They are particularly vulnerable because they have no individual rights to the land. The trauma of resettlement is also exacerbated for indigenous communities because of their strong spiritual ties to their land. Vulnerable groups, other than the women and indigenous people, faced many hardships too as projects often tended not to take into consideration their special needs and problems. Although efforts are underway to provide them assistance, generally these remain limited in their impact (Mathur 2006).

(e) Compensation: Compensation is one of the most deliberated upon issue in any resettlement planning. It is the yardstick through which success of any resettlement programme is generally gauged. Traditionally, the project executing agencies have understood compensation as synonymous to the resettlement. It was in the 1990s that both the terms were conceptually understood. Shihata (1993:45) explains:

> *Compensation is what the owner of property, unilaterally acquired by the government, receives in lieu of that property. It can be made in cash or in kind, and is usually based on a standard of valuation provided by law. Rehabilitation, on the other hand, constitutes a series of measures, including but not limited to monetary compensation, aimed at affording the affected population the possibility to become re-established and economically self-sustaining in the shortest possible period.*

It is important to understand that compensation is usually provided only to the people who lose their land, while rehabilitation is for those too who are indirectly affected by the project. Though cash has been the most popular mode of compensation, there are various other methods to compensate the project affected people. All these modes of compensation have their own strengths and challenges. Some of these have been discussed in detail.

Cash Compensation: Cash compensation has been the most widely used mode of compensation. It has one major advantage; that is, it provides liquidity and consequent flexibility to those displaced. Once cash compensation is made, people have a freedom to move anywhere as per their choice rather than restricting themselves to the relocated sites offered by the government. Studies have shown that many people were able to prosper better as they could invest the cash along with their own savings in some trade/craft. While cash compensation offers flexibility, the case studies have shown that the way this has been executed has led to multiple problems for the affected communities. Firstly, the simple cash payment to the affected people provides them with the means to use it for consumption purposes, while discouraging a return to productive lives. Secondly, traditional cash compensation is given only to those persons whose properties the project acquires, ignoring others who lack ownership rights, although in occupation of the assets which they depend on for their living. For instance, agricultural laborers, sharecroppers, landless workers, tribal people, hunters, nomadic herders and other such people who often constitute large groups severely affected by displacement, are not entitled to compensation (Mathur, 2006). Thirdly, the amount of cash paid is not enough to enable them to purchase lands and other assets of comparable worth (Cernea 1999). Fourthly, the compensation has generally been made in instalments over a period, which prevents the affected people from moving to the new place, and resettle as quickly as possible. This defeats the very flexibility of cash compensation. Fifthly, there is a lengthy bureaucratic process involved in claiming the compensation. Lots of paperwork makes it impossible for already confused illiterate people to claim compensation. Lastly, the cash compensation becomes a problem for tribal people which had only customary rights rather than formal title on their land and who many a time do not know how to use/invest the money they received. In such situations, they are swindled by middlemen and crooks. Money is thus frittered away in ways which do not support them in reestablishment. Empirical evidence from many countries indicates that compensation in cash usually does not ensure the replacement of the lost land. Many dispossessed farmers remain landless forever. Agricultural laborers, including tenants, whose livelihood depends on being hired by landed agriculturists (who themselves get displaced), may end up relocated at sites other than those of their former employers and so are uncertain of retrieving the old, or finding new work (Parasuraman 1996). Despite these drawbacks, the projects continue to focus on cash compensation, ignoring that there are other better ways to assist those in need.

Land based Compensation: Land is another common form of compensation. Land compensation has been one of the most propagated modes of compensation especially in the projects where agricultural land has been acquired. Land, besides giving a sense of security to the displaced, helps in maintaining a kinship structure as they are resettled as a community at the new site. This may also mitigate the effect which Downing mentioned in the form of 'dissonant culture'. Studies substantiate the fact that resettlers have generally resettled well when land has been provided as compensation. As per the IFC's resettlement guidelines, 'in land-for-land compensation, it should be ensured that the new land is equivalent or superior in productive potential to the land from which people will be displaced; it should be located in reasonable proximity to land from which people will be displaced; no transaction cost such as registration fees, transfer taxes, or customary tributes must be charged; and new land should be prepared (cleared, levelled, and made accessible) for productive levels similar to those of the land from which people will be displaced' (IFC 2002:45). However, in practice, this mode of compensation has its own share of problems. *Firstly*, as productive land is already in scarcity, finding fertile land for the resettlers has been a challenging task for the government. *Secondly,* ownership disputes have occurred in many of the resettlement projects where land was given. There are case studies to prove that people did not get legal entitlements of the land even after 20 years of resettlement. As a result, land continues to be in the possession of some other people, with the allotment of land remaining in the names of the displaced only on paper. *Thirdly*, in case, the land is given at a faraway place from the original site, the very advantage of land compensation is defeated. *Fourthly,* in many projects, women are exempted from compensation of land. The payment of compensation to legal titles is intrinsically gender biased. Because land and property are mainly registered in the name of males, women are usually excluded from receiving compensation (ADB 2003: 3). Despite many problems that come with new land, it can prove to be one of the best resettlement options for people displaced from their lands in rural areas.

Job Opportunities: In most of the recent projects, jobs have been offered to the displaced along with the other modes of compensation. In most of the cases, people who get permanent jobs have better chances to resettle more quickly than those who get land. This is due to many advantages of a job as compensation such as security of income, annual increments, leave, education allowance and post retirement pension benefits. The benefit generally valued most by resettlers is wage employment, which yields a steady income flow and a sense of control over their lives. Even temporary wage-earning during project construction ensures much needed income during the transition period. But in an era of downsizing and technological innovations, with emphasis on automation reducing job opportunities, it is becoming extremely difficult to provide employment to the displaced (Hasan 2006). However, finding an adequate job is always a challenging task for the project executing agencies. The nature of the job (skilled or unskilled) makes a lot of difference. For the affected people, the government sector jobs mean a lot, not only due to a permanent source of income, but also as a status symbol (Mathur 2001, 2006b).

Apart from above mentioned modes of compensation; the project authorities have also adopted many other additional reliefs/assistances such as training for self-employment and monthly payments for a time period. This additional assistance helps the relocated people to settle in their new places more comfortably. All these modes of compensation have their own sets of limitations and challenges. However, it is the responsibility of the project executing agencies to ensure that appropriate modes of compensation are adopted keeping in mind the best interest of the affected people. The ultimate goal of any resettlement effort must be to ensure a sustainable livelihood for the displaced. A livelihood is sustainable when it can cope with and recover from shocks and stresses; sustain its capabilities and resources, without significant negative effects on the natural resource base (Chambers and Conway 1992:5). The last but most critical aspect is effective involvement of all the stakeholders (including women) in relocation planning, site selection as well as in its development. In cases where compensation packages were negotiated with project affected people and other stakeholders, the process has resulted in fewer instances of injustice and better outcomes for the resettlement process. Even where everyone may not see negotiated compensation as the most appropriate or effective option, affected people tend to feel more satisfied for having engaged in the negotiation process (Robinson 1999).

(f) Legal and Institutional Mechanism: A comprehensive legal and institutional framework is critical for any resettlement programme. In the absence of any legal and policy framework, the projects address the resettlement matters as they arose in a purely impromptu manner by promulgating instructions that were specific to the project causing displacement. This leads to an improper resettlement and consequent impoverishment of those displaced. In the 1970s when the dam construction steeped, there were no laws that specifically dealt with the resettlement issues. The focus of the prevailing laws was the acquisition of land. As far as resettlement is concerned, they restrained themselves to the payment of cash compensation that too only to those who actually lose a land or house due to acquisition. 'Lack of an official resettlement policy that defines institutional responsibilities, rights of those displaced, financing mechanisms, land acquisition, compensation, indemnification, and titling is one of the most common problems in resettlement planning' (Mejia, 1999:166). Hence, the emphasis was laid to introduce resettlement policy guidelines at the international level in order to plan and implement involuntary resettlement adequately. The first policy statement on involuntary resettlement was issued by the World Bank in 1980. Subsequently policy guidelines were issued by the Asian Development Bank (ADB), the Organisation for Economic Cooperation and Development (OECD), the International Finance Corporation (IFC) and other international development agencies. The large funding agencies persuaded and demanded that developing nations must frame their own resettlement and rehabilitation policies. These generic guidelines and tick-box approaches, however, could not ensure adequate resettlement of the affected communities leading to rising dissatisfaction among project-affected people. There have been various reasons for the same. Firstly, a legal and institutional mechanism will be effective only when good quality of personnel is hired for the implantation of the plan. As resettlement requires specialist expertise, an interdisciplinary team that includes social scientists and community development experts should be in charge of resettlement during the entire implementation phase (Mathur 2006). Besides recruiting the right persons on the job, it is also significant to train them.

(g) **Coordination:** The resettlement is a cumbersome task and cannot be handled by any single agency. The coordination with many state and non-state agencies are required to successfully carry out a resettlement plan within the decided timeframe. Some of the agencies which are directly related to the resettlement process are civil works, engineering, personnel, finance and law. Besides this, some other agencies which come to play a major role once the relocation has taken place are: health, education, agriculture, small-scale industry, social welfare and counsellors. Furthermore, it is important that all the stakeholders are actively involved in the coordination committees formed for the rehabilitation of project affected people. Although resettlement heavily depends on the close relationship of the resettlement agency with many other agencies, inter-agency coordination problems are a perennial feature in most projects. A strong coordination mechanism must also be in place to deal with the issues that arise in harmonising the activities of several agencies, each with its own exclusive sphere of activity (Mathur 2006).

(h) Resettlement Costs and Budget: There is a general tendency in large projects to overestimate the benefits and under estimate the cost of the project. The same holds true in the case of large dams. One of the reasons for this is that project cost is generally estimated in terms of cost incurred in the construction of dams and related infrastructure. The resettlement cost of the project is never estimated (same holds true about environmental and social costs of the dams). Inaccurate assessment of the costs of land acquisition, compensation, and resettlement gets the whole project into trouble at the later stage. The underestimation of resettlement costs, leading to insufficient allocation of financial resources, remains a major cause of most impoverishment that occurs amongst the displaced people (Cernea 1999).

(i) Grievance Redressal Mechanism: Involuntary resettlement itself leads to grievances among the people who have been adversely affected by the same. Hence, it becomes the responsibility of the project executing agencies that grievances, if any—such as the amount of compensation, eligibility criteria for relocation, the quality of basic amenities at the relocated sites—must be addressed as a priority. Timely redressal of grievances is important for the satisfactory implementation of resettlement and for the completion of the project as per the schedule. However trivial the grievances might appear; it is unwise to ignore them. The weak grievance redressal mechanism leaves the affected people with no other option than to seek other means for resolution of their problems (Mathur, 2006). Establishing a grievance redress mechanism is therefore in the best interests of the project itself.

(j) Role of NGOs in Resettlement Process: The critical role played by NGOs in the resettlement process is now well documented. There are two key contrasting functions that NGOs have been performing in the resettlement process. Firstly, they are acting as a pressure group on resettlement agencies so that rehabilitation is carried out in an effective manner. Secondly, they are facilitating the state by bridging the gap between government agencies and the affected people. Experience has shown that local NGOs can often provide valuable assistance and ensure viable community participation. Government agencies themselves have now become more aware of their limitations in managing resettlement. This is a task that requires live contact with the people to be resettled on an almost daily basis, and NGOs known for their closeness to the people definitely appear better suited for it. NGOs have played a useful role in reconstructing livelihoods of the affected people. The NGO presence in many project areas has made people more vocal in demanding their rightful claims (Mathur 2006). Many NGOs have proven themselves very effective in designing resettlement plans and realistic options, acceptable not only to the people but also to governments, and in mobilising the energies of the resettlers for better implementation and monitoring of those plans (Cernea 1996). The NGO involvement in resettlement operations can be particularly helpful in areas such as carrying out socio-economic surveys, facilitating the construction of housing at relocation sites, promotion of welfare activities, or the monitoring of the implementation of resettlement plans.

(k) Monitoring and Evaluation: Continuous monitoring of the project leads to early identification of issues/problems, if any, which if unresolved can lead to serious problems at the later stage. Regular monitoring provides periodic checks to ascertain whether resettlement activities are proceeding according to the plan. It provides both an information management system for project managers as well as a channel for the affected people to make known their needs and reactions to resettlement implementation. Evaluation, on the other hand, is an exercise usually undertaken towards the end of the project to assess whether the plan achieved its intended goals (Mathur 2006). The monitoring and evaluation carried out by independent/external agencies always gives a fairer view regarding the functioning and success of the settlement programme. External monitoring is often needed to periodically assess resettlement implementation and impacts, verify internal reporting, evaluate qualitative aspects of the resettlement program, and suggest adjustments to the delivery mechanisms and procedures, as required (World Bank 2004). No monitoring will be complete without the participation and feedback from the affected people. No one else can analyze the efficacy of a resettlement plan better than those who are affected by it the most.

Summing up

It was often erroneously assumed that the resettlement process ends once the affected people have been moved to the new site. It should however, be understood that the resettlement is not only relocation. In fact, this is the beginning of the most important phase in resettlement. The challenges go far beyond the mere physical relocation of the population. For the population involved, resettlement must result in a clear improvement of their living standards, because the people directly affected by a project should always be the first to benefit from it (Warren 1999). Successful resettlement takes time. At the very least, it should be implemented as a two-generation process. If success cannot be passed on by the first generation of resettlers to their children, then resettlement has failed (Scudder 1997). The process must include not only protective measures but also the provision of new rights, resources and strategies for the sustainable improvement of both subjective and objective indices (Bartolome et al. 2000:27). For resettlement to lead to the development of those resettled, the process has to address the complexities of resettlement itself and to effectively engage the full range of political and institutional actors. A positive outcome requires several enabling conditions such as a low level of displacement, resettlement as development policy with supporting legislation, a combination of land and non-land based sustainable livelihood provisions, strong community participation and accountability and commitment from government and project developers. Providing a legal framework that governs the process of displacement is important for protecting rights of affected people (WCD 2000).

The process of restoring livelihoods may require a strategy built around short-term survival and long-term adoption under different conditions, based on the existing economic pattern with a strong social base of cooperation, mutual help and self-help. It needs no further emphasis that the involuntary resettlement programme be treated as a development activity in itself, rather than as a relief or salvage operation. This requires concerted efforts to move away from the R&R package to a development strategy that could help resettlers improve, if not restore, their livelihood. Empowering people, particularly the economically and socially marginalized, by respecting their rights and ensuring that resettlement with development becomes a process governed by negotiated agreements is critical to positive resettlement and rehabilitation (Sorensen 1999).

'An unsuccessful resettlement scheme creates new inequalities by depriving the displaced only of income and wealth but also of social goods in two other ways: liberty and opportunity and social bases of respect' (Drydyk 1999: 1-8; Rawls 1971). It is therefore high time that resettlement planners do not take resettlement merely as damage control exercise intended to neutralise its more visible negative impacts.

SECTION II:

DAMS, DISPLACEMENT AND RESETTLEMENT: INTERNATIONAL PERSPECTIVE

CHAPTER 4

FORMULATION OF INTERNATIONAL STANDARDS

Since the 1950's, when dam construction started in developing countries, the biggest challenge was mobilizing the financial resources for these large projects. It was at this juncture of development that multilateral and bilateral development banks came forward by providing the much-needed assistance for large projects. The World Bank began financing large dams in the 1950s by committing an average sum of over $1 billion per year. For the period from 1970 to 1985, this amount rose to $2 billion per year. Adding in finance by the Asian, Inter-American, and African Development Banks, as well as bilateral funding for hydropower, suggests that the total financing for large dams from these sources was more than $4 billion annually at the peak of lending during the period 1975-84. The total investment in dams by the multilaterals and bilateral processes is approximately $125 billion (WCD 2000:194). These agencies not only provided finances but also provided technical assistance to conduct feasibility studies, and to create institutional frameworks to plan and execute these projects.

However, in the late 1980s and early 1990s, these funding agencies started facing increasing public scrutiny and criticism from the civil society organizations. The growing controversy over Bank funded projects and criticism of these projects at a grassroot level led to the commissioning of the first independent review of the World Bank in 1992. In June 1994, 326 activist groups and NGO coalitions from 44 countries signed the Manibeli Declaration which called for a moratorium on World Bank funded large dams until a comprehensive, independent review of all Bank funded dam projects had been conducted. It was followed by the report of the World Bank's Operations Evaluation Department (See OED 1996), an internal review of the performance and impacts of a sample of 50 Bank funded large dams. The desk study observed that 90 percent of dams reviewed met the Bank's standards for resettlement at the time they were built, but 75 percent failed to meet the Bank's latest standards.

By the late 1990s, it was becoming clear that the cost of controversy could seriously affect future prospects for dams and stall efforts to finance other non-dam water and energy development projects. By 1997, suspicion and mistrust between proponents and critics of large dams threatened to dominate and undermine the wider discussion needed to reach agreements on ways to improve access to water and energy services. One such major resistance was in the case of Word Bank funding in the Sardar Sarovar Project in India. The criticism was not only for improper execution of resettlement plans in World Bank funded large infrastructure projects but also due to growing recognition of the severity of the social and environmental impacts of dams. It was felt that there was a need to have a policy guideline to protect the rights of internally displaced persons (IDPs) due to these large dams.

The forced displacement as a violation of human rights has been implicitly mentioned in many of the documents of international human rights law such as the International Bill of Rights. The Universal Declaration of Human Rights (1948) proscribes arbitrary interference with an individual's home (Article 12) and depriving people arbitrarily of property (Article 17). The International Covenant on Civil and Political Rights (ICCPR 1966) and the International Covenant on Economic, Social and Cultural Rights (ICESCR 1966), though are general in scope, apply to Internally Displaced Persons (IDPs). Both instruments contain guarantees of rights implicated in any situation of displacement, such as an individual's right to an adequate standard of living and the sanctity of the family unit. While the ICCPR provides that citizens shall have freedom of movement and choice of residence, the ICESCR provides for the right to education and the right to work. Both these documents permit limitations to these rights only in a very specific number of situations (Gross 2009). Despite various international instruments implicitly referring to the rights of IDPs as well, international instruments have not adequately protected IDPs. In the absence of binding law to specifically protect IDPs, national and international bodies have had difficulty determining which human rights guarantees apply to IDPs and how to apply them effectively (Price 2009). In response to this mounting pressure, the World Bank issued its first policy on involuntary resettlement in 1980.

Another major effort in this direction was made in 1998 when the United Nations Guiding Principles on Internal Displacement came into existence. These principles recognized IDPs as a population distinct from traditional refugees and sought to apply some of the protections of international instruments to IDPs. It provided protection for displaced persons and sought to avoid displacement altogether. The Guiding Principles address the proper treatment of IDPs at all the stages of displacement, these are: protection against displacement; protection during displacement; provision of humanitarian assistance; and protection during return, resettlement, and reintegration. The close relationship between the Guiding Principles and existing international law allowed the Guiding Principles to serve an indicative function (Lavoyer 1998). The Guiding Principles also provided a proportionality test for determining the acceptability of the displacements in development projects. According to the Principle 6(2)(c), the project must meet the 'requirements of necessity and proportionality' to show 'compelling or overriding public interests' (UNHCR 1998). Although the Guiding Principles were not binding international law, both states and non-state actors widely respected them. It is, however, considered a weak document as it allows displacement resulting from large development projects if the projects provide sufficient benefits for the public (Gross 2009). It was followed by a comprehensive policy on involuntary resettlement by the World Bank in 1996.

Considering the World Bank policy guidelines as a 'good practice' model, many other international agencies, including the Asian Development Bank (ADB), the Organization for Economic Cooperation and Development (OECD) and International Finance Corporation (IFC) also formulated their own resettlement policies. This chapter has analyzed the resettlement policies of some of these agencies in detail.

World Bank

The World Bank is the greatest single source of funds for large dam construction, having provided more than US$ 50 billion for construction of more than 500 large dams in 92 countries by the year 1996. The World Bank has been directly or indirectly associated with around 10 percent of large dams in developing countries. In the period from 1986 to 1993, involuntary resettlement was a part of 192 projects, displacing a total of 2.5 million people over the life of those projects (World Bank 1996a:20). From 1990 to 2010, a total of 1,423 projects were approved by the Bank, with 431 closed projects, 747 active projects, and 245 projects in the pipeline. The increasing trend is not only in absolute numbers, but also in the percentage of projects with involuntary resettlement in relation to the overall Bank portfolio (World Bank 2012). According to the World Bank's estimate (1993), around 10 million people are displaced annually because of dam construction and urban infrastructural projects.

The World Bank issued its first policy on involuntary resettlement in 1980. The purpose of this policy was to provide broad guidelines to its own staff to look after the interests of displaced people at the project site. The guidelines conceived displaced people as a group temporarily victimized by development and therefore, to be provided with specific measures recognizing their losses and the significance of their socio-cultural milieu due to involuntary resettlement (Price 2009). The first standard Operational Manual Statement 2.33 of the World Bank, 'Social Issues Associated with Involuntary Resettlement in Bank-Financed Projects' (1980), later became its Operational Policy 4.12 on Involuntary Resettlement in 2001. In 2016 (taking effect in 2018), it was transformed into the 'Environmental and Social Standard 5: Land Acquisition, Restrictions on Land Use and Involuntary Resettlement'. These subsequent modifications in the policy required all displacement to be conceived and executed as development programmes with time-bound action plans detailing how those displaced would be provided with adequate investment resources and opportunities to share in the project benefits (World Bank 2001: paragraph 2). According to this policy, 'involuntary resettlement may cause severe long-term hardship, impoverishment, and environmental damage unless appropriate measures are carefully planned and carried out.' For these reasons, the basic elements of the Bank's resettlement policy have been:

- Involuntary displacement should be avoided or minimized whenever possible, because of its disruptive and impoverishing effects.
- Where displacement is unavoidable, the objective of Bank policy is to assist displaced persons in their efforts to improve, or at least restore, former living standards and earning capacity.
- Displaced persons should be: (i) compensated for their losses at replacement cost, (ii) given opportunities to share in project benefits, and (iii) assisted in the transfer and in the transition period at the relocation site.
- Moving people in groups can cushion disruptions. Minimizing the distance between departure and relocation sites can facilitate the resettlers' adaptation to the new socio-cultural and natural environments. The trade-offs between distance and economic opportunities must be balanced carefully.
- Resettlers' and hosts' participation in planning resettlement should be promoted. The prevailing social and cultural institutions of those resettled as well as the host communities should be taken into consideration while carrying out the transfer and reestablishment process.

- New communities of resettlers should be designed as viable settlement systems equipped with infrastructure and services, able to integrate in the regional socio-economic context.
- Host communities that receive resettlers should be assisted to overcome possible adverse social and environmental effects from increased population density.
- While the Bank's policy is to ensure the pre-project living conditions for the displaced people, the emphasis is to extend protection to vulnerable sections whose hardships are often overlooked. In particular, such groups include: (i) persons losing assets who are not eligible for compensation for want of formal title; (ii) persons not losing assets but losing access to income generating opportunities, notably wages, sales, rent, etc. and (iii) persons compensated for assets but unable to restore incomes because opportunities to replace assets or economic alternatives are either not available or not attainable.

Although the World Bank policy lacks legal enforceability, as a major funding agency, the World Bank has enough leverage to ensure that resettlement is carried out by borrowers in accordance with its own resettlement policy. It is significant to mention here that the adoption of involuntary resettlement policy in the World Bank was not as smooth and easy as it seems. Social scientists including the initiator of the Bank's resettlement policy, Michael Cernea, had a hard time convincing the Bank on social costs of large projects. The policy was often attacked on the ground that the costs of compliance with this policy will increase the costs of doing Bank business (Likosky 2005). Anthropologists and other social science advocates within the World Bank took a cue from the available case studies enumerating displacement disasters to formulate guidelines for the Bank's operational manual.

Though the formulation of a resettlement policy was a great leap forward, the real challenge lies in the implementation. Mathur (2015), through his study on Bank funded projects, realized that the World Bank, often in a hurry to disburse loans, regardless of their social and economic consequences, soon began ignoring, project after project, compliance with its own resettlement standards, and as a result, an otherwise well-meant resettlement policy has achieved much less than it initially promised. The biggest example of this has been the Sardar Sarovar dam in India which generated a lot of controversy due to the wide performance gap between the policy guidelines and their compliance. The borrowing agencies have also shown their casual approach as far as compliance to the resettlement norms prescribed by the World Bank has been concerned. It is mainly because the minimum resettlement standards set in the World Bank policy are on a higher side than those in the national laws (Price 2008).

Subsequent refinements of the World Bank's policy on involuntary resettlement though used a stronger wording than the earlier formulation, the bottom-line objective still remained 'at least restore', not 'must improve', the economic and social base of those displaced (Price 2009). The Operations Evaluation Department (OED) of the Bank itself found that income restoration was the weakest part of planning and the results have been the least satisfactory so far. Many critics have asserted that the World Bank's policy, OP 4.12 adopted in 2001 is weaker in comparison to its predecessor (OP 4.30). The new policy has been criticized as formalizing a structure and process that potentially violates human rights (Downing 2002a; Goodland 2007). Despite the World Bank's previous operational policy considered involuntary resettlements as development programmes in their own right, in reality the World Bank hardly lived up to its own prescription. The revised version, however, omitted this definition completely, leaving no scope for further discussion (Downing 2002a).

The revision of the World Bank's Environmental and Social Framework (2014) has also been criticized by social scientists and civil society organizations. The Bank has been accused of weakening land rights protection for poor and vulnerable communities. In a joint statement of more than 100 civil society organizations in 2014, the World Bank was criticized for: (1) providing an 'opt-out' clause on safeguards for indigenous people; (2) diluting involuntary resettlement policy; (3) excluding land administration projects from resettlement safeguards; and (4) providing insufficient protection to farmers, pastoralists, and indigenous people against land grabbing (Inclusive Development International 2014). Indeed, the safeguards seem to be at odds with the spirit of the 'Voluntary Guidelines on the Responsible Governance of Tenure of Land, Forest and Fisheries' (2012). The guidelines developed under the leadership of the Food and Agricultural Organization and officially endorsed by the Committee on World Food Security have been considered as a major milestone in the effort to contain the global land rush, as they emphasize the need to respect customary land rights and invoke human rights principles of protecting vulnerable and marginalized groups against dispossession and displacement (Brüntrup et al. 2014). Some observers believe that the World Bank's attempt to exonerate itself from its obligations to people at risk of displacement and resettlement, and to give its borrowers more discretionary power in dealing with the displaced, is a reflection of its aim to enhance funding of private and public mega-projects and a response to growing competition from newly emerging lenders and private investors not tied to safeguard regimes (Pred 2014; Connell 2015).

Despite the gaps, the World Bank resettlement policy has indeed played a significant role in improving resettlement outcomes overall (Mathur 2015). The adoption of this policy changed the Bank's operational approaches and public response about population displacement and cast it into a new conceptual framework (Cernea 1996).

Asian Development Bank

Similar to that of the World Bank's policy on involuntary resettlement, the Asian Development Bank's (ADB) Policy on Involuntary Resettlement was adopted in 1995 and became operational in January 1996. The Policy required that involuntary resettlement be an integral part of project design, dealt with from the earliest stages of the project cycle. The policy aimed to avoid involuntary resettlement wherever feasible and to minimize resettlement where population displacement is unavoidable by exploring all viable project options. It further provided that if, nonetheless, individuals or communities must lose their land, means of livelihood, social support systems, or way of life they should be (ADB 1995):

- Compensated for lost assets, loss of income and livelihood;
- Assisted for relocation;
- Assisted so that their economic and social future will generally be at least as favorable with the project as without it;
- Provided with appropriate land, housing, infrastructure, and other compensation, comparable to the without-project situation;
- Fully informed and closely consulted on various alternatives of resettlement and compensation.

The Policy also specified that lack of formal legal title to land is not a bar to compensation and other assistance. This may apply to a range of people affected, e.g., informal dwellers, land users with traditional or customary rights, squatters or those with adverse possession rights but no formal legal title to land and assets.

The ADB's original Policy on Involuntary Resettlement (ADB 1995: Paragraph 33) had similar wording to that of the World Bank, requiring that 'displaced people receive assistance [...] so that they would be at least as well-off as they would have been in the absence of the project'. Only in the case of the poorest affected persons did ADB's policy specifically require improvements, in paying 'particular attention [...] to the needs of the poorest affected persons including those without legal title to assets, female-headed households and other vulnerable groups, such as indigenous peoples' (ADB 1995: Paragraph 34). This policy was superseded by the Safeguard Policy Statement (SPS) approved by the Board of Directors of ADB in 2009 (came into effect in 2010). The key policy principles of the Safeguard Policy Statement (ADB 2009:17) are:

1. Screen the project early on to identify past, present, and future involuntary resettlement impacts and risks.
2. Carry out meaningful consultations with affected persons, host communities, and concerned nongovernment organizations. Pay particular attention to the needs of vulnerable groups, especially those below the poverty line, the landless, the elderly, women and children, and indigenous peoples, and those without legal title to land, and ensure their participation in consultations.
3. Improve, or at least restore, the livelihoods of all displaced persons through land-based resettlement strategies, cash compensation, replacement of assets, and additional revenues and services through benefit sharing schemes where possible.
4. Provide physically and economically displaced persons with needed assistance.
5. Improve the standards of living of the displaced poor and other vulnerable groups, including women, to at least national minimum standards.
6. Develop procedures in a transparent, consistent, and equitable manner to ensure that those people who enter into negotiated settlements will maintain the same or better income and livelihood status.
7. Ensure that displaced persons without titles to land or any recognizable legal rights to land are eligible for resettlement assistance and compensation for loss of nonland assets.
8. Prepare a resettlement plan elaborating on displaced persons' entitlements, the income and livelihood restoration strategy, institutional arrangements, monitoring and reporting framework, budget, and time-bound implementation schedule.
9. Conceive and execute involuntary resettlement as part of a development project or program. Include the full costs of resettlement in the presentation of the project's costs and benefits.

Though the ADB's Safeguard Policy Update (ADB 2009:17) contains similar wording as of its 1996 policy, 'to enhance, or at least restore, the livelihoods of all displaced persons in real terms relative to pre-project levels; and to improve the standards of living of the displaced poor and other vulnerable groups', it has certain noteworthy additions to the earlier document. *Firstly*, it consolidated three previous safeguard policies (environment, involuntary resettlement, indigenous peoples) within one policy framework. *Secondly*, a new section was added describing the conditions, procedures and processes for the use of country systems in ADB supported projects. *Thirdly*, it explicitly mentions the strengthening of borrowers and/or clients' safeguard systems and developing their capacity to manage environmental and social risks. *Fourthly*, it mandates a requirement for a final resettlement plan based on detailed design and semi-annual monitoring for all social safeguards.

Despite being a comprehensive policy, it has been criticized by experts for not incorporating additional social dimensions such as core labor standards or gender as explicit safeguard policies, as some other multilateral financial institutions have done (Brubaker and Linda 2018). Many social scientists believe that the revised Safeguard Policy Statement is a major dilution of ADB's involuntary resettlement policy. The revised policy has the same faulty economic assumptions that Cernea (2003) and others (Picciotto et al. 2001) have been criticizing for years. Downing (2002a) and Scudder (2005) stated that this policy will generate rather than reduce poverty in the projects funded by ADB.

International Finance Corporation

The International Finance Corporation was founded in 1956 as the World Bank Group's private sector investment arm. Its purpose is to promote economic growth by providing sustainable private sector development in developing member countries. The IFC had initially declined to follow the World Bank's policy on resettlement. A major anthropological evaluation study by Downing (1996) revealed a displacement disaster in IFC's Bio Dam project in Chile which resulted in a disastrous, and unmitigated, impact on the indigenous people (Price 2009). The World Bank's involuntary resettlement policy principles were adopted by ten major investment banks with the adoption of the Equator Principles in 2003 (Price 2009). These Principles have been based on the IFC's environmental and social safeguard performance standards, including on involuntary resettlement. This is a voluntary code that depends on the commitment and transparency of each signatory financial institution (Oliver-Smith 2009). The standards have been periodically updated and are known as the International Finance Corporation Performance Standards on social and environmental sustainability and on the World Bank Group Environmental, Health, and Safety Guidelines. The latest revision of the Equator Principles was in July 2020. The IFC also developed a Performance Standard for Land Acquisition and Involuntary Resettlement in 2006. The IFC's basic principles for addressing the adverse effects of involuntary resettlement associated with its investment projects have lots of similarity with the principles declared by the World Bank (IFC 2002: 30-31). Such as:

- Involuntary resettlement should be avoided.
- Where involuntary resettlement is unavoidable, all people affected by it should be compensated fully and fairly for lost assets.
- Involuntary resettlement should be conceived as an opportunity for improving the livelihoods of the affected people and undertaken accordingly.
- All people affected by involuntary resettlement should be consulted and involved in resettlement planning to ensure that the mitigation of adverse effects as well as the benefits of resettlement are appropriate and sustainable.

It further provides that:

- The involuntary resettlement policy applies under all conditions of potential physical or economic displacement resulting from the acquisition or use of land for a project regardless of the total number of people affected or the significance/severity of anticipated impact.
- For land-based resettlement, the IFC Handbook recommends that new land should be (a) equivalent or superior in productive potential to the land from which people will be displaced; (b) located in reasonable proximity to land from which people will be displaced; (c) provided free of any 'transaction costs' such as registration fees, transfer taxes, or customary tributes; (d) prepared (cleared, levelled, and made accessible) for productive levels similar to those of the land from which people will be displaced.
- The client will take possession of acquired land and related assets only after compensation has been made available and, where applicable, resettlement sites and moving allowances have been provided to the displaced persons in addition to compensation (Paragraph 9 of IFC Performance Standard-5). It further requires that any loss of asset is compensated at full replacement cost, and that

assistance to help displaced persons to become re-established is provided.

IFC further provided eight Performance Standards on Environmental and Social Sustainability (2012) that the client is to meet throughout the life of an investment by IFC: Assessment and Management of Environmental and Social Risks and Impacts; Labour and Working Conditions; Resource Efficiency and Pollution Prevention; Community Health, Safety, and Security; Land Acquisition and Involuntary Resettlement; Biodiversity Conservation and Sustainable Management of Living Natural Resources; Indigenous Peoples; and Cultural Heritage. These eight Performance Standards establish standards. They aimed to achieve positive development outcomes and have been the reference point for many large-scale projects, irrespective of whether they have IFC funding or not. The IFC Performance Standards (sometimes together with the Equator Principles) have been widely accepted by industry as being the 'gold standard' for social and environmental performance (Reddy et al. 2015; Lambert 2015). These standards have also been widely accepted by many large consulting firms, corporations and industry bodies as a voluntary standard or benchmark they apply internally or acknowledge that it will be the standard external stakeholders use to evaluate them. Though IFC Performance Standards are reasonably aligned with human rights expectations, to be human rights compliant, they have to be regarded as the basic minimum requirement (Ploeg and Vanclay 2017a).

The Compliance Advisor Ombudsman of IFC examined the impact and effectiveness of the IFC's Safeguard Policies three years after their specific adoption by the Board (IFC 2003). The report argues that it is not the existence of the minimum standards that puts a brake on business in most cases, but the cumbersome way in which the standards are sometimes implemented. It further reported that the accountabilities that exist within IFC to date do not reinforce the message from the top that the Safeguard Policies and their values are everybody's business, regardless of whether they are a staff or manager's function. It asserts that for a development bank, environmental and social performance matter as much as financial rate of return. The conclusions of this study suggest the next step for IFC by stating that for the Safeguard Policies to maximize their potential as standard setters and multipliers, for them to make a real difference on the ground in the way they are applied, the institution must move towards accountability for performance, not just process compliance.

Organisation for Economic Cooperation and Development

Founded in 1961, the Organisation for Economic Cooperation and Development (OECD) is an intergovernmental economic organization with 38 member countries. Its primary purpose is to stimulate economic progress and world trade. The Development Assistance Committee of the Organisation for Economic Cooperation and Development (OECD-DAC) has been producing guidelines on development-related topics over several decades. The OECD Guidelines for Multinational Enterprises (original 1976, current 2011) provided recommendations on responsible business conduct and voluntary principles on topics such as employment and industrial relations, human rights, environment, information disclosure, combating bribery, consumer interests, science and technology, competition, and taxation (OECD 2011). However, they have been silent on matters such as land acquisition, resettlement, expropriation, and fair compensation. In 1992, for the World Conference on Environment and Development in Rio de Janeiro, the OECD-DAC prepared a series of guidelines related to aid and the environment. The third guideline in that series, Guidelines for Aid Agencies on Involuntary Displacement and Resettlement in Development Projects (OECD-DAC, 1992), intended to assist project developers to ensure that the population displaced by a project received benefits and were properly re-established (Vanclay 2017b). According to the guidelines, the primary objective of adopting policy guidelines for resettlement activities was to ensure that project designers and implementers follow the best practices in such situations so that the population displaced by a project receives benefits from it and are re-established on a sound productive basis. It further elaborated certain principles of resettlement planning (OECD-DAC 1992:6-7):

- Involuntary population displacement should be avoided or minimized whenever possible by exploring all viable alternative project designs. In every case, the alternative to refrain from carrying out the project (the ‘non-action’ alternative) should seriously be considered, and people’s needs and environmental protection must be given due weight in the decision-making process.
- Where displacement is unavoidable, resettlement plans should be formulated with due care given to peoples' needs and to environmental protection.
- All involuntary resettlement should be conceived and executed as development programmes, providing sufficient investment resources and opportunities for resettlers to share in project benefits.

- Displaced persons should be (i) enabled to reconstruct a land-based or employment-based productive existence; (ii) compensated for their losses at replacement cost; (iii) assisted with the move and during the transition period at the relocation site; and (iv) assisted in their efforts to improve their former living standards, income earning capacity, and production levels, or at least to restore them.
- Participation by environmental agencies and community participation in planning and implementing resettlement is essential and should include women.
- Host communities that accept resettlers should be involved in the planning process and assisted to overcome possible adverse socio-environmental consequences from the resettlement.
- Indigenous groups, ethnic minorities, and pastoralists who may have informal customary rights to the land or other resources taken for the project must be provided with adequate land, infrastructure, and other compensation. The absence of legal title to land by such groups should not be a bar to compensation.
- Since women are, to a great extent, responsible for making the natural resource base productive (with their knowledge, skills, and labor) and thereby contribute significantly to the well-being of their families, communities and national economies, planning for relocation should consider their preferences and should address their specific needs and constraints.
- The implementation of the resettlement plan is to be effectively supervised.

It further emphasized the involvement of non-governmental organizations (NGOs) in planning, implementing, and monitoring resettlement and the importance of socio-economic survey. The guidelines specifically mention that cash compensation alone should generally be avoided, except in well justified instances, as it typically leads to impoverishment. The guidelines have largely been consistent with the standards of the World Bank and IFC Performance Standards and therefore have been somewhat percipient.

Summing Up

Following the footsteps of the World Bank, the African Development Bank Group (AFDB) approved an Integrated Safeguards System in 2013 with a consolidated Policy statement and five operational safeguards. The European Bank for Reconstruction and Development (EBRD) approved an integrated Environmental and Social Policy with ten Performance

Requirements in 2014, which bears some resemblance to IFC's policy architecture. The new Asian Infrastructure Investment Bank (AIIB) approved its Environmental and Social Framework in 2016 with a consolidated policy, i.e., Environmental and Social Policy and three Environmental and Social Standards (Brubaker and Linda 2018). The Inter-American Development Bank (IDB) has five safeguard policies: Environmental and Safeguards Compliance Policy; Natural Disaster Risk Management Policy; Involuntary Resettlement Operational Policy; Operational Policy on Gender in Development; and Operational Policy on Indigenous Peoples.

The emerging transnational efforts of international financial institutions to promote accountability has created new openings for local perspectives. Social researchers, barely acknowledged a decade ago, have found a place in these organizations. Participation is now acknowledged as an integral part of resettlement planning even though local procedures may favor restricted use of simple questionnaires. Grievance redressal mechanisms have been put in place. Independent monitoring panels have been established. These international policy standards have persuaded various national governments to supplement their national laws, especially for those projects using international financing. The focus of planning has moved beyond compensation to restoration or improvement of the economic and social base of those displaced (Price 2009).

While it is generally agreed that the adoption of a policy is an important step forward, experience indicates that compliance with the policy often remains problematic (Likosky 2005). World Commission on Dams (WCD) in its report (2000:188):

> *Despite these changes, the banks' policies, like the national regulatory systems, are more concerned with project planning, design and financial management than with options assessment or with the operational phase of a large dam project. In addition, they have paid more attention to monitoring the planning and construction phases than the operation of the project, which is often left to national governments. Post-implementation monitoring is generally discontinued at most five years after project commissioning. Even then, the main focus has been on comparing the project proposals with the project outcome. Weak treatment of social and environmental impacts at appraisal leads to weak assessments of outcomes at evaluation*

'Indifference about the extent and seriousness of the impoverishment effects on the tens of millions of displaced people led to a "business-as-usual" approach, which prevailed because of the powerlessness and marginalized position of these people' (Scudder 2005). One blatant example of such indifference of the international financing agencies towards the resettlement is visible from their non-acceptance to the WCD report. WCD, after carrying out the social, environmental, and economic consequences assessment of options and institutional processes in 150 dam projects, published a Report on Strategic Priorities, Criteria and Guidelines (2000). Though the report was not officially binding, the actual test of the Report's worth was its potential acceptance by global funding agencies such as the World Bank. However, despite an initial warm response and commendation of the Strategic Priorities, the report and its Guidelines never got legally adopted by the World Bank (Dubash et al. 2001; Fujikura and Nakayama 2009). In fact, after deferring the construction of mega dam projects for a decade, the World Bank, in its 2003 water strategy paper, showed its intent to resume funding of large dams (Goodland 2007). The Asian Development Bank never wholly recognized the WCD Report (Dubash et al. 2001). It, furthermore, publicly released a gap analysis comparing the Report against its own involuntary resettlement policy (ADB 2002). The big resettlement nations such as China and India swiftly rejected the Report (McDonald and Webber 2010).

Even if international financial institutions are present, it is now evident that they cannot compensate for the absence of essential legal frameworks, lack of transparency, cumbersome bureaucratic procedures, lack of commitment to funding, little or no institutional capacity, and, above all, absence of political will and commitment to the principles of equity and justice in the project executing country (Jayewardene 2008). Moreover, projects financed by international financiers may use international standards, but a huge number of nationally financed projects continue to operate on the old laws and regulations. For a vast number of projects not financed by international financiers, the national legal frameworks apply (Price 2009). This calls for reform of the policy principles that apply not just to international policy standards for involuntary resettlement, but also to the national legal and regulatory frameworks through which they are implemented (Price 2008).

CHAPTER 5

RESETTLEMENT EXPERIENCES OF SOME CONTROVERSIAL HYDROELECTRIC PROJECTS: ASWAN, THREE GORGES, ILISU AND BELO MONTE

Discussing the dams from a human rights perspective is not an easy job. There are various reasons for this. One of the most prominent reasons has been that there have been contrasting perceptions regarding the feasibility of these projects as well as its impact on the displaced community and the ecosystem. On the one hand, there are reports of the state sponsored agencies, supported by various studies, which not only justify the construction of these dams but also over emphasize the achievements of these projects. There are project specific reports which show that many of these projects could achieve their predetermined targets of electricity generation, irrigation as well as control of floods and droughts. These reports further highlight specific achievements of certain projects in improving the living standards of the resettled people as well as in the overall growth of the region. On the other hand, there are reports from non-state agencies which showcase how these hydroelectric projects have wreaked havoc on the local ecosystem as well as on the life of those displaced due to these projects. For instance, WCD's report drew the conclusion that 40-80 million estimated Global Dam resettlers have rarely had their livelihoods restored let alone improved (WCD 2000: 129). Some assessments are potentially biased by politics and such bias tends to lead to inappropriate assessment methodologies and, subsequently, to erroneous conclusions. In this chapter, effort has been made to present a balanced view about the benefits as well as the social and ecological consequences of some most controversial hydroelectric projects across the world.

The objective of discussing these case studies is not to provide a comprehensive bibliography of pro-dam or anti-dam studies, but to highlight the acrimony of the debate and the existence of highly polarised positions, even among those who claim to be providing disinterested scientific analysis. These case studies show that though there are wide variations across the countries as far as resettlement policy framework and its implementation is concerned, there are commonalities cutting across projects and regions. The sequence on the basis of which case studies have been presented here is the years of construction, to ascertain whether there has been any shift in policy as well as the process of resettlement with the changing time.

Sr. No.	Name of Dam	No. of Resettled people (approx.)	Years of Construction
1.	Aswan High Dam (Egypt)	100,000	1963 -1969
2.	Three Gorges Dam (China)	1,200,000	1994-2003
3.	Ilisu Dam (Turkey)	78,000	2006-2018
4.	Belo Monte Dam (Brazil)	20,000	2011-2020

Aswan High Dam (Egypt)

Egypt is called the gift of Nile because the river Nile has been the lifeline of the otherwise rainless Egypt, lying in arid and semi-arid zones. The river has sustained Egypt as well as its neighbouring states by being a source of transport, commerce and irrigation. The first Dam to harness the river was constructed in 1889. The height of the dam was raised twice in 1912 and 1933. However, the dam was not able to fulfil the requirements of Egypt in the later years. The population of Egypt increased by 96 per cent in the 50 years between 1897 and 1947. On the other hand, the increase of croplands during the same period, by conversion from basin irrigation to perennial irrigation, was only 36 per cent. As a consequence, the per capita area of farmland declined by 33 per cent during this period (Shibl 1971). The expansion of the production base for agriculture in order to cope with the increasing population therefore had the highest priority for Egypt. This led to the conception of the Aswan High Dam.

Geographical and Historical Context

Though the initial feasibility studies of the Aswan High Dam were carried out in the late 1940s, the project has been controversial since the very inception of the idea of this multipurpose project. The dam is closely linked with the political aspirations of Egyptian leader Gamal Abdel Nasser who, in the 1950s, intended to build a dam on the river Nile to generate electricity as well as to control annual flooding. Nasser's much-quoted dictum (1958) declares:

> *For thousands of years the Great Pyramids of Egypt were foremost among the engineering marvels of the world. They ensured life after death to the Pharaohs. Tomorrow, the gigantic High Dam, more significant and seventeen times greater than the Pyramids, will provide a higher standard of living for all Egyptians* (Joesten, 1960:59).

The project was initially proposed to be financed by the United States and Britain, however, due to Suez Canal controversy and changed diplomatic relations between Egypt and the USSR, the project was finally started with financial and technical assistance of the USSR. The construction process of the Aswan High Dam was carried out between 1960 to 1970. After the sudden demise of President Nasser in 1970, the reservoir created under the project was named Lake Nasser.

The dam is located at the border between Egypt and Sudan. The dam is 4.8 kilometres wide, and 100 meters high, and around 57 million cubic yards of earth and rock were used to construct the dam. With a length of 563 kilometres and a width of 64 kilometres, Lake Nasser is considered as one of the largest man-made lakes in the world. It is a multipurpose project built to ensure hydro power, sustainable irrigation, secure food production and to improve the standard of living. Its hydropower station capacity is 10^9 kWh per year. The Dam is known as the 'High' Dam to distinguish it from the lower Aswan Dam which was built by the British in 1902. The High Dam is more than twice the length of the old Aswan Dam. 10 million Egyptian Pounds was an estimated cost of the project. This included compensation, transportation, construction of homes and the initial payment to the farmers for their resettlement as well as the cost of construction of new canal and electrical installations. Another 15 million Egyptian Pounds was paid to the Sudan government as compensation for the forced removal of their people as a result of flooding (Beddis 1963).

Displacement and Resettlement

As the Dam had the political support of the Egyptian government, all the efforts were made to carry out the project including resettlement in an effective manner. A national level body named the 'Aswan High Dam Ministry' was created to take care of the project. The Aswan project was made an integral part of the Aswan Province's programme of economic development, this meant greater government commitment to the project, with resulting greater availability of funds and therefore of recruited staff—which meant that the line ministries did not have to take on a huge new task with existing staff complements (de Wet 2000). Therefore, though the financing of the project was shared by several government departments, each with their own responsibility, and overall coordination and responsibility was with the office of the Governor of Aswan Province. The recruited personnel were given significant salary increments to keep them motivated (Fahim 1983).

Around 100,000 local inhabitants known as Nubians residing along the stretch of the Nile River were displaced. These Nubians were primarily settled cultivators and pastoralists. The Nubians have been relocated four times in less than a century. Firstly (in 1902), during the construction of the first Aswan Dam, and twice again (in 1912 and 1933) on account of increasing the height of the dam, and finally (in 1963) as a consequence of the building of the Aswan High Dam (Dafallah 1975). Initially 40,000 feddans (roughly equivalent to acres) of land was set aside to resettle the displaced persons in other parts of Egypt: Kom Ombo, Esna, Radissieh, Dar el-Salam, and Bayadieh (Joesten 1960). A comprehensive plan was prepared for the movement and the resettlement. People's participation was ensured while preparing the resettlement plan and the villagers were told the purpose of the move and were taken into confidence while making arrangements for their livelihoods. Some 25,000 houses were built in 33 villages which were given the same names as the old Nubian villages. The villages were built in the same order as beforehand (Zeid and Shibini 1997). To maintain their social set up, people were allowed to move as communities. The government arranged the transportation of animals and the possessions of the people getting displaced (Beddis 1963). However, the resettlement was not smooth in the initial phase. During the first relocation campaign, there was a delay in construction of the houses which inconvenienced the resettlers (Grimm 1991; Fahim 1983).

A combination of cash and kind was adopted for the compensation for houses. It included a house for the displaced as well as cash to facilitate the resettlers in improving their houses (Fahim, 1983). However, delays in the compensation at Aswan were recorded in various studies. Fahim (1981) stated that at Aswan, by 1979 (15 years after relocation), only 60 percent of resettlers had received available land; Fernea (1998:7) identified that to this day, Nubians still cannot get titles for their land or houses. Though people were compensated for crops in their old fields, customary ownership issues were raised while compensating for land. As stated by Murdock (1989:60):

> *...in the case of Aswan at New Halfa, the government did not compensate the Arab pastoralists coming on to the scheme (other than giving them a tenancy on the scheme) as it felt it did not owe them anything as their lands had not been individually registered and by implication were state property. By contrast, the Nubians coming onto the scheme, who had owned freehold land before resettlement, were given not only houses and tenancies on scheme, but double the hectare they had previously held*

As Nubian landowners received larger tenancies than former laborers (Fahim 1983), the compensation scheme reinforced inequity already existing in Nubian society. Similar differentiation was witnessed between men and women and between settlers and hosts.

The Egyptian government resettled many in 'New Nubia', north of Aswan, providing education, healthcare, and land, requiring them to raise sugar cane, an unfamiliar crop. For Nubians, it was an alien environment too far from the Nile. Though efforts were made to identify areas where the climate and general living conditions were similar to those of Nubia, the Nubinas lost their ancestral land and their social fabric based on joint ownership of waterwheels and palm trees. Many Nubians also found their new houses lacking aesthetically and tried to decorate them with traditional Nubian motifs (Fekri 2007).

Sudan moved its Nubians to settlements near Khashm el Girba. They received community services and leased land, and were directed to raise cotton and peanuts. Herding nomads who already used the land resented the intrusion. Many Nubians avoided resettlement areas, seeking city jobs (Donald 2000). Others refused to leave Nubia, or returned to their Homeland and established villages on the shores of lake Nasser (Walton 1981).

Economic and Social Impacts

Agriculture: Increased agricultural productivity was one of the core objectives of constructing the Aswan High Dam. Prof. Ragaei El Mallakh, in 1959, very enthusiastically stated that the dam would serve agriculture by providing cheap electricity for irrigation and drainage pumps. This would: increase production, cut down production costs and release dairy animals from farm work and thus raise their meat and milk production. As predicted, the dam enabled Egypt to shift from basin irrigation (one crop per year) to perennial irrigation (two or more crops per year). The cropping area has risen to about 14.0 million acres compared with about 9.3 million acres in 1952. Around 2.5 million acres of land were transformed from seasonal to year-round irrigation. They were now no longer dependent on the yearly flooding of the Nile (Walton 1981). Higher yields and production led to an improvement in the living standards of the people. In addition, about 100,000 acres of desert land was reclaimed for cultivation. Despite some problems in irrigation agriculture, with better irrigation facilities, the land became more productive and due to multi cropping, the tenants were able to produce crops for their own consumption as well as for sale (Fernea 1998:4,8). Despite these advantages, a few studies (Beddis, 1963; Zeid & Shibini, 1997; Nakayama & Fujikura, 2001) pointed out that there has been a gradual decrease in the fertility of agricultural lands in the Nile delta, which used to benefit from the millions of tons of silt deposited annually by the Nile floods.

Job opportunities: Though the agricultural scheme itself was a source of job-creation and a growth-point (Murdock 1989), besides the tenancy under the scheme, the Arab pastoralists continued to maintain their herds off-scheme (Sorbo 1985). This made the scheme viable for them and enabled them to continue a settled existence on the Scheme, thus also benefiting from improved commercial, social and educational services (Sorbo 1985). Similarly, in the Kom Ombo Scheme, the Egyptian Nubians continued their pre-resettlement tradition of working as labor migrants in Egyptian towns, while subcontracting out their tenancies on the scheme (Fahim, 1981). This ensured better economic conditions for these resettlers.

Improvements in infrastructure and services: The power generated from the project has been used to provide electricity in Egypt' s countryside (for around 4500 villages) as well as to operate factories and pumping stations for irrigation and drainage. This further accelerated the pace of industrialization and a rise in standards of living, promoting culture, education and civilization throughout Egypt, particularly in rural areas. The availability of schools in Kom Ombo led to better job prospects for the Nubians. Better education further improved their mobility. With more disposable income in hand, they could avail better services. At Aswan, despite apprehensions about the increased instances of diseases, various reports show that there has been a lower rate of Schistosomiasis among the Nubians. This may be due to the better availability of pipe water. With more money in hand, they were able to hire workers to till it, which further decreased their exposure to snails and irrigation canals (USEPA 1978). Improving navigation was one of the core aims of the Aswan High Dam Project. The dam led to better navigation, both upstream and downstream of the dam to the Mediterranean. This further resulted in better economic prospects from transport. Though the end of flooding had sharply reduced the number of fish in the Nile, many of which were migratory, Lake Nasser has been stocked with fish with annual production of about 35000 tons. It propelled the mushrooming of fishing and packaging industries in the surrounding areas.

Monuments and Archaeological Sites: The preservation of the legacy of mankind is as important as the construction of dams, the erection of factories and the greater prosperity of the people (Säve-Söderberg 1987:90). The Aswan Dam site has historical significance for Egypt as there were around 17 important temples and monuments of common heritage such as Abu-Simbel, Philae, Kalabsha, Amada which had to be preserved (Zeid and Shibini 1997). An international rescue effort involving UNESCO was initiated known as 'The Nubia Campaign' to save the archaeological sites (Fekri 2007). Many monuments were transferred to higher elevations by UNESCO in coordination with donors and the Egyptian authorities. This included relocation of the ancient Egyptian temple complex of Abu Simbel, built in the thirteenth century B.C.

The resettlement in the Kom Ombo led to social and cultural empowerment not because of positive relocation experience, but due to the integration of Nubians with a wider political economy. The project led to the strengthening of the Nubian identity and greater collective self-respect. While arising out of the scheme, this has been an unanticipated consequence (de Wet 2000). The electricity (10 billion kilowatt-hours annually) provided a tremendous boost to the Egyptian economy and introduced twentieth-century life to many villages. The Aswan project fulfilled half of Egypt's entire energy needs and helped in massively modernizing Egyptian political traditions. The movement of communities out of relative isolation into a wider socio-political context led to better opportunities for employment, education, participation in community affairs, and travel for women (Fahim 1983:54).

Environmental Consequences

The High Aswan Dam, since its inception, was perceived as an environmental disaster. Some of these identified consequences were: salt build up in the soil; shore line erosion; change in the water table; and a need to use chemical fertilizers. Many articles appeared in newspapers and journals within the United States from the late 1960s to early 1970s substantiating this perception (see Sterling 1971 a-f, 1972). The predictions were supported by many Japanese researchers and journalists (Mikiyasu and Fujikura 2001). However, these claims were refuted by many researchers asserting that these reports were politically biased. Though the political biases against the dam cannot be ruled out, there is no denying the fact that the dam had adverse ecological impacts, similar to other dam projects around the world. The most serious ecological factor has been that as the sediment and nutrients carried by the river settled out in the reservoir at 130 million tons each year leading to the filling up of the reservoir, windblown sand dunes spilled into the reservoir, adding to fill and altering chemical composition (Moattassem 1994; Stanley and Wingerath 1996). Pearce (1994:30), in his study, pointed out that in Cairo, the water table was only 81 centimetres below the surface; 90 percent of cultivated land in Egypt has been waterlogged; and 35 percent has been salinized. When water evaporates from soil without adequate drainage, salts accumulate at as much as a ton per hectare per year. Since perennial irrigation provides no nutrients, fertilizer is applied, and the rate has increased exponentially (Pearce 1994: 30). The reduction of waterborne nutrients flowing into the Mediterranean is suspected to be the cause of a decline in anchovy populations in the eastern Mediterranean. Besides this, the occurrence of moderate earthquakes of magnitude 5.3 about 55 km south-west of the High Aswan Dam in 1981, generated significant concern among the Egyptian people with regard to safety of the dam.

There are different schools of thought regarding the success or failure of the project. On one hand, there are academicians who consider the project as one of the landmarks in Egypt's struggle for social and economic development. They assert that the dam has played a significant role in comprehensive control of the Nile flow and strengthening the water management and optimization of its use. These achievements have had positive impacts on agricultural production, with horizontal expansion in newly reclaimed and irrigated land and new communities and employment opportunities. Sufficient, steady and timely water availability, with cropping pattern flexibility and diversity, has brought great benefits to the agriculture sector (Zeid and Shibini 1997). The Executive Meeting of the International Commission on Large Dams (ICOLD), held in Cairo 1993, where the environmental, social and economic aspects of the dam were thoroughly discussed by worldwide experts, gave support to the project as a vital achievement in a documented report and certificate of excellence.

On the other hand, various studies highlighted the issues such as siltation, salinization and use of fertilizers peculiar to the dam. Waterbury (1979:5), while terming Egypt's policies leading to the dam 'short-sighted' and 'non-integrated', observed that, 'The history of this project is testimony to the primacy of political considerations determining virtually all technological choices with the predictable result that a host of unanticipated technological

and ecological crises have emerged that now entail more political decisions'.

There is no denying the fact that the Aswan High Dam protected Egypt from the dangers of high floods that would have ravaged Egypt in 1964, 1975 and 1977 and the water stored in Lake Nasser is shared by Egypt and the Sudan and was crucial during the African drought years of 1984 to 1988. It also saved expenditure necessitated by flood precaution. The dam's clean, sustainable and clean energy in turn enhanced tourism, paved the way for export crops, and increased fishery production. Fahim, while pointing to the tensions around the issue of resettlement of the displaced, argues that while the resettlers have clearly undergone significant suffering as a result of the dam at Aswan, one also needs to keep a wider national perspective in mind when evaluating the overall success of the Aswan High Dam Project (Fahim 1981:45-46).

Three Gorges Dam (China)

China has constructed almost half of the world's large dams since 1950. The Yangtze River basin alone has around 45,700 dams with 220.0 billion m^3 of total capacity (Yang and Chang 2009). With the height of 594 feet and the length of 7,770 feet, the Three Gorges Dam is the largest hydroelectric project in the world till date. The Three Gorges Reservoir has a surface area of about 1,045 square kilometres and extends upstream from the dam about 600 kilometres with the water storage capacity of 39.3 billion m^3. The dam stretches approximately two kilometres across the river Yangtze. This $24 billion project has been presumed to be a major source of renewable power for an energy-hungry nation. The dam promised to generate 84.7 billion kwh electricity per year, which is the capacity of 18 nuclear power plants (Yang 1992: 44-49). The project however, has been in controversy from its very inception due the human rights violations of those displaced as well as the ecological impact of the project.

Geographical and Historical Context

The Yangtze is the longest river in China. Harnessing the power of the Yangtze was first envisioned in 1919 by the Nationalist leader Dr Sun Yat-sen. Mao Zedong, the father of China's communist revolution, in his poem entitled 'Swimming' written in 1956 rhapsodized the dam. Mao declared:

> *Walls of stone will stand upstream to the West/to hold back Wushan's clouds and rain*' (Lee, 2014).

The project, however, could not be realized during his lifetime, due to financial restraints posed by the failures of the Great Leap Forward in the 1950s and Cultural Revolution in the 1960s and 1970s. Four decades later, the project was finally approved by the National People's Congress. In March 1992, when the proposal was submitted to the Fifth Session of the Seventh National Congress, it was approved by only two thirds of the delegates, which in the Chinese context is the slimmest of margins. The evident concern was ignored and decision-making reverted to the autocratic style typical of centralized planning in previous decades (Sukhan and Sleigh 2001). However, during its relatively long construction period of 17 years, the Three Gorges Dam has been considered a catalyst for institutional changes in China.

The dam development has been at Sandouping in western Hubei Province, just below the famous Three Gorges—Qutang, Wu and Xiling. The key purpose of the dam has been to control flooding. Frequent floods in the region had claimed more than one million lives in the past 100 years. The severe floods on the Yangtze caused more than 30,000 deaths in 1954. The major flood in 1998 led to 14 million being homeless and economic losses of $24 billion (Yin et al. 2007). Therefore, the potential of the dam to mitigate major floods provided a powerful argument for building it. The dam aimed to protect 75 million people in Hubei and Hunan, and three million hectares of farmland in the middle Yangtze, subject to annual flooding because the land lay several metres below the flood line. The dam was expected to regulate 60 to 90 percent of the floodwater at the middle reaches. As 80 percent of electricity supply in China came from burning coal, the dam claimed to provide a cleaner source of energy and to increase China's total energy supply by 10 percent. The dam with increasing ship size from 2000 ton to 10,000 ton was also desired to improve river transport by connecting the East Coast to industrial Chongqing. Furthermore, the dam was also expected to help in overcoming the chronic water shortage in the Yellow River by connecting the dam with the Yellow river through a canal (Sukhan and Sleigh 2001).

The finances for the Three Gorges project came from three sources. Firstly, a Three Gorges Dam Construction Fund was collected through a nationwide levy of 0.015 yuan/kW of electricity sold annually to raise a total of 30 billion yuan for the first 11 years (CWRC 1994). The second source of revenue was from the Gezhouba Hydro Dam situated 40 km downstream from the Three Gorges. Thirdly, domestic loans were obtained mainly from the China Construction Bank, and partly from bonds and shares in the Three Gorges Project and Gezhouba Co. Ltd. (China Daily 1998).

Displacement and Resettlement

China has a poor record in relocating people displaced by several hydroelectric projects built since 1949. By 1996, there were 118 large and medium hydropower dams across China's seven major rivers and their tributaries with an estimated total of 10.2 million displaced people (Jing 1997). With the past neglect, coercion and suppression accompanying construction of China's big dams, there were obvious reasons for the academicians and civil society organizations to worry about the fate of those displaced due to the Three Gorges Dam.

The dam has displaced around 1.2 million people in 277 towns and 1680 villages in 20 districts (counties) in China's Hubei province and Chongqing municipality (CWRC 1993). Many studies suggest that the total population to be relocated, including natural growth over the 17 years of construction, may be 20 to 30 percent higher than this original estimate. Out of those displaced, 59 percent were urban (498,800) and 41 percent were rural (348,700). Estimates of lost assets in the area included 466,300 mu farmland (around 76,817 acres), 134,730,000 m^2 of housing, 1599 factories and numerous infrastructure facilities (CWRC 1993). Opponents of the project from the very beginning questioned the capacity of the Chinese Government to reconstruct the livelihoods for such a large number of people, citing the terrible failure of earlier resettlements in restoring livelihoods of those displaced.

The official estimated budget for resettlement was over 100 billion yuan (US$ 11.76 billion). Funding for the resettlement had two components. The first one provided some 40 billion RMB for the restoration and re-establishment of the reservoir economy. This included compensation for those displaced (excluding the provision for interest and inflation). The second component was for the implementation of development assistance measures such as tax exemptions for industries as well as financial assistance beyond the construction stage of the Project (Duan and McDonald 2010).

To guide this mammoth undertaking, the Central Government created 'The Three Gorges Project Construction Committee' as a supreme policy-making body to ensure long-term economic development for the people in the region. 'The Regulations on Resettlement for the Construction of the Three Gorges Project on the Yangtze River' (1993) had two significant programmes: 'The Partnership Support Programme' to ensure funding to improve infrastructure and create employment opportunities within new enterprises; and 'The Development Assistance Fund' which channelled revenue generated by the operational dam into six main areas: production, living standards, education, health services, subsidies for resettled people, and vulnerable groups (the poor, the elderly and the disabled). Funds were also directed into key industries such as oranges, animal husbandry, tourism and fishing (Brooke and Hulten 2017). The Three Gorges Project Resettlement Development Bureau was set up for planning, decision-making, and supervision of population resettlement in the reservoir area. Furthermore, China Yangtze River Three Gorges Project Development Corporation (CTGPC) was set up in 1993 as an autonomous entity with fixed assets of 3.9 billion yuan (US$ 672 million) and ownership of the Three Gorges Dam (China Daily 1993:2).

With the exception of a few who arranged their own resettlement with the help of relatives and friends, all of those displaced were resettled by the Chinese government. About 85 percent of the population was relocated to towns newly built nearby or moved to villages higher up in the mountains (Wu and Liao 1999). The remaining 15 per cent (around 190,000) of the area's rural residents were moved out of Hubei and were resettled in other provinces under a government-organized programme (Xu et al., 2013; Wang et al. 2013). The efficacy of this resettlement policy, however, needs to be elaborated further.

Rural to Rural Resettlement

The cash compensation of 5,460 RMB per household member was given for rural-to-rural resettlement. As per the regulations (1993), the rural resettlement was planned to be land-based (Shi et al. 2012) with a focus on reconstructing rural livelihoods through the intensification of agricultural practices and the clearing of reclaimable land. In consonance with the plan, resettled rural households converted steep forested land into farmland, despite it being unsuited for farming. However, with the floods in 1998, it was realized that deforestation had increased the risk of flooding and erosion. The National Forest Conservation Program restricted further deforestation and required the reforestation of the steeper cleared land (McDonald et al. 2008). In 1999, the Central Government responded by adjusting the rural resettlement policy. Under the new policy, the government prohibited the opening of new land on slopes greater than 25 degrees and those affected by the project were encouraged to move outside the region to protect the fragile ecosystem. Under this policy, 196,000 people were resettled to the lower reaches of the Yangtze River, to cities along the east coast, and western and southern China (TGPCC 2009; Steil and Duan 2002). This, however, only increased the miseries of those displaced as the region was already densely populated leading to soil erosion and land degradation (Yuefang and Wilmsen 2012).

Rural to Urban Resettlement

About 190,000 rural residents were resettled out of the region in eleven provinces through a government-organized program (Xu et al. 2013). Resettlement began in 1993 under Sichuan Province but in 1997 the task was transferred to Chongqing Municipality. The newly-created Chongqing Municipality with no experience or skilled manpower had to bear the burden of resettling 84 percent of displaced people. Government planned to relocate 180 factories to Chongqing to resettle 67,000 displaced people (Sukhan and Sleigh 2001). However, the Chongqing industries, who were already facing a challenge to absorb 100,000 unemployed residents found it impossible to employ displaced persons from the Three Gorges area. This led to high unemployment rate in the region (Chongqing Statistical Bureau 1998; China Daily July 22, 1998). In Chongqing Municipality, out of 4,000 farmers who were moved off the land into the secondary or tertiary sectors, 90 per cent had to find other jobs with the closure of the small enterprises due to economic and/or environmental reasons. This further reduced the potential for jobs (Tan et al. 2003). Rural-to-urban households received the largest amount of cash compensation i.e., 9,917 RMB per household member. However, despite the higher levels of average compensation provided to the rural-to urban households, the impoverishment took place due to lack of employment opportunities. Low educational levels aggravated the situation. Establishing new livelihoods in a competitive urban environment that valued education and prior work experience put many rural people at a disadvantage. Older, less educated people and those who relied exclusively on farming before resettlement found the transition to urban life more difficult (Ong 2014). For this group, retaining even a small piece of farmland as a safety net could have helped in supporting incomes and averting food insecurity.

Another issue of concern in the resettlement has been the livelihood of secondary migrants. Secondary migrants have been the peasants who did not live below the inundation line, but in areas which were used for the reconstruction of towns that were inundated by the reservoir. These peasants lost their homes and farmland to the reconstruction. Many of these were given work in a factory. These were left with no other option than to look for new occupations or steady employment. They survived on funds that the authorities provide each month, and on ad hoc construction work in the area. Their average income came down to 30-40 yuan per month (Gu and Huang

1999), which was half the amount regarded as the standard, basic cost of living, not including fees for school, doctor or other expenses.

Social and Economic Impact

The project is China's largest engineering and infrastructure project since Liberation and is estimated to have affected the lives, habitat or economy of at least 20 million people above the dam and another 300 million downstream. It took 17 years to complete and relocated 1.2 million people to make way for the construction and the reservoir. Despite its scale and notoriety, information on the expected socio-economic impact is lacking. To date, Three Gorges resettlement is managed by engineers and no baseline information on the dam-affected people has emerged in the public domain. The Canadian Government's feasibility study of the project carried out in late 1980s was rejected by civil society organizations by declaring it as biased, ignoring the socio-economic impact of resettlement, and lacking crucial baseline information on sociology and demography (Barber and Ryder 1993).

The Three Gorges Dam flooded nearly 34,000 ha of agricultural land: 50 percent rice fields, 22 percent garden plots, one percent fishponds and ten percent forests (Zhu et al. 1996). The project area had been one of the most densely populated regions in China with a population density of 283 persons per km^2 (2.07 times the national average and four times the density of other mountainous regions) in 2006 (CWRC 2007). The land inundated by the project was highly fertile. With the inundation of the fertile plains due to the construction of the project, the shortage of farmland became more vivid. The economic cost of submerging farming land is high in China. Furthermore, decline in the quantity and quality of the farmland challenged the capacity of the rural resettlers to derive an income from the land-based occupations (Yuefang and Wilmsen 2012).

Various studies on the project highlighted the human rights issues in the resettlement process such as change in the resettlement policy in 2000; relocating people within the reservoir area to moving them to distant provinces (Heggelund 2004); the impacts of resettlement on villagers' livelihoods due to insufficient provision of cultivated land in the inundated area; the difficulty of transferring rural migrants to secondary and tertiary industries (Tan 2008); and faulty estimates by government officials of the population to be relocated (Jing 1997).

The displacement always leads to emotional and psychological consequences on the displaced. To fill the vacuum and to connect migrants with their past, some resettlement sites were named after the former villages or towns; in other cases, the word 'new' was added in front of the old name. As their old neighbourhoods, former landscapes and everyday lives were totally immobile, it created a collective nostalgia among those displaced by the Three Gorges project. Many younger resettlers experienced ambivalence between longing for better work opportunities and nostalgically recalling their hometowns; and older migrants both wish to stay with their migrant children and long to move back to their places of origin, both during life and after death (Dan et al. 2021). One of the key components prominent to the resettlement policy in China has been the 'hukou status' (one's access to almost all local public services, such as schooling, social insurance and social welfare) (Zhu and Qian 2021). The resettled people in China lose their former hukou status and are assigned hukou status at their resettlement site. This restricted the mobility of the Three Gorges migrants and prevented them from returning to their places of origin (Dan et al. 2021).

The project had many serious issues related to restoring the livelihood of those displaced. The land and jobs promised to migrants were often unavailable. The land which was offered—in the resettlement sites uphill or in distant places outside of the Yangtze Valley—was, in most cases, infertile or uncultivable. The availability of virgin lands for the displaced was insufficient (Duan and Steil 2003). Duan and Steil (2003) also showed that, in the early phase of the resettlement plan, the government tried to transfer rural migrants to secondary industries by offering jobs in township and village enterprises. However, as many of these industries closed down, the unemployment rate in the region multiplied. Apart from fair compensation, another issue of concern has been the decline in the government investment in the region many years before construction as the area was to be flooded. This led to the residents having a much lower standard of living when compensation was calculated than they would have if the dam had not been planned at all (Sukhan and Sleigh 2001).

The studies further stated that women encountered discrimination in the resettlement process due to a gender-segregated labor market. For instance, in construction and transportation, jobs were more readily available for men. With higher unemployment among the relocatees, women suffered more due to their low educational level and lack of skills. As a result, displaced women were confined to working in farms tending livestock and crops. The low quality of cultivated land uphill in the reservoir area led to limited income for the family. This 'increasing feminisation of agriculture' put women in an unfavourable position (Tan 2008:145-159). Peculiar to all the dam construction sites, there have been many health concerns for the Three Gorges project too. The decreased flow downstream from the dam led the snails to breed unchecked, which led to a spike in schistosomiasis cases as well as other parasitic diseases, such as paragonimus and malaria in some areas (IRN 1997).

There were many instances of embezzlement of resettlement funds by local officials which led to inadequate compensation. For instance, in Yunyang County, out of the officially stipulated RMB 29,000 (US$ 3,625), villagers who organized their own resettlement received RMB 20,000 and those who went through government-sponsored relocation received only RMB 6,773 (Yi 2003). According to a newspaper report on the Three Gorges Dam project, township and county governments devised their own separate schemes for compensation (South China Morning Post 1999a). In January 2000, the National Audit Office announced that US$ 62.5 million had been embezzled in 1999 by 14 officials. Despite reports that part of the amount had been retrieved, RMB 350 million was eventually reported as having been embezzled (Heggelund 2004:110-111). Two international organizations, known to be opposed to the dam, also highlighted the widespread corruption among local resettlement officials including bribes for construction contracts and bureaucratic mismanagement of resettlement funds (Wu 1998).

Environmental Consequences

Regardless of the contribution made by the project for the national economic development by reducing floods, boosting national electricity output and conserving water to take care of the water shortages in the North of China (CWRC 1994; Martellaro 1991), the ecological consequences of the project have attracted significant attention from researchers. The dam has flooded a large area of farmland and withheld fertile silt from downstream areas. A scientific report indicated that the dramatic recession in China's largest freshwater lake, Poyang Lake, has a strong linkage with the Three Gorges Dam regulation (Han et al. 2018). The construction of the Three Gorges Dam has greatly reduced the downstream sediment discharge, which in turn has changed the morphological evolution of the river channel and the hydrological regime of Dongting lake wetlands (Zhandong et al. 2012). The loss of populations and species has been a serious issue of concern as the 'Three Gorges Reservoir Area' has been located within the biogeographic area known as the Mountains of Central China, which is considered one of the three most important hotspots of biodiversity in the country (Ying et al. 1993; Li et al. 2003). As this region acted as a refuge for life during the late tertiary and the quaternary cold periods, many endemic and ancient species can be spotted in the reservoir region (Ying et al. 1993).

The Three Gorges Dam will not only affect terrestrial ecosystems in the reservoir area but also those located downstream, in the middle and lower reaches of the Yangtze River (Jordi and Ren 2009). The Yangtze River is one of the richest rivers in Asia and it harbours over 350 species of fish (Huang 2001; Fu et al. 2003). The dam imperils this delicate fish population in the Yangtze. The decreased flow of fresh water also means that saltwater from the East China Sea now creeps farther upstream. This, in turn, seems to be causing a rise in the number of jellyfish, which compete with river fish for food and consume their eggs and larvae, thereby threatening native populations that are already dwindling as a result of overfishing (Lee 2013). The project has already contributed to the decline of the baiji dolphin, which is so rare that it is considered functionally extinct. As 40 percent of China's sewage and effluents are dumped in the Yangtze (despite sewage treatment plants being built along the river), the aquatic biodiversity will also be adversely affected due to river pollution (Dudgeon 2005; Müller et al. 2008; Stone 2008). The Three Gorges area alone accounts for 20 percent of Chinese seed plants—more than 6,000 species. Economic development has spurred deforestation and pollution in surrounding provinces in central China, endangering at least 57 plant species, including the Chinese dove tree and the dawn redwood. The reservoir created by the Three Gorges Dam threatens to flood the habitats of those species along with over 400 others, says Jianguo Liu, an ecologist at Michigan State University and guest professor at the Chinese Academy of Sciences who has done extensive work on biodiversity in China (Hvistendahl 2008).

One of the core purposes of the project has been to prevent floods. However, recent studies show that dams are spurring drought in central and eastern China. *China Daily* (China's largest English-language newspaper) reported that the Yangtze had reached its lowest level in 142 years (Lee 2013). Another fear is that the dam may trigger severe earthquakes, because the reservoir sits on two major faults: the Jiuwanxi and the Zigui-Badong. Chinese Academy of Engineering scholar Li Wangping reports on the CTGPC's website that the area registered 822 tremors in the seven months after the September 2006 reservoir-level increase. Though none have been severe enough to cause serious damage, as the dam's water level set to be raised to its full 575-foot capacity and then lowered about 100 feet (30 meters) during flood season; increase in water pressure, in water fluctuation and in land covered by the reservoir, makes for a 'very large possibility' that the situation can worsen (Hvistendahl 2008).

The effects of the dam's disturbance of whole ecosystems could reverberate for decades. A study conducted by the Institute of Mountain Hazards and Environment (CAS) in Chengdu revealed that the negative impact of the reservoir would far outweigh its benefits (Lei 1998). Several environmental non-government organizations and numerous scientists (both from China and abroad) have heightened the controversy by warning of the serious environmental risks of building the Three Gorges Dam (Jordi and Ren 2009). In a statement made by International Rivers Network (IRN 1997) and Friends of the Earth which appeared in the New York Times, it stated that:

> *The dam would be ineffective in controlling the Yangtze floods, and it would not produce sufficient electricity to remedy China's power shortage. The reservoir, moreover, would lose its function within 50 years because of siltation, which made it unreasonable to commit US$75 billion – almost seven times the US$11 billion official projection made in 1992 and three times the updated estimation of US$25 billion – to build the dam. In short, according to the campaigners, the scheme would be an ''economic and ecological catastrophe* (IRN, 1997: 108).

In 2020, extreme floods which hit China's Three Gorges Dam reaffirmed the fears of ecologists and social scientists about the dam. A breach of the dam, a controversial and unprecedented feat of engineering along the Yangtze River, would be embarrassing for China, which took 17 years to build the megaproject, displacing millions and submerging swathes of land (Lily 2020). The way the project was carried out led to the opposition of the project by many. The resettlement programme was conducted 'in an atmosphere of officially orchestrated secrecy and intimidation' (Lee 2013: 114; Yi 2003). Oustees were not allowed to talk to the media; the protests were suppressed by the use of force; and petitioners were imprisoned (Yi 2003). Various reports (Sukhan and Sleigh 2001) have highlighted the human rights violations during the resettlement such as coercive eviction; forced migration to inhospitable localities; living amongst hostile host populations; and variable compensation causing widespread resentment. After the 1989 Tiananmen crackdown, all opposing voices were suppressed more. Furthermore, with individual peasants having little or no formal political power, a land market being virtually absent and compensation for resettlement usually kept secret (Sukhan and Sleigh 2001), the chances of rights of the displaced getting ignored are more.

With rising dissatisfaction and complaints in some locales, the State Council devised a Working Plan to address the grievances and for the development of the region by improving the resettlers' production conditions; creating employment opportunities by developing training and environmentally friendly industries; and protecting the resettlers' basic living standards by establishing a social safety net (Duan and Wilmsen 2012). However, how effective these strategies would be in ensuring better living standards of those displaced would be a matter of inspection and analysis in the coming years.

Ilisu Dam (Turkey)

Turkey has always played a significant role in world politics due to its ideal geographical location; its sound links with Europe and United States; and its good relations with the countries of the region. However, the world oil crisis of 1973, followed by hikes in oil price in 1980 put Turkey into the worst economic crisis in its history. Besides this, an increase in population led to increasing demand for energy in Turkey (Demirbas 2002a). In the 1990s, the energy production in Turkey increased about 4.4 percent per year, with electricity consumption growing at an average annual rate of about 8.5 percent (WECTNC, 1998). As the energy demand of Turkey was expected to increase fivefold between 2000 and 2025 (Demirbaş 2002), emphasis was shifted to meet the energy needs of the nation using various sources such as natural gas, solar and wind (Demirbas et al. 2004). This led to the initiation of GAP project in Turkey.

The South-eastern Anatolia Project known as GAP in Turkish (Güneydoğu Anadolu Projesi) is one of the largest power generating, irrigation, and development projects of its kind in the world (Demirbas et al. 2004). This infrastructure development program on the Euphrates and Tigris rivers and their tributaries encompasses 22 dams and 19 hydroelectric power plants and irrigation schemes on an area extending over 1.7 million hectares. The total installed capacity of its power plants is 7,476 MW, which means an annual production of 27 billion kWh (Kaygusuz 1999). The estimated total cost of the GAP on completion is US$ 32 billion, 85 percent of which has to be financed by the state.

Major Turkish hydro dams as part of the GAP include: Ataturk (2,400 MW capacity), Karakaya (1,800 MW), Ilisu (1,200 MW), Cizre (240 MW), Silvan/Kayser (240 MW), Hakkari (208 MW), Alpaslan II (200 MW), Batman (198 MW), Konaktepe (180 MW), and Karkamis (180 MW) (Demirbas 2002). The area to be irrigated accounts for 19 percent of all the economically irrigable area in Turkey (8.5 million hectares), and the annual electricity generated would account for 22 percent of the country's economically viable hydroelectric power potential (Balat 2003). The Ilisu Dam has been in controversy since its inception for multiple reasons: displacement of Kurdish people; environmental concerns; danger to cultural heritage; as well as transboundary water dispute between Turkey, Iraq and Syria.

Geographical and Historical Context

The Tigris River is one of the two main constituents of the Tigris-Euphrates River System. It is the second-largest river in Western Asia, after the Euphrates. It originates near Lake Hazar in eastern Turkey and follows a south-eastern route of 523 km to Cizre, where it forms the border between Turkey and Syria for 32 km before entering Iraq (Altinbilek 2004). Investigations related to the Tigris River project go back to the 1950s. After the establishment of the State Hydraulic Works (DSI) in 1954, basin-scale surveys were initiated. The reconnaissance studies on the energy potential of the Tigris River focused on the use of elevations between 500 m and 370 m by the Ucagac, Celikhan and Cizre Dams (FPGA 1968). The feasibility report for Cizre Dam suggested a new system composed of two dam projects, namely Ilisu and Cizre (Ilisu Hydropower Consultants 1983). With a height of 135 metres, 1,200 MW capacity and an estimated cost of $2 billion, the Ilisu has been the largest hydroelectric power project on the Tigris River. This dam is located on the River Tigris, 65 km upstream from the Syrian and Iraqi borders at the village of Ilisu, between Mardin and Sirnak (ECGD 1999).

Originally planned as a Build-Operate-Transfer (BOT) scheme, the project failed to find a bidder. In 1997, the government, through the State Hydraulic Works (DSI), the government agency responsible for the construction of dams, invited Sulzer Hydro of Switzerland to form a construction consortium of private companies to build the power plant at Ilisu. The consortium was comprised of Balfour Beatty (UK and USA), Impregilo (Italy), Skanska (Sweden), ABB Power Generation, Sulzer Hydro (Switzerland and Austria) and the Turkish companies: Nurol, Kiska and Tekfen. Each contractor approached their government's Export Credit Agency (ECA) to underwrite support for their involvement in the project against the risk of non-payment. The consortium disbanded in 2001 and resulted in the Ilisu dam being put on hold. Despite this setback, the state remained determined to build the dam to supply the energy requirements needed to sustain economic growth.

Displacement and Resettlement

According to the estimates, the dam involved the flooding of 300km^2 in the Kurdish region of Turkey, including the historic town of Hasankeyf displacing up to 78,000 people. However, as the impact area of the Ilisu dam fell within five provinces: Diyarbakir, Mardin, Batman, Siirt and Sirnak with a total population of 3 million, 90 percent being ethnically Kurdish and 10 percent being Arabs and Turks, the impact was estimated to be much higher. The civil society organizations opposing the project asserted that the state agencies have underestimated the number of local people eligible for displacement compensation because of inadequate demographic data on the 'empty' villages (Morvaridi 2004). DSI data and the Resettlement Action Plan (RAP) survey estimated that 184 villages would be affected. Of these, around 85 were supposedly empty due to displacement as a result of security conflicts (Morvaridi 2004). According to Morvaridi, (2004), three options were offered to people as compensation for loss of assets. These were:

- **Cash compensation for lost assets:** Each household would get on average US$ 25,000 depending on the value of their house, land and other resources. This was a kind of self-resettlement with no further support from the State.
- **Government-assisted resettlement:** This included new housing and land in an urban or rural area, which was designated for the purpose. This was financed through expropriation of the compensation that displaced people would have received, plus loans as necessary. The average household resettlement cost/compensation was estimated to be US$ 35,000.
- **Credit assisted resettlement:** A package that allowed people to keep their expropriation compensation and also to have access to a mortgage.

A household survey was carried out to know the preference of the displaced. The survey revealed that 78 percent of households opted for monetary compensation, 17 percent for government-assisted resettlement and 5 percent for credit assisted resettlement (ECGD 2002). This was surprising as in most of the case studies of resettlement projects, the majority of the households always opt for land-based resettlement rather than compensation. The reason for the same may be that the nature of information related to government assisted resettlement circulated among the people by the resettlement authorities which somehow led to a perception among the displaced that cash compensation would be more beneficial than other options.

Though various risk mitigation measures were initiated to restore income and securing livelihoods for those displaced, these were majorly for government-assisted resettlement. As only 17 percent households opted for government-assisted resettlement, the majority of the displaced were left out. Particular to the issue of cash compensation, many problems were encountered in self resettlement such as: delays in compensation and money not well spent due to lack of knowledge about their new chosen field. Some started businesses but lacked experience and lost everything while others left their money in the bank; however, due to high inflation rates, their money quickly devalued (ECGD 1999: 48).

The region already had grave inequalities as far as land ownership has been concerned with high levels of landlessness (approximately 35 percent) and small number of families (called 'Aga' in the region) possessing all the cultivated land. The majority of households owned small plots of land. The Ilisu Resettlement Plan provided compensation to only those households on whose name land deeds were registered. However, due to lots of land disputes, around 50 percent of rural people in the dam area did not have registration deeds and hence, could not prove ownership (Morvaridi 2004). The administration of expropriation and compensation became more complex where family land had not been re-registered after farms were broken up through inheritance, or areas of farmland that were in joint ownership but where the deeds had not been amended to reflect this. Women and adult children who resided on family land were not entitled to get compensation as individuals (Morvaridi 2004). Land issues were further complicated as Turkish national legal framework ignored the issue of access to common property resources and therefore no compensation was given for the loss of income due to inaccessibility of pastoral land used for grazing livestock.

One of the key components of any successful resettlement policy is the participation of the communities affected by the project. As far as the Ilisu dam project was concerned, communication or transparency in information sharing was found to be missing. The project design work commenced in the 1950s, with site investigations and feasibility studies approved by the government in 1982. The local people were neither informed nor consulted regarding the project until late 1990s when an international funding consortium for the dam was already in place. This led to frustration and misconceptions about the potential impacts of the project. Morvaridi (2004:733), in his study, pointed out that 'The main implementing agencies have had little direct involvement with the local people, other than a one-day public awareness meeting attended by thirty-two village heads (of a potential 184) in 2000, at which sketchy information about the dam and resettlement packages was shared. Even the environmental impact assessment reports commissioned by the Consortium and their ECAs were published in English and are not available in Turkish or Kurdish languages, thus excluding the local and national NGOs from this information'.

The avenues of protest or opposition to the state have always been limited in the Kurdish region. The reasons for this can be traced back in 1923 to when the political establishment tried to consolidate Turkey as 'one nation'. To enforce this, the government-imposed uniformity on the Kurdish people through steps such as renaming Kurdish villages with Turkish names in the 1960s and banning many Kurdish cultural institutions, including language, clothes, music and religious practices. This led to a violent conflict between the Kurdish Workers Party (PKK) fighting for an independent Kurdistan and the state. Most of the Kurdish region, including the Ilisu dam area, has been under Emergency Rule since 1980 and civil rights and liberties which exist elsewhere in the country have been curtailed in this region (Morvaridi 2004). Demonstrations are not allowed and critics of the dam have been subjected to intimidation or accused of belonging to the PKK, a crime punishable by up to 15 years' imprisonment (KHRP 1999: 38). Many people from the region assert that the main aim of the project was not to produce electricity but was political and militaristic (Kitchen and Ronayne 2002). It has been a way to control the Kurdish communities by getting them out of their traditional set ups and scattering them in urban areas. The project would further transform the geography of Turkish Kurdistan and would deny the Kurdish guerrillas the environment in which they operated (KHRP 1999:14).

Social and Economic Impacts

The dam has been opposed by a number of affected communities. More than 350,000 people in Southeast Anatolia have already been displaced by other GAP projects and there has been ample evidence that inadequately conceptualized or negotiated resettlement has resulted in impoverishment and social disruption (Morvaridi 2004). The resettlement plans have ignored the impact of displacement on the Kurdish women. With the legal titles being intrinsically gender biased, women were usually excluded from receiving compensation (ADB 2003:3). High level of illiteracy among Kurdish women made them more vulnerable. Ronayne (2006) in her study specifically mentioned the adverse impact of the project on the women in the Kurdish region. According to her, most Kurdish women carry a heavy workload as housewives, bringing up large families and working on the land to feed whole villages. The war in the 1990s between the Turkish State and the PKK (Kurdistan Workers' Party), which led to internal displacement of an estimated three million people (KHRP et al. 2003: 13), increased the vulnerability of women. Most of these women found work in low wage jobs in the informal sector such as agricultural labor. Some women displaced by conflict also worked as prostitutes. The dam induced displacement put them in higher risk of domestic violence and murder. This violence has been supported by the practical actions and/or inaction of the State, landlords and religious hierarchy (Ronayne 2005: 24).

Another controversial issue which led to the opposition of the project across the globe has been the submergence of international heritage, Hasankeyf, an ancient settlement in the reservoir area of Ilisu Dam. In 1978, the Turkish government declared Hasankeyf a site for conservation and thus legally protected. This designation put a halt to the dam project. However, in the 1980s the Turkish government reversed its earlier order and approved the hydroelectric dam. No significant efforts were made to ameliorate the adverse impacts of the project on the cultural heritage of the region during planning. Human habitation along the river dates back at least 12,000 years (Emrah and Tigrek 2016). The remains of structures built by Romans, Abbasids, Eyyubies, Akkoyunlus, Artuks and Ottomans could be seen in Hasankeyf and there were several tumuli waiting to be uncovered. The inundation of these archaeological sites around Hasankeyf due to the dam has received criticism from national and international groups (Basgelen 2006; KHPR 1999). According to archaeologists, Hasankeyf was one of the oldest continuous settlements on earth. This ancient Mesopotamian city has spanned nine civilizations. It also functioned as a Muslim pilgrimage site and held great significance for its residents and for many Kurdish people worldwide (Ronayne 2006). However, the dam would flood the area and bury the homes, the caves, and the antiquity of more than three hundred medieval monuments and 83 archaeological sites of Hasankeyf under the waters of the Tigris (Ackerman 2009).

The cultural heritage damage wrought by GAP, including the Ilisu Project itself, has been justified by state agencies on the pretext of social and economic benefits to the large numbers of impoverished people who live in the Kurdish regions of Turkey (Kitchen and Ronayne 2002). However, the recent studies have highlighted that the local people would receive little or no benefit from the project and it would lead to impoverishment among the Kurdish community. Of most concern to people is the break-up of communities as a result of the dam (Ronayne 2002:133-36).

Environmental consequences

The Euphrates-Tigris River system is among the most intensely developed freshwater resources worldwide (Bremer 2016). GAP's project has led to a drastic ecological change in the Euphrates and the Tigris region due to multiple dams that have been planned or already constructed. The Euphrates River has been gradually transformed by dams between the period 1975-2000. The portion of the Euphrates from its source to the Turkish-Syrian boundary has lost its quality of being a river and turned into a series of reservoirs (Demirsoy 1996). Ilisu would inundate the Tigris Valley, which consisted of deep canyons with undamaged banks that built an exceptional natural landscape and irreplaceable habitats for wildlife. The reservoir area would inundate up to 170 km of the river course (Derneği 2006).

Due to various common characteristics in their recent geological past, the Tigris and Euphrates Rivers are mostly considered as elements of a single stream system. That is why several habitats and their reliant organisms that were lost in the Euphrates could still be found in the Tigris Basin, such as the highly endangered Euphrates Softshell Turtle (Taçkavak and Atatür 1995). The Tigris in Turkish territory formed exceptional riparian habitats, especially in this area, and sheltered many bird species as a natural migration corridor (Welch, 2004). The area provided essential stopover habitat for migrating birds, most conspicuously in spring (Kasparek and Bilgin 1996). Hasankeyf and its surrounding area comprised a crucial part of an Important Bird Area, declared as 'Dicle (Tigris) Valley IBA' (Kiliç and Eken 2004), and also of key biodiversity areas in the region (Eken et al. 2006) including globally threatened bird species: Falco naumanni (vulnerable); Coradas garrulus, and Emberiza cineracea (both near threatened); Neophron percnopterus, Hieraaetus fasciatus and Apus affinis (endangered) (Biricik and Karakas 2012). However, an array of ongoing dam projects threatens the biodiversity of the Tigris.

Development planners proclaim that the Ilisu dam has been the most eco-friendly way to fulfil the increasing national demand for energy. Many local activists asserted that the government must reduce the elevation of the Ilisu dam from 526 to 496 metres to reduce its adverse impacts (Morvaridi 2004). On the other hand, the government claimed that reduction in the height of the dam would reduce energy supply by 50 percent making it less feasible and would defeat the whole objective of building the dam (ECGD 1999). It is noteworthy that the Dam was considered to be economically viable because of its high electricity generation capacity i.e., 3833.5 GWh/y. However, as a large number of dams and additional activities upstream, there would be a considerable decrease in the total energy production (Yalcin and Tigrek 2016) making it less viable.

In southeast Turkey, there has been a recent proliferation of human rights NGOs ('Stop Ilisu Dam' and 'Save Hasankeyf') dealing with the displacement of people as a result of the series of dams built there since the 1960s (Kitchen and Ronayne 2002). Despite this resistance, the state agencies maintain that the Southeast Anatolia Development Project (GAP) will lead to increase in per capita income, will reduce economic inequalities and ensure political stability in the region. The dam has also received global attention in recent years due to the fear that it may lead to potential water wars in the Middle East (Dolatyar and Gray 2000; Marsh n.d.). Transboundary water relations in the Euphrates-Tigris (ET) basin has often been marked by political confrontation and rivalry between Iraq, Syria and Turkey (Kibaroglu and Sayan 2021). Despite the construction of the dam being completed in 2018; Turkey stopped filling the reservoir behind the dam due to severe drought and water scarcity in Iraq that resulted in violent protests in Basra. Although both Iraq and Turkey support intergovernmental cooperation, Turkey's water development ventures continue to raise concerns in Iraq (Klimes 2020).

Belo Monte Dam (Brazil)

The Amazon region is considered to have the highest potential of hydroelectricity with an estimated potential to produce 77 GW from water resources (Brasil 2007). Due to its abundant natural resources, Amazonia was viewed as a potential region for facilitating Brazil's economic development. Brazil has one of the cleanest electricity matrixes in the world, with 65.2 percent of its total electricity supply coming from hydropower (Empresa 2015). The Brazilian government planned to build additional hydroelectric dams to meet the country's rising demand for energy (Ministerio de Minas e Energia 2012). As the Rio+20 (United Nations Conference on Sustainable Development) utilized the green economy discourse internationally, the Brazilian government advertised the Belo Monte project as a green economy initiative.

Described as the world's third largest hydroelectric dam, the Belo Monte dam (2011-2020) constructed in the State of Para in the Brazilian Amazon is one of the controversial projects of the Brazilian government. Since the initial proposal, the Belo Monte dam has been fiercely opposed and has witnessed innumerable controversies, protests and a long legal battle that challenged laws, as well as the social and environmental impacts of the project. It further led to the involvement of multifarious agencies such as the Supreme Federal Court, Public Prosecutor's Office, Regional Courts, International Labour Organization, and the Inter-American Commission on Human Rights. As well as civil society organizations such as the Socio-Environmental Institute, Greenpeace, and the Coordination for the Indigenous Organizations of the Brazilian Amazon, etc. (Cândido and Almeida 2013: 145).

Geographical and Historical context

The idea of the Belo Monte Dam was first articulated by the military dictatorship of the nation in late 1970s for promoting economic growth and national security. The perceived need to raise energy production was furthered by blackouts and energy rationing in the early 2000s. In 2009, a transmission line failure from the Itaipu Dam resulted in a blackout in 18 of Brazil's 26 states, affecting the cities of Sao Paulo and Rio de Janeiro for several hours and enhancing the argument for national electric grid stabilization (Patel 2010). The initial proposal required the submergence of around 20,000 square kilometres of area, including the entire Paquigamba indigenous reserve. The project witnessed resistance from the civil society organizations as well as the indigenous community of the region since the 1980s when the plan was shared in public domain. This led to change in the initial plan of six dams along the river Xingu to one dam to avoid flooding of indigenous areas. The project was renamed 'Belo Monte'. The resistance against the project, however, continued despite project revisions which lessened its impact.

The Belo Monte Dam has been one of the flagships development programmes (known as PAC, Programa de Aceleração do Crescimento) launched by the Brazilian President Luiz Inácio Lula da Silva (popularly known as President Lula) in the years 2007-2010 to boost Brazilian infrastructure and to create jobs. The initial approximate cost of the project was US$ 15 billion. The project has to be financed by the World Bank. However, rising social movements and consequent international pressure led to the World Bank withdrawing itself from the project which delayed the process of construction. The construction work finally began in 2011. The work was frequently halted due to labor disputes and occupations of the site by indigenous protesters. Finally, the project was funded by the Brazilian Development Bank (BNDES) and government pension funds. The most important feature of the project was the role played by the private sector. Energy sector was partially privatized in Brazil during the President Cardoso (late 1980s and early 1990s), including hydroelectric projects

(PACa 2013). Therefore, the project was built by a consortium of companies known as the Belo Monte Construction Consortium (CCBM), which included the giant civil construction firms Andrade Gutierrez, Odebrecht, and Correâ Camargo, as well as a number of state-owned and state-run companies and pension funds that hired contractors to complete the work (Bratman 2015).

Displacement and Resettlement

The dam was expected to displace around 20,000 people with 82 percent (approximately 16,400) being from urban Altamira and 2,800 from rural surroundings including Vitoria do Xingu (Eletrobras 2009). The official Environmental Impact Report revealed that around 138,407 people living in the submerged areas, construction site and maintenance areas would be directly influenced by the project while another 317,472 dwellers would be indirectly affected by the plant (Eletrobrás and Ministério das Minas e Energia 2009). The Brazilian government asserted that the resettlement would be done in the most efficient manner. The then President, Luiz Inácio Lula da Silva (2010) declared in a speech at Altamira:

> *Let us use clean energy and preserve the environment. This is my commitment [...] We do not want ever again a hydroelectric plant that commits a crime of insanity such as Balbina [...] We don't want to repeat Tucurui, we want something new* (Atkins 2018: 235).

Nearly US$ 2 billion was invested in programs to reduce the negative social and environmental impacts and construct schools, hospitals and other projects to develop the infrastructure of the region. Approximately US$ 250 million was to be allocated by a participatory decision-making space—the Steering Committee of the Regional Sustainable Development Plan of the Xingu (CGDEX)—comprised of representatives from civil society of 11 dam-affected municipalities and officials from federal, state and municipal government (Klein 2015). The Basic Environmental Plan (Piano Basico Ambiental, PBA) proposed that rural displaced population will be given options such as (Norte Energia S.A. 2010):

- Monetary compensation for their land and assets;
- Assisted relocation to a property in the same region;
- Resettlement assistance for rebuilding a home on the same property if it is partially flooded; or
- Resettlement in a planned community in the region for smallholder farmers or those without property rights.

Randell (2016), in his survey of displaced people, highlighted that the majority of the population chose monetary compensation (landowners) or credit payments (landless households) so that they could use the same to purchase titled property. Compensation was based primarily on productive assets (e.g., cacao trees, other fruit trees, and crops) as well as pasture, homes, and infrastructure on the property. According to the dam timeline, after the initial assessment, the company was required to return to the farmer with a proposal within 90 days. This first step, however, often experienced long delays. After receiving the proposal, farmers could either accept it or request a new assessment if they found that assets were not included (e.g., if the company failed to account for a portion of the cacao trees). Upon receiving the updated proposal, the households had a short period of time to evaluate it before signing the agreement. If farmers did not accept the second proposal, they were told that they must go to court, an expensive and time-consuming process that few farmers chose to pursue. Those who did not own land were provided with credit for R$ 132,000 (Brazilian currency), which they could use toward buying documented land with a definitive title or public deed. In addition, farmers whose assets had been valued at less than R$ 132,000 could opt for this credit instead of their compensation payment. However, landless sharecroppers were constrained by both low compensation amounts and the fact that they were compensated in credit that had to be used toward land with a legal title, which was scarce and expensive in the region. Rising land prices in the region due to population resettlement as well as in-migration for dam-related employment opportunities restricted a household's ability to find suitable land. The involvement of a private agency (Norte Energia) having more than one hundred lawyers restricted the people's capacity to negotiate for better compensation amounts (Randell 2016).

While urban resettlement was not without its problems, rural resettlement provision was chaotic and badly planned. Xingu being one of the most important rivers in the Amazon region, is a source of life for indigenous communities from the states of Mato Grosso and Pará, as well as riverside dwellers, fishermen and family-based farming populations, who survive on the river and use the river as a means of transportation (Bermann 2007; Júnior and Reid 2010). Inadequate and delayed compensation, the failure in providing alternative farmland, and many other problems disrupted their livelihoods. Social and environmental mitigation enjoyed low official priority within Eletronorte. It was only after a series of local protests in the early 1980s that some further concessions in the form of new settlements, relocation and infrastructure provision was given to people (Hall and Branford 2012).

After the state's return to democracy, Brazil's 1988 Constitution recognized many rights of the indigenous people. Article 231 of the Constitution recognizes the indigenous people's rights to the lands they occupy, and states that it is the Union's responsibility to respect and protect all their assets (Brasil 2007). It also prohibits removing indigenous peoples from traditional lands except when epidemics or catastrophic events present imminent threats to the populations, or in the interest of national sovereignty, that too temporarily. It further states that 'Hydric resources, including energetic potentials, may only be exploited [...] after hearing the communities involved, and the participation in the results of such mining shall be ensured to them, as set forth by law' (Brasil 2007).

All these constitutional provisions were ignored in the case of Belo Monte. The democratic participation of the affected community was found to be much problematic. The Brazilian state did not take effective measures to ensure that the Xingu communities were fully aware of Belo Monte's possible impacts. A 20,000-page Environmental Impact Assessment page was made publicly available only two days before holding public meetings. This made it virtually impossible for attendees to become properly acquainted with the highly complex project before engaging in the dialogues. The meetings were held in urban areas difficult to access by the affected communities, who reside in more remote locations (Anaya 2010). During a public audience Norte Energia held in July 2012, the company evidently took advantage of attendees who spoke little Portuguese by allowing biased translations to distort their messages to the company's president (Amazon Watch 2012). Company was also accused of attempting to 'buy [them] off cheaply, by offering televisions, boats, and other perks while refusing to address the various legally required social and environmental conditions the company has yet to fulfil' (Amazon Watch 2012).

Though some indigenous groups living nearby in the Xingu basin agreed to the project on the pretext of getting better houses, boats, food, and infrastructure, the majority of them resisted the construction. The Xikrin tribe along with nine other indigenous groups halted the construction work at site for three weeks (June 22 to July 12, 2012) asserting a number of demands on behalf of the communities (Perkins 2012). In a collective statement in the Tirncheira-Bacaja indigenous territory:

> [...] *Stop this and let the river run so that our children can drink and bathe in its waters. If they build this dam the river will become ruined, its waters*

will no longer be good. The river will be dry; how will we be able to navigate and travel? (Amazon Watch 2012a).

Leaders from the Xingu River Basin asserted that their right to consultation on Belo Monte as spelled out in the Constitution, UNRIP, and ILO 169 has not been honoured (Diamond and Poirier 2010).

Social and Economic Impacts

In the initial years of the construction of the Belo Monte Dam, there were significant changes in the dynamics of the labor market. With the construction sector absorbing a large number of workforces, the demographic boom in Altamira city boosted the local economy leading to a significant increase in employment generation in other formal sectors. A large proportion of workers were hired by the industry and service sector that provided services to the Belo Monte construction company. However, soon after the concrete placement stage of the dam, which is a labor-intensive activity, was completed in 2017, the formal employment rates returned to the levels prior to Belo Monte Dam in all economic sectors. Therefore, very little new formal jobs were created permanently by the dam (Calvi et al 2020). Secondly, an important part of the workforce available in rural areas was directly mobilized to build the dam or drawn to commercial activities and services in urban areas. This situation led to a labor shortage, pushing production costs in rural areas, which affected the entire agricultural sector of the Altamira region. Rural establishments with lower financial capacity and low available family labor were the most affected (Calvi et al 2020).

A large number of local residents living in the city of Altamira were directly affected by the dam. As Altamira city has been the administrative headquarters of Belo Monte; there has been a rising migration of people seeking employment opportunities in Altamir (G1 2010; Paulo 2011). Altamira's population grew from 77,439 (in 2000) to 109,938 (in 2016). Though some positive changes occurred in the Altamira region, especially with regards to infrastructure—such as temporary improvements in the quality of roads which were previously unpaved and impassable in the rainy season (Bro et al. 2018)—this unplanned migration led to crumbling down of the health, education and sanitation systems of the city. Irregular water service delivery or no connection to the local water distribution system led to an increase in shallow dug wells. As septic tanks remained the main wastewater disposal system throughout the city (Pessoa 2016), it was feared that septic tank discharges to the ground coupled with shallow wells and an increase in water pumping due to greater water demand could lead to septic tank contaminants reaching water wells, putting the health of the population at risk (Ministerio Publico Federal 2016). This was one of the core reasons why, in 2017, Brazil's Federal Public Ministry suspended a license to operate the project until the sanitation crisis was fully addressed (Ministerio Publico Federal 2016 and 2017; Pessoa, 2016). Such a population influx also caused extensive issues and a number of controversies, with larger numbers straining local infrastructure, increasing rents and living expenses, and leading to increased violence and social problems in the region (Leite et al. 2013).

The project has the potential to generate an average of 11,233 MW per hour of operation, which would be distributed to seventeen Brazilian states, serving approximately 18 million residences (an estimated 60 million people in total). People resisting the dam assert that the local people would not benefit much from the project as most of the electricity would go to local mining operations before being routed to the metropolitan areas of Rio de Janeiro and São Paulo, about 1,800 miles away.

International Rivers (2012), in its report, stated that though the ecological hydrograph should guarantee the minimum water quantity on the Xingu River, specifically a 100 km stretch known as the Xingu's Big Bend, as formerly fertile sections of the Xingu Basin and home to 800 indigenous people would be without water threatening the food and water security for indigenous groups living in the area. The dam's effects on the flow of the Xingu will also lead to the deterioration of water quality and the growth of aquatic plants harmful to humans and the fish they consume (RIMA 2009). It will further lead to decrease in the number of fishes, extinction of some species and lower agricultural production. Reduced stream flow and drought would lead to the disappearance of transportation through the river consequently leading to difficulties in selling and buying in the nearby cities and will isolate them geographically from commercial centers, schools, and social service providers located in urban areas. This will also have implications for upstream communities like the Kayapó, whose dietary staples include migratory species (Diamond and Poirier 2010). The loss of access to local markets and medical facilities will become particularly problematic given the dam's projected effects on public health and rural food security (Inter-American Commission on Human Rights 2011).

The Xingu River Basin is of utmost significance due to its cultural and biological diversity. 'It is considered a historical regional system and ethnographic complex, with different traditions, distinct languages and internal variants of each language' (Franchetto 2011:230). The word Xingu means 'house of God' to indigenous and region's native peoples regard the Xingu as the birthplace of civilization; its destruction would thus constitute a 'cosmological catastrophe' for local groups like the Arara and the Jumna (Diamond and Poirier 2010).

Environmental Consequences

The Brazilian Amazon has been a focal region for sustainable development debates globally. The region's 'glocalized' sociological and environmental issues involve repercussions that are simultaneously national, regional, and hyper-local (Brown and Purcell 2005). The run-of-the-river generation power plant has no doubt reduced the adverse impacts of the dam; it will have many ecological consequences in the Amazon region. Prior to the dam's construction, the Amazon rainforest area had already been deforested for soy production, logging, livestock production and human occupation. The project further led to submergence of around 516 km^2, of which 44 percent correspond to a river and 56 percent is divided into forests, urban areas, pastures, crops, and other areas (Eletrobrás and Ministério das Minas e Energia 2009). It has diverted more than 80 percent of the Xingu River's flow. The Xingu River Basin comprises 27 million hectares of high priority land for biodiversity conservation, housing 30 indigenous reserves and 12 protected areas. Big Bend, a 62 mile stretch of river that serves as an ecological hotspot will be adversely affected. Changes in landscape, loss of vegetation and natural environment and damage to the archaeological heritage due to the flooding, and vegetation removal to construct the dam and for urbanization are some of the factors that cause serious environmental impacts and the biome of the region (Issa et al. 2015).

The ecologists have apprehensions about the economic viability of the project. The Belo Monte hydropower plant has the capacity to generate approximately 11,233 MW. However, the actual energy produced will be 4,500 MW, around 60 percent less than the estimated due to the seasonal pluvial conditions (Júnior et al. 2006; Castro et al. 2011; Leite et al. 2013; Bratman 2014). Secondly, due to initial change in the plan (from six dams to one), the energy prices will be between US$ 28 and US$ 41 per megawatt hour (MWh), which is only slightly below the average costs of hydropower generation (Diamond and Poirier 2010). Fearnside (2006) asserted that the dam would be viable if other dams are built upstream, which would lead to more environmental impacts in the region. Another issue prominent in all the hydro projects has been emission of methane gases due to submergence of the forests in the flooded areas leading to adverse environmental consequences. Due to its disastrous environmental impacts, people have started calling it a 'monster dam'.

Though the Brazilian Ministry of the Environment required thorough evaluation of potential environmental impacts before any Brazilian hydropower plant project is approved (Sperling 2012), the project was started on the basis of 'Partial Installation Environmental License' which was not as per the Brazilian legislation. As per the law, there have been 29 environmental and social conditions that have to be met by the developers before the commencement of the construction process. These conditions included: regulations concerning health, education, sanitation infrastructure, and the protection of indigenous land (Amazon Watch 2011). As the construction continued with little progress in meeting the environmental or the indigenous conditions in the construction licenses, there were renewed court requests to halt the project (Ascom MPF 2012). The Pará Federal Court suspended the license in 2011; however, the Federal Regional Court authorized the release of the same (Paulo 2011). Due to the increased political aspirations associated with the project, the project was approved in the National Congress of Brazil in less than a month without consulting the indigenous groups affected by its development. The government asserted that as no indigenous peoples will be displaced due to the project, therefore, it was unnecessary to consult the indigenous community staying in the area (Inter-American Commission on Human Rights 2011). The Inter-American Commission on Human Rights (IACHR) in April 2011 also demanded suspension of the environmental licensing process and construction of the dam based on violations of the free, prior, and informed consent and environmental impact study in the communities. However, the Brazilian government responded strongly to the same by suspending the nation's payment of $800,000 to the Organization of American States, and by temporarily withdrawing its ambassador (Soltis 2011).

There is no denying the fact that the Belo Monte Dam will stimulate economic growth of the region with consistent supply of electricity and will ensure energy generation during dry seasons; however, its adverse impacts overweigh the positive impacts. Some of these are: disruption of social-cultural-historical relations; uncertainty in income generation and local subsistence; ecological imbalance and its consequent impact on social economic life of the natives.

Summing up

The resettlement experiences of four of the most controversial hydro power projects have been discussed in this chapter. Though there are wide variations in the resettlement policies as well as its implementation across the countries, certain similarities can be drawn in the resettlement experiences in all the above discussed case studies. Firstly, in the case of all these dams, the ambitions and the interest of the political leaders (President Lula in the case of Belo Monte; Mao Zedong in Three Gorges; Gamal Abdel Nasser in Aswan High Dam) led to going ahead with the projects despite the controversies and resistance at the local and international level. The interest of the central agencies, nonetheless, ensured better financial and institutional mechanisms to implement the projects. This involvement of the political heads of the states in the conception of the projects, however, could not be replicated with the matching interest in the resettlement of the affected communities. Though, some positive features were there in all these resettlement policies such as provision of land-based compensation, taking landless persons into consideration as well as provision of social services; the study found numerous gaps in the policy implementation which consequently led to unsatisfactory social infrastructure services and inadequate income restoration. The compensation and restoration of livelihood remained a challenge in all these projects leading to the impoverishment of the affected communities. The effective participation of the indigenous/minority communities was missing in all the projects. Similarly, the resettlement policies missed acknowledging the specific resettlement needs of women, which in many cases increased the vulnerability of this group (for instance in the case of Ilisu dam). Conceptualizing resettlement as a development opportunity rather than an obligation seems to be existing only on policy guidelines rather than in reality. The social-psychological impacts of these projects on the locals, changing the way they live and relate to each other, causing them to lose their historical-emotional-cultural relations have not been the concern of any of these projects. Furthermore, all these projects, despite having environmental laws obligating the EIA, have somehow overlooked the ecological consequences of these projects.

All the resettlement planning in principle must be primarily based on the guidelines of the World Bank as well as Cernea's risk model; however, various field studies have highlighted that the planners have been selective in its application and narrow in their conceptualization of developmental objectives for local people. The very first principle of World Bank Model that 'displacement should be minimized and its adverse impacts should be mitigated' (World Bank 2001) was ignored in the resettlement planning

(Morvaridi 2004), in all these projects except in the case of Belo Monte where the initial proposal of six dams was changes to one dam under public pressure.

While a number of those dams may be seen to have achieved the main goal for which they were constructed, they have also been instrumental in causing severe socio-economic hardships for those who have to make way for these large dams. The affected persons in reality have the least chances of getting benefits out of these projects as in most of the cases the electricity generated by these dams often benefited urban elites leaving the local people more impoverished. It is, however, common to ignore the plight of communities surviving on these rivers, when the dams are constructed with national development as a core objective in the mind of planners.

SECTION III:

DISPLACEMENT AND RESETTLEMENT IN INDIA: LEGACIES, CHALLENGES AND SOLUTIONS

CHAPTER 6

RESETTLEMENT LAWS AND POLICIES IN INDIA[1]

The focus of post-colonial independent India was to accelerate the pace of development. It was done through the introduction of five-year plans. Nehru's vision of modern Indian society led to focus being shifted to heavy industries, power, mining and hydroelectric projects for creating productive resources. Named as 'temples of modern India', these dams generated hope among the people about the resurgence of 'New India'. Many large-scale hydroelectric projects were started in the 1960s and 1970s to fulfil these aspirations. Some of these were: Hirakud Dam (Orissa), Ukai Dam (Gujarat), Rihand Dam (Uttar Pradesh), Kutku Dam and Damodar Valley Project (Bihar), Koyna Dam (Maharashtra), and Upper Krishna Irrigation Project (Karnataka). A prerequisite for making these projects a reality was to make the land available with displacement of people through land acquisition being the only option left. Hydroelectric and irrigation projects have led to the largest number of displacements and destruction of habitat. The magnitude of displacement due to the development projects can be gauged from its scale itself. While there is a lack of reliable estimates of the total number of persons displaced so far, non-official estimates place them around 2.13 to 3.5 crores between 1951 and 1990. The number increased to 6 crores by the end of the year 2000 (Fernandes 2004). In India, around 50 million people were already displaced due to development projects by the end of the year 2013 (Government of India Report 2013). In addition to this number, lakhs of people have been (indirectly) displaced from land and livelihood owing to the impact of project activities which have not been even taken into account for computing the number of displaced persons (Saxena 2008b). Nehru himself acknowledged the displacement caused due to these projects while speaking to villagers who were to be displaced by the Hirakud Dam in 1948 by stating that:

[1] Some portions of this chapter have been extracted from my article "Development Induced Displacement and Resettlement in India: Laws and Policies" published in Social Justice and Human Rights in India Ed., New Delhi: Rawat, 2020

If you are to suffer, you should suffer in the interest of the country
(Purohit 2016)

While these projects accelerated the pace of economic development in India, the suffering caused to those who got displaced because of these projects must not be overlooked. Each nation has its own framework of laws and regulations that apply to land acquisition and compensation that are often strongly influenced by the pedigree of their legal system (Price 2009). Since the first guidelines for development-caused involuntary resettlement were adopted by the World Bank in 1980, a large number of national governments, including India, have enacted resettlement guidelines and legislation requiring compensation and post-resettlement support that is more commensurate with replacement (Price 2008). While early approaches prioritised financial compensation for restoring original standards of living, more recent policies have acknowledged the social, health, and livelihood costs of displacement by seeking to prevent or minimise displacement when possible and adopting a 'resettlement with development' approach (Neef and Singer 2015). To understand the issue of development induced displacement in the Indian context, it is important to understand the origin of the land acquisition laws in the colonial era.

The Land Acquisition Act, 1894

The Act was enacted during colonial rule to enable the State to acquire land with minimal compensation payment in order to keep the state exchequer rich. Hence, many issues such as what type of land can be acquired, the purpose of acquisition and the process of acquisition and compensation were actually not spelt clearly. It was left to the state to decide on all such issues. The irony is that in post-colonial India, the governments failed to bring any significant change in this law. However, before critically analysing the law, it will be important to understand the land acquisition process enumerated under the Act (Land Acquisition Act 1894).

Preliminary investigation: If the Government is satisfied that the land in any locality is required or is likely to be required for any public purpose, a notification to that effect shall be published in the Official Gazette and in two daily newspapers circulating in that locality of which at least one shall be in the regional language. The designated official then can conduct a survey of the land (Section 4).

Hearing of objections: Any person interested in any land which has been notified under section 4 within 30 days from the date of the publication of the notification, may object in writing to the Collector (District Magistrate) to the acquisition of the land. The Collector, after giving a personal hearing, will refer the case to the appropriate Government along with his recommendations on the objections (Section 5A).

Declaration of intended acquisition: If the appropriate Government after considering the objections still decides that any particular land is needed for a public purpose, a declaration shall be made to that effect by the concerned Government. The notification is required to set out the details of the area to be acquired as well as the public purpose for which the land is acquired (Section 6).

Declaration: After declaration, the Collector proceeds with the acquisition of land and land is marked out, measured and planned (Sections 7 and 8).

Notice to persons interested: Public notice is issued for the claims to compensation before a notified date (Section 9).

Enquiry and award by Collector: The Collector decide the value of the land (at the date of the publication of the notification under Section 4), the actual area of the land to be acquired, the compensation amount and the apportionment of the compensation among all the claimants (Section 11).

Urgency Clause: It provides Special powers to the Collector to take possession of land in case of urgency within 15 days from the publication of the notice under Section 9 (Section 17).

Compensation: In determining the amount of compensation to be awarded for land acquired, the Collector (or the Court as the case may be), shall take into consideration the market-value of the land at the date of the publication of the (notification under Section 4); the damage sustained to the standing crops/trees at the time of taking possession; the damage sustained by the person interested, at the time of taking possession of the land; the damage to the property, movable or immovable etc (Section 23). This section also provides for an additional payment of 15 percent of the market value in view of the compulsory nature of acquisition.

The main philosophy behind the Act has been that the state has power of eminent domain. The doctrine was part of the common Law of England and was applied to all the British colonies, including India. The government after independence continued with the practice of this doctrine for acquisition of land. As per this doctrine, the state may directly own land through acquisition, purchase, etc, or by default. This means all lands which are not privately owned, are owned by the state and the state has power of eminent domain on privately owned land too (Dwarkadas Shrinivas vs Sholapur Spinning and Weaving Co Ltd. 1954). The legal rationality of the Eminent domain created such a tilt in favour of the state that it became immune to the challenge in the Court as well. The Act further had many legal controversies and left many substantial questions unanswered as far as the process of land acquisition and provision of compensation was concerned. Some of these were (Desai 2011):

What constitutes public purpose? The definition of public purpose in the Act has been vague. This has led to the acquisition of land by the government for any purpose. The colonial government used it primarily for the requirements of the government and its agencies. However, after independence, the scope of public purpose was broadened to include manufacturing, trade and commerce as well. It was further extended to the needs of the corporate sector working purely on the profit motive. Even the inconsistency between the actual and stated purpose was not considered as an infringement of public purpose. It led to the discretionary power used by the state to take away the livelihood sources of poor and indigenous people. It further raised a question about who would decide what the public purpose is. Courts time and again upheld that it was the prerogative of the State to decide whether a public purpose would be met with the acquisition of a particular land or not.

Who is entitled to the compensation? The law used the expression 'person interested' for the identification of a person, eligible for compensation. However, the same was not precisely defined by the law. Hence, in practice, landowners, whose rights were entered in the record of the concerned village, got compensation. Forest dwellers and tribals were not covered under this category, as they did not possess any occupancy rights to land or habitat as they only possessed customary ownership to these resources. It also ignored the dependents on such lands such as landless laborers and an artisan as far as compensation was concerned. This duality of property rights had no legal or constitutional justification and, therefore, were most discriminatory (Singh 1989).

What will be the mode of compensation? First, the connotation of compensation in the law had a limited meaning. As the Act was understood, it was assumed that it only mentioned monetary compensation for the land acquired by the State. It did not make up for the whole range of losses: social and economic, resulting from the forced eviction. No value was attached to these losses in the computation of compensation. Secondly, it excluded from its purview the loss of rights collectively enjoyed by the community at large over these lands and resources. Thirdly, it did not specify any mode of compensation and in the absence of any clear direction under the law, the practice was to give cash compensation as it was considered the simplest and cheapest method to discharge its responsibilities by the state. This narrow understanding led to total ignorance to the multiple dimensions of sufferings associated with displacement. 'Implicitly it was also assumed that land is a commodity, that property rights over such land are well defined, that a market for land exists and that market prices approximate the scarcity value of the land to the society' (Goyal 1996: 1463). It was further silent about the rehabilitation of those displaced.

Hence, it can be stated that the Land Acquisition Act, 1894, restricted itself to land acquisition and related processes. It protected the interests of the state but not the citizens. There were no provisions for rehabilitation, protection of community rights and consent, and the rates of compensation were nominal (Nielsen 2011). The Collector had unlimited powers under Section 9 of this Act. Settling compensation claims, deciding on the value of land and the mode of compensation were solely under their preview (Desai 2011). The compensation amount was not adequate, partly because the local market price of land, which was used to decide the compensation amount, was typically lower than the value at which land transfers actually took place, and also because no attempt was made to compensate for the loss of assets on the acquired land (Ghatak and Ghosh 2011). The job of the state was assumed to be done, once the land was acquired and the compensation amount was paid to the claimants. Under the guise of compensating for lost assets, these laws externalised much of the costs on those displaced while limiting the legal responsibility of the state to cash compensation for a limited set of assets (Jayewardene 2008). The framework of law, therefore, was in conflict with the overall framework of social justice enshrined in the Constitution and expressed through various instruments, national and international, of human rights (Baxi 1989).

The rising public concern against this colonial law led to many movements and litigations against forced eviction since the 1990s. It was asserted that involuntary displacement has been the very negation of the Preamble to the Constitution which focused on commitment to justice—social, economic and political. It also violated certain Fundamental Rights such as right to reside and settle in any part of the territory guaranteed under Article 19 of the Constitution and right to live with dignity under Article 21. It also compromised the Directive Principles of State Policy enshrined in Article 39 (b) and (c). Besides this, special protection provided to the Scheduled

Tribes in the Constitution were also getting infringed, as development projects led to eviction of the affected tribals from the project areas (Saxena 2008b). The particular issue raised was - absence of any comprehensive law or policy regarding the compensation and resettlement of those displaced due to development projects. The World Bank also expressed its grave concern for the sufferings of the displaced persons.

Prior to 2003, India did not have any resettlement and rehabilitation policy at the national level. While the pressure from the World Bank hastened the formulation of the first ever National Policy on Resettlement and Rehabilitation for Project-Affected Families, 2003, the policy was criticized by civil society organizations engaged in this field asserting that the policy failed miserably to fulfil the aspirations of the displaced. This led to policy being replaced by ‘National Policy on Resettlement and Rehabilitation’ in 2007. However, the need was felt to have a combined law which makes resettlement and rehabilitation as a compulsory component of the land acquisition process. This led to the formulation of ‘The Right to Fair Compensation and Transparency in Land Acquisition, Rehabilitation and Resettlement Act, 2013’ (MoRD 2013). The key features of the Act along with the subsequent developments have been discussed below.

The Right to Fair Compensation and Transparency in Land Acquisition, Rehabilitation and Resettlement Act, 2013

The Act came into force in January 2014 and endeavoured to regulate land acquisition and laid down rules for compensation, resettlement and rehabilitation for the affected people. The Act replaced the 120 years old Land Acquisition Act, 1894. Some of the key features of the Act have been:

Definition of public purpose: Section 2(1) of the Act prescribed list of public purposes for which land can be expropriated. This list included: military/national defence projects; infrastructure projects including mining, agriculture, water harvesting and water conservation structures, sanitation and industrial corridor projects; housing projects; urban development projects; and residential projects. A clear list of public purposes restricted the government’s authority, in comparison to the provisions of Land Acquisition Act 1894, which provided unlimited powers to the government by stating that land could be expropriated ‘whenever it appear[ed] to the [appropriate Government] that land in any locality is needed or likely to be needed for any public purpose [or for a company]’.

Urgency clause: The Act (Section 40) restricted the use of the urgency clause (the provision by which land expropriation may be expedited) in emergency circumstances to situations involving India's defence, national security or for emergencies due to natural calamities, and any other emergency that too with the approval of Parliament.

Provision of the Consent: The Act provided that the consent of at least 80 percent and 70 percent of the project affected families should be obtained when the government acquired the land for private companies and for public-private projects respectively. However, the consent of the land owner should not be required when the government acquired land for public purpose and shall control the land directly.

Social Impact Assessment (SIA): Section 4(4) of the Act mandated the conduct of Social Impact Assessment (SIA) to assess whether a proposed acquisition served a public purpose. The SIA must also include an estimation of affected families displaced, the extent of lands likely to be acquired, whether the amount of land proposed to be acquired is the absolute bare minimum level required for the project, whether land acquisition at a different place has been well-thought-out, and a description of the nature of the social impacts and overall costs vis-a-vis the benefits of the project. It further provided that the SIA report should be appraised by the expert group who would ensure that land has been acquired only when it was necessary. However, the SIA requirement could be avoided in cases of 'urgency'.

Establishment of Land Acquisition, Rehabilitation and Resettlement Authority (LARR): The Act provided the mechanism for the establishment of a Land Acquisition, Rehabilitation and Resettlement Authority by the state government as a 'One Person' authority with powers of civil court for development projects.

Participation of all the stakeholders: The Act required the LARR Authority to hold a public hearing at the affected area as a means of ascertaining the viewpoints of affected families. It further mandated consultation with the concerned panchayats and municipality and conducting public hearing in the concerned area.

Grievance Redressal mechanism: Unlike the Land Acquisition Act 1894, the Act under Section 16 provided an effective grievance redressal mechanism for affected persons. As per the Act, the Collector should hear objections of the aggrieved persons and should submit a report of the same to the Government.

Return of unutilized land: The Act required that if the land acquired under the Act remained unutilized for five years, it should be returned to the original owners or the land bank.

Definition of 'land owner': The Act broadened the definition of land owner by including persons granted forest rights under 'The Scheduled Tribes and Other Traditional Forest Dwellers (Recognition of Forest Rights) Act, 2006'; person who has been entitled to be granted *Patta* rights; or any person who has been declared as such by an order of the court or Authority.

Limits on acquisition: The Act forbids land acquisition when such acquisition would include multi-crop irrigated area. In case of acquisition for emergency purposes, the concerned authority should set up a cultivable wasteland of equivalent area.

Compensation: Section 26 of the Act defined the method by which market value of the land should be computed under the proposed law. The market value of the land has to be determined by the average sale price for similar types of land situated in the nearest village or nearest vicinity area. This sale price has to be assessed, by considering one-half of the total number of sale deeds or the agreements to sell, in which the highest price has been mentioned. The market value would be multiplied by a factor of, at least one to two times the market value for land acquired in rural areas and at least one times the market value for land acquired in urban areas. The compensation could also be a consented amount, in case the land has been acquired for private companies or public-private partnership projects.

Rehabilitation and resettlement: The Act under Section 3 broadened the definition of affected family. Under the Act, the 'affected family' besides including a family whose land or other immovable property has been acquired, includes, among others, agricultural laborers, tenants, share-croppers or artisans or who may be working in the affected area for three years prior to the acquisition of the land, whose primary source of livelihood stand affected by the acquisition of land. The Rehabilitation and Resettlement entitlements of livelihood-losers consisted of a job or a lump-sum payment in lieu thereof, resettlement allowance and one-time financial assistance for loss of cattle sheds and petty shops. The artisans, small traders, self-employed persons and owners of non-agricultural land or institutional, commercial and industrial structures must also be provided a one-time financial assistance. The agricultural tenants have been entitled to a portion of the cash compensation accruing to the landowners. In the event of involuntary displacement, transportation allowance and a one-year subsistence grant should also be offered. The 'affected family' that did not own a homestead but had been residing continuously in the affected area for three years prior to the acquisition should be provided a house at the relocation site (Das 2020). In addition to the above-mentioned compensation and entitlements under the Act, scheduled caste and scheduled tribe (SC/ST) families have been entitled to several other additional benefits as per Schedule II.

The new legislation having many positive features was welcomed by social activists as well as civil society organizations. However, many procedural difficulties were reported in the acquisition of lands while implementing a project in the field. For example, it became difficult to acquire land in various states (such as Punjab and Haryana) where most of the land has been irrigated. Besides this, payment of compensation based on the market price of land could not ensure social justice and efficient use of resources as there was huge difference in the rates at which actual transfer of land takes place and the amount that was registered. The implementation also varied from state to state as the 'acquisition and requisitioning of property' being in the concurrent list in the Indian Constitution, both the central and state governments have power to make laws/rules over the same, though, state-enacted rules must comply with central laws. Due to this federal-state issue, the implementation of the LARR Act has not been consistent across India's 29 states; many states chose to waive certain requirements established in the LARR Act (Kohli et al. 2017; Ramesh et al. 2016). In Maharashtra, for example, only private projects must adhere to consent and SIA requirements; in Tamil Nadu, many expropriations carried out under state laws were exempted for SIA and consent requirements. Andhra Pradesh reduced the notice period for public hearings that must be conducted as part of SIA. In Jharkhand, there has been no requirement to return the land to its original owners if the expropriated land remained unused for five years (a requirement established in the LARR Act) (Mahaprashasta 2016).

Therefore, the government of India introduced certain amendments in the Act. Stating it to be an urgency, these were brought about by an Ordinance on December 31, 2014 (Government of India 2014). Subsequently, an Amendment Bill was passed by the Lok Sabha to replace the Ordinance. This included some more changes to the Ordinance. The important changes brought about by the amendment have been:

- The Bill created five special categories of land use: national security projects, rural infrastructure including electrification, affordable housing and housing for poor people, industrial corridors, and infrastructure and social infrastructure projects where the central government owned the land. This conceptualization of five categories of projects has been severely criticized by the social activists asserting that the categorization is loose and vague, lacks precision and clarity and can be misused by including any project under one or the other category (Yadav 2015).

- These five special categories have also been exempted from the provision under the LARR Act 2013 which mandated the consent of 80 percent of land owners for private projects and that of 70 percent of land owners for PPP projects. The relaxation of the condition of consent has left almost no activity requiring consent, defeating the very purpose of the consent.
- The Bill also exempted projects in these five categories from undertaking Social Impact Assessment. This created the situations similar to the prior to the enactment of 2013 legislation with no accountability of the state agencies to those affected by the projects.
- The 2013 Act had imposed the restrictions on the acquisition of irrigated multi-cropped to safeguard food security. The new bill, however, removed this provision as well. This would adversely affect food security. Furthermore, it enlarged the ambit of dilution by leaving it to the state governments to fix the limits of such acquisition for each district or state. The conditionality of developing an equivalent area of cultural wasteland as a compensating mechanism for such acquisition has also been relaxed by providing the alternative in the form of monetizing in case this was not possible.
- The terminology used in the 2013 Act, for the applicability of acquisition of land has also been changed from ‘private companies’ to ‘private entities’. This enabled the acquisition of land by the state, even for registered societies, co-operatives, trusts, proprietorships, partnerships, non-profit organizations etc.; therefore, increasing the magnitude of displacement manifold.
- The Act had excluded private hospitals and private educational institutions from the ambit of infrastructure projects for which land could be acquired without the consent of the affected persons. As per the bill, these two exclusions have been omitted, thereby allowing compulsory acquisition by the state for these two purposes as well.
- As per the proposed bill, the period after which unutilized land has to be returned would be the later of: five years, or any period specified at the time of setting up the project. This would enable the project agency to retain the unutilized land for a longer period and

would deprive the land losers of the benefit of return of land because it empowers the acquiring authority to 'specify an extremely lengthy and generous period for completion of any project without any accountability' (Ramesh 2015). This may further lead to unutilized land being diverted for other uses. The proposed amendment would fail to check the tendency of project authorities to acquire large areas of land much in excess of requirement (Saxena 2015).

This proposed dilution of the provisions of the mandatory consent and social impact assessment resulted in an unrest. Civil Society Organizations asserted that the amendment has been proposed only due to the pressure of corporations, bureaucrats, politicians and neoliberal economists who considered the 2013 Act unworkable and a serious bottleneck to economic growth (Chakravorty 2015). Due to the rising resistance against the proposed bill, the government referred it to the Standing Committee of parliament for its consideration. The bill is still to be passed in the upper House of the parliament. In the meantime, many state governments (Madhya Pradesh, Andhra Pradesh, Tamil Nadu, Punjab) have enacted their own laws and policies for land acquisition.

Even if the new legislation and its subsequent amendments attempt to introduce a right based approach in the process of acquisition of land; the success of the legislation in doing so will be evaluated in the years to come. Issues such as corruption and late payments need to be resolved. Efforts must be made to restore or replace lost livelihoods. It is also important to keep in mind that besides focusing on proper resettlement and rehabilitation of the displaced population, moreover, to rethink the causes and consequences of displacement in the paradigm of development. The dominant paradigm of development today is growth-centric and market-centric. It is a double-edged sword; it definitely benefits a few. While we cannot do away with the current development paradigm, an effort needs to be made to examine the problems caused by the current development model and to make it more inclusive and sustainable.

> ***Let it not be said of India, that this great Republic in a hurry to develop itself is devastating the green mother earth and uprooting our tribal population.***
> —From the Speech of the President of India, K.R. Narayanan 25th January 2001 (MoEA 2001)

CHAPTER 7

DISPLACEMENT AND RESETTLEMENT IN INDIA: CASE STUDIES

The first recorded dam in India was on the Cauvery River, the southernmost of the three great river catchments draining the Deccan Peninsula, in the second century AD. The dam is still in use though massively altered and reinforced, and is just one of the many ancient dams subsequently reconstructed throughout India, with a particularly pronounced period of dam building as long ago as the thirteenth century AD (Everard 2013). Independent India undertook development projects to improve the quality of life of its people through planned development under the successive Five-Year Plans. Such projects included dams, power, mining, industrial and allied infrastructures, transport network, urban development, commercial forestry and other projects. However, these projects often came at significant human cost, exemplified by inadequate compensation, insufficient consultation and improper resettlement.

In the absence of firm project wise data, the estimates of the total numbers displaced by planned development interventions from 1951-1990 range from a conservative 110 lakhs to an overall figure of 185 lakhs. These figures do not include the sizable number of people who are not acknowledged as being 'project affected' (i.e., by loss of livelihood caused by natural resource extraction or degradation), those displaced in urban areas and those victimized by the processes of secondary displacement. If these are tallied, the number of those displaced since independence would be as high as four crores (Kothari 1996). The majority of this displacement has been due to multipurpose mega-dams. 'India with more than 4000 dams is one of the top five dam-building countries which account for nearly 80 percent of all large dams worldwide. India and China have built around 57 percent of the world's large dams and account for the largest number of people displaced. In India, estimates of the total number of people displaced due to large dams vary from 16 to 38 million people' (WCD 2000:9).

Most adversely affected by such displacement have been indigenous and tribal communities. This can be substantiated from the fact that despite indigenous communities being only eight percent of the population in India, 40-50 percent of those displaced hail from indigenous and tribal communities (Mathur 2013). As the demand for energy grows and with the emphasis of the government on energy production through coal-fired power plants and hydroelectric dams, the displacement is going to multiply in the decades to come. Hence, the issue of development-induced displacement in India is situated at a critical intersection of cultural identity, human rights, development aspirations, social conflict, and national security concerns (Neef and Singer 2015).

Many large hydroelectricity projects in India have faced lots of resistance from displaced people as well as from the civil society organizations. The Tehri, Pong, Kosi, Ganghak, Bodhghat, Narmada, Bedthi, Bhopalpatnam and Ichampatti, Tungbhadra, Malprabha and Ghataprabha river basin projects have all faced resistance (Biswal 2015:465). The multiple issues raised were: location and design of the projects, social and ecological consequences of these projects as well as the issue of inadequate compensation and improper rehabilitation of those displaced. This chapter endeavors to analyze the efficacy of resettlement policies in two most significant hydroelectric projects in India. The first one is Bhakra Dam Project as it was one of the largest investment schemes in newly independent India and there was least resistance from displaced people. The second one is the Sardar Sarovar Project, a project which has generated lots of controversy both at the national and global level.

Bhakra Dam Project

> *When I walked around the site, I thought that these days, the biggest temple and mosque and gurdwara is the place where man works for the good of mankind. What place can be greater than Bhakra Nangal, where thousands of men have worked or shed their blood and sweat and laid down their lives as well? Where can be holier than this; which can we regard as higher?*
> —Prime Minister Pandit Jawaharlal Nehru's famous comment (cited in Singh 1997: 55)

Nehru's famous and often repeated utterance describing dams as 'temples of modern India' on the opening of the Bhakra project in 1954 are still widely quoted in Indian school textbooks, despite the fact that Nehru came to regret his statement within his own lifetime (Everard 2013:28). The evaluation of socio-economic and environmental impacts of the Bhakra Dam has been a difficult task as long time has passed since the project came into being and it was difficult to retrieve baseline data to compare the socio-economic scenario and ecological characteristics of the area before and after the construction of the dam. This is one of the reasons why there has been scarcity of research on the environmental as well as socio-economic impacts of the dam. One literature available is the report released by Bhakra Beas Management Board (BBMB) titled '*Socio-Economic and Environmental Impacts of Bhakra Beas Project – An Assessment*' in 2001 (Duggal 2001). The report listed many benefits of the project; however, it is interesting to note that the report did not mention even a single negative impact of the dam. In a populist government structure, this seems to be the natural and expected outcome of any report released by a government agency. Besides this, Rangachari's (2006) defence of the Bhakra project is one of the popular works on evaluating this iconic dam. Dharmadhikary's (2005) '*Unravelling Bhakra: Assessing the Temple of Resurgent India*' provides a compelling alternative analysis, based on a detailed three years study. Though both the studies have been carried out almost at the same time, Dharmadhikary's study contradicted the facts presented by Rangachari as well as by BBMB and enumerated multiple devastating impacts the project had on local community as well as on ecological system. Considered a great triumph at the time of construction, the project has come under criticism for various reasons in the subsequent years. One of the major reasons was that the resettlement process remained incomplete even decades after the displacement. The project has also witnessed a long period of wrangling between Haryana, Punjab, Rajasthan and Himachal Pradesh, the states affected by the project in one or other way, over what the proper distribution of costs ought to be (Verghese 1994:16). Though the projected outcomes of any hydroelectric projects such as irrigation, flood control, employment generation, land reclamation, fishing as well as tourism could not be ignored; it would be important to note some of the major socio-environmental impacts of the project.

Historical and Geographical Perspective

'The world's toughest' as applied to the Bhakra Dam is no misnomer. Every contractor who visited the project has agreed that nowhere have the problems of supply, river division, labor and topography been more difficult (World's Business 1958). Built on the river Satluj in Himachal Pradesh, just before it enters into Punjab, the project was considered the largest single investment scheme in newly independent India. The earliest reference to the Bhakra project can be traced back in 1908 when Sir Louis Dane, the then Lieutenant Governor of Punjab, made a reference regarding the same in a note. The proposal was revived in 1915 and a comprehensive project report was prepared in 1919. The initial literature mentioned it purely as an irrigation project to overcome the devastating effects of famine in that area. However, the conflict between the princely States and later due to partition of India in 1947, the government considered suspending the proposal until a dispute with Pakistan, over how the waters of the Indus and its tributaries would be divided, was resolved. With the Partition of Punjab, almost 80 percent of the irrigation system went to Pakistan along with a large portion of fertile agricultural land. This provided another justifiable reason to go ahead with the project. Instead of letting the job by contract, the Indian Government decided to undertake it herself. The project was made a showpiece, proudly displayed to visiting foreign dignitaries. Various agencies and experts including United States Bureau of Reclamation (USBR), Harvey Slocum (who built the Grand Coulee, Bull Shoals and other great dams in the US) and J. L. Savage were involved in various capacities; though the overall direction remained clearly vested in CWPC (Central Water and Power Commission) (World's Business 1958; Klingensmith 2007).

When the construction of Bhakra Nangal project began, Bilaspur (or Kahlur) was an independent hill State and Raja Anand Chand was the last ruler. In 1954, the state was merged with the Union Territory and later became part of Himachal Pradesh (Singh et al. 2014). The dam has a height of 226 meters. A reservoir named Gobind Sagar is spread over an area of 168.35 sq. km with the water storage capacity of 9340 million cubic meters. The dam's powerhouses have a combined generating capacity of 2880 MW and it generates about 14,000 million units (kWh) of electricity in a year. The work of the dam was completed in 1963.

Displacement and Resettlement

According to the official data (BBMB, 2002b), the dam led to the submergence of around 44153 acres of land and the displacement of 36,000 persons (7206 families) in 371 villages. This included the submergence of Bilaspur town. Out of 36000 people displaced, 34.8 percent (12514 persons) belonged to tribal communities (IIPA 2002). Three modes of compensation and resettlement were adopted:

Payment of cash compensation to resettle by their own choice: 37 percent of those displaced opted for cash compensation. Those getting cash compensation were left to fend for themselves. Most of these were oustees chose to continue to live in Himachal Pradesh itself—simply moving up the slopes of the hills on the side of the river—as they had no other place to go. They received cash compensation at the rate of Rs. 100-500 per acre depending upon the quality of the soil (Dharmadhikary 2005). Since the people who settled along the mountain slopes had no lands, they faced serious economic difficulties as the major source of their income was acquired. As there were no banks at the time when the compensation was given, many of them deposited their money with the local *Sahukars* (money lenders) who never returned the money. Jobs became their main source of survival. Some people got work at the dam site while some continued to get jobs in the army as per the tradition of the area (Dharmadhikary 2005). The residents were also not happy with the amount of cash compensation they received. As the compensation was given on the basis of household, the traditional joint family system with many adult children staying under the common roof proved to be a disadvantage for most of them. The cash compensation was soon spent on meeting the expenses related to shifting from the old to the new place, settling down there and other household expenses. Though a Tribunal was established by the government for the redressal of grievances related to rewards, the lack of leadership and education among the displaced led to only a few people approaching the Tribunal for redressal of grievances.

Settled by Himachal Pradesh (HP) government in its own area: 33 percent of those displaced opted to be settled by HP government in its own area. As the town of Bilaspur was to be fully submerged, a new town was therefore built on the slopes of the adjoining mountains. The markets were situated at the foot of the mountain, while the government offices and residences were built higher up the mountain. Each family was given a plot of land. There were three categories of plots: House plots (10x10 sq. ft.), Commercial Plots and House cum Shop Plots (37x38 sq. ft). While the cost of plots was Rs. 4000, the families were charged Rs. 226 per plot. The families were given rehabilitation grants for the construction of their new homes. The facilities provided for those settling in Himachal Pradesh, according to BBMB, were free fishing licenses in the reservoir for three years; new ferries, roads and village paths; employment at the construction site and training for the skilled jobs.

Resettled by the government by acquiring land: One of the requests made by the displaced persons (around 30 percent displaced persons) was that they should be rehabilitated on lands to be irrigated by the new canals and should be settled at one place to restore community ties. Around 13200 acres of land was acquired in 30 villages of Hisar district (now in the State of Haryana) to resettle the displaced. The resettlement site was over 200 kms away from their original homes. The policy was that no oustee would be given more than 25 acres of land, but also not less than his acquired holding, subject to his compensation amount being adequate to meet the cost. In other words, it was not really a land-in-lieu-of-land policy. The oustees were paid cash compensation, and they were to pay for the new lands from this. The oustees were not to be given any proprietary rights to these lands till they had fulfilled all the conditions of resettlement and paid all sums due from them. Among the conditions was that if any Court decision led to an increase in the price of lands allotted to them, the oustees would compensate the Government for the same. Landless tenants were also declared eligible for allotment of land equal to the extent of their submerged tenancy subject to a maximum of five acres (BBMB 2002b). It was also decided to allot half an acre of land free of cost to each artisan and laborer of the rural area who did not own or cultivate land provided he shifted and settled to the Hisar district (BBMB 2002b). For the oustees resettled in Hisar district, mud huts were provided to serve as shelter accommodation; drinking water supply was ensured by repairing of existing wells and providing new wells; new canals were constructed; loans were given for the construction of houses and arrangements were made for easy supply of building material and transport.

The policy was hardly fair or adequate, both, in its conception and implementation. Various gaps were identified in the implementation of the resettlement plan. The representative team of the project-affected persons, when taken to Hisar to show the sites proposed for rehabilitation, did not approve the site stating various reasons such as bad quality land, overgrown with bushes and undergrowth. The resettled people had to put lots of effort into making the soil arable. There were many wild animals and snakes, making habitation on these plots very dangerous. Besides this, ignoring the requests of displaced people to settle at one site, people were settled in 33 villages spread over a wide area.

The landowners in Hisar from whom land had been acquired for resettlement of oustees were dissatisfied with the compensation given to them, and went to court. In many cases, the courts granted substantial increase in the prices. As per the earlier agreement, the arrears had to be paid by the resettled people, leading to an additional burden on them. To make the situation worse, the basic civic amenities such as drinking water, electricity, schools, colleges, or dispensaries were missing at relocated sites. The lack of post offices in the region made communication with their original homes very difficult. As the Land was allotted under the Colonization Act, 1912, they did not receive title deeds for their lands. Most of the people received proprietary ownership only in 1980. Due to the uncertainty regarding ownership, they could not invest in the land and were not able to get loans against the land. In a few cases, the house plots were forcibly occupied by the residents of the original villages. When the oustees complained against this, the locals lodged false cases against them, and the whole administrative machinery being in favor of the locals, resulted in a lot of harassment to the oustees (Dharmadhikary 2005).

Peculiar to the dam induced displacement, most of the oustees had difficulties in readjusting to the resettlement sites. Business was slow during the period, therefore, many had to switch over to new types of businesses. While the younger generation was able to cope up with the challenges to resettlement, the elderly people were found to be nostalgic about their old ways of life and environment. They have fond memories of how natural springs were used for getting water for drinking, how their old land along the river bank was cultivated soon after the river spill subsided and how they had enough brushwood for cooking purposes (Dharmadhikary 2005).

Although the cases of oustees reached Apex court, no fixed timeline was given by the court for settling the claims of the oustees while framing guidelines for the same. The Bhakra Dam Oustees Association has been found to be pursuing the issue with the resettlement committee till date (2020) despite it being more than 58 years when the project was dedicated to the nation in the year 1963. The recent communication of Bhakra Dam Oustees Association (dated March 12, 2019) addressed to the Chairman BBMB stated that people are still struggling for the basic human rights such as drinking water, school for children and community centres etc. Even the land titles have not been transferred in the name of some of the oustees till date. They are still asking for proprietary rights. They all had a general grievance that their sacrifice for the nation had not been fully recognized by the people who are benefited or even by the project authorities (Dharmadhikary 2005).

Social and Economic Impact

The project is stated to be the lifeline for the states of Punjab, Haryana, Rajasthan and Himachal Pradesh. Many studies (Bhatia et al. 2007) affirmed that the dam has increased the gross irrigated area by 7.1 million ha yr^{-1} and consequently led to the increase in food grain production by 25 million tons yr^{-1}. Furthermore, a large number of migratory workers from underdeveloped areas of Bihar and Uttar Pradesh have sent large amounts of remittances creating further multiplier effects in those regions. As much as 55 percent of the total increase in food grain production in the country over two decades (1961-80) came from the Bhakra dam. As a result of such a high increase in domestic production, the net imports of food grain declined substantially from 10.3 million ton in 1966 to almost zero in 1972. The Bhakra system canals and recharge of groundwater have played a very significant role in the availability of drinking water supplies in rural and urban areas of Punjab and Haryana. The system has also provided water supplies needed for industries, small establishments and household enterprises in these two states. The Bhakra Dam system is a major source of drinking water supply for Delhi, providing about 900 million liters per day (MLD), or 40 percent of the total surface water supplies of Delhi (Bhatia et al. 2007).

However, what has gone unreported or underreported has been the overall impact on the people who were displaced due to the project. The entire economic structure of the region was overhauled after the construction of the dam. Fishing activity which was essentially carried out in an informal and unorganized manner before the dam, was transformed into a commercial activity with no one being allowed to fish without a license. Commercialization and licensing of fishing rights took away the livelihood of local communities who had been carrying out fishing in that area in an unorganized and informal manner for a long time. As the government did not allow fishing activity in the reservoir during the first 2-3 years after the construction of the dam, this proved detrimental to the fishing communities in the region.

Farming was the major occupation of the region. The plains on the banks of the river were extremely fertile. Both the kharif and the rabi crops could be cultivated. Irrigation was done with water from the Sutlej and the large number of natural streams flowing into the plains from the mountains. A variety of crops like corn, wheat and cotton grew there. Most people also owned orchards and sold the fruits as their livelihood. The corn that was cultivated in the region was sent to Punjab and Haryana. Synthetic fertilizers or pesticides were not used at all. Apart from income from agriculture, there was a substantially large cattle economy in this region. All these economic activities were adversely affected at the resettlement sites. Hissar being a semi-arid region, agriculture became extremely difficult for those resettled. With no other jobs and no provision of reservations for oustee families in the case of government appointments, the majority of the resettled had to spend many years trying to scrape up enough for minimum sustenance.

The reservoir has also led to the significant changes in the micro-climatic conditions in that area which has adversely affected the health and well-being of the local community. The dependency of people on lake water and public water supply systems, instead of fresh water earlier, has increased the intensity of many diseases such as gastroenteritis, enteric fever, viral hepatitis, malaria (due to mosquito breeding) and many more. The area covered by the reservoir as well as nearby areas has thick fog almost throughout the day in the winter season which leads to respiratory diseases (Dharmadhikary 2001).

The resettlement also proved to be detrimental to the cultural bond between those resettled in Bilaspur and in Hisar and hampered the liberty of women. The loss of esteem at relocation sites curtailed the prospects of future grooms. Families living in Himachal no longer preferred to marry their daughters into the families relocated in Hisar due to contrast climatic conditions and poor economic status. Furthermore, the dislocation from their safe native villages to a strange land led to multiple restrictions on the women's freedom to move.

Environmental Consequences

When the studies of ecological impacts of large dams started getting carried out, the initial emphasis was on immediate impact on the ecology of the local area. However, the recent studies on dams have studied thoroughly the consequences of dam construction both upstream and downstream. As is true with other hydroelectric projects across the globe, the biggest environmental impact of the Bhakra project has been the submergence of around 168.35 sq. km of land area to create a reservoir 'Gobind Sagar'. Furthermore, 1000 acres was acquired to establish a township in Nangal. The area had been very fertile and was well irrigated by river Satluj as well as due to the flow of many natural streams flowing from the mountains in that area. Out of the total submerged area, 5750 hectares consisted of forest land which was rich in biological diversity (Singh et al. 2000). Another consequence of the construction of the dam has been the loss of native fishes. '32 species of fish are near threatened, 20 species became vulnerable, and 12 and 2 species have been put into the category of endangered and critically endangered respectively due to the project' (NBSAP 2001: 194). One of the most famous native species of fish '*Mahseer*' was put onto the threatened list.

During the construction of Bhakra Dam, the diversion of river water was started in the mid-1880s with the opening of Sirhind Canal on the river

Satluj. The impact of the dam on downstream areas was obvious and could not have been ignored by the policy makers at the time of the inception of the project as well. This could be substantiated from the fact that the First Five Year Plan mentioned the need to protect down streams in its chapter 26 on 'Irrigation and Power' as early as in 1950. The same, though, has not been put in practice while conceptualizing the hydroelectric projects in India till date. The most visible downstream impact of the Bhakra Dam has been the disappearance of grey canals. Out of the total 17 MAF (Million Acre Feet) flowing into Govind Sagar, only 1.4 MAF remains in the river to flow down to Harike, which is just eight percent of the total inflow into the reservoir (Anand 1956). This led to the loss of natural fertility of agricultural land due to annual floods. This has further led to the increased dependence on tube well irrigation and excessive use of fertilizers to retain the productivity of the land. This along with populist government policy of free electricity and water to farmers have led to the depletion of groundwater resources as well as the high incidence of cancer and other diseases due to excessive use of chemical fertilizers and pesticides. This raises another big question mark on the current development paradigm which has long term serious and irreversible environmental and health consequences.

The last and most significant issue regarding the large dam projects has been the sedimentation and siltation in the reservoir area. The issue is important from an economic perspective as well, as it impacts the performance of the dam. In fact, when the Bhakra complex celebrated its first decade in October 1973, the reservoir was found to have already lost nearly 14 percent of its storage capacity because of silt. Bhakra officials did not concede this and contended that actual power generation at the Bhakra complex has been greater than the initial estimates (5,916 MU in 1973-74 against the original estimate of 4,000 MU). The Bhakra Board contended that silt-clearance operations have always been going on and that the dam's life- span would be unaffected. They even claim that, at the present siltation rate, the life-span of Bhakra would be 780 years against the wide-ranging life-estimate of 550 to 730 years arrived at in the original Project Report (EPW 1974). The government reports substantiate the fact that silt deposited in Bhakra Reservoir in live storage has been 9.70 percent of live storage capacity (Duggal 2002). The 10 percent reduction in storage capacity has serious repercussions not only on the life of the dam but also poses questions such as: 'how high will the river then flow, how much will it spread, what will happen in downstream area and what will happen when the life of the dam will be over' (Dharmadhikary 2001: 200). Most of these questions not only remained unanswered but were also ignored at policy making level. According to a 1999 report from the International Water Management Institute, 'In the

Bhakra Irrigation System, the practice of allocating and distributing canal water supplies [...] leads to the current high productivity of water. The long-term sustainability of agricultural productivity seems threatened. In some areas, saline water tables are rising, and soils are becoming sodic, while in areas that have fresh groundwater, water tables are falling. There is an urgent need for the farm, regionally, and system wide' (Sakthivadivel et al. 1999: 20-21).

There has also been a dam-induced flood management problem. The sudden release of large flows from the dam may have devastating impacts on downstream communities and especially on those, who, believing themselves to be protected by a dam, have moved onto previously flooded alluvial soils. In the case of the Bhakra project, McCully wrote 'In 1978, nearly 65000 people in the Punjab were made homeless by floods exacerbated by forced discharges from Bhakra Dam... Eleven years later a similar flood occurred' (McCully 2001: 147). The year 2019 again witnessed the similar flood when due to heavy rains; the dam crossed its critical mark of 1680 feet. The flood gates of the Dam were opened putting the life of people staying in 300 villages downstream areas at risk.

The displacement and resettlement in the case of Bhakra Dam project has been unique as there was negligible resistance to the project even from the oustees. The biggest reason for the same was that the dam was constructed at the time when the excitement for the newly found independence was quite high accompanied by patriotic sentiments. By the 1950s, India had a political 'culture of demonstration', as Itty Abraham (1997) has called it, in which the regime identified itself with spectacular technological projects and thereby demonstrated its modernity and hence its legitimacy (Klingensmith 2007: 267). 'The Bhakra project was implemented under unique circumstances. These were the circumstances due to which it got not just the cooperation of the oustees but also their blind faith to the extent that no other project in India got' (Dharmadhikary 2001: 224). The nostalgia regarding the project can be seen from the statement regarding the project in the Editorial of The Economic Weekly (1954):

> *WHERE great construction works bring to the service of man the melting snows of the Himalayas and the rain waters that run to waste or spell death and destruction in untamed floods—these are the places of modern man's workshop*

However, whether the future generations will also be under the same rhetoric about the dam or not is a question to ponder upon.

Sardar Sarovar Project

In the last few decades, the debates on the viability of large hydroelectric projects in India have been dominated by the most controversial, the Sardar Sarovar Project. The strong civil society led movement has opposed the project tooth and nail. Numerous local and international environmental and human rights organizations such as Narmada Bachao Andolan, the US' Environmental Defense Fund, Friends of the Earth, Japan's Tropical Rainforest Action Network, the UK's Survival International, and Sweden's The Swallows have opposed the project (Payne and O'Bannon 1994). This resistance to the construction of huge dams on the river Narmada signifies the struggle for a society based on the principle of justice and equity in India (Friends of River Narmada 2008). These movements further questioned the presumptions made by the State and asserted that its planning has been unfair, and the construction has caused large-scale abuse of human rights along with serious and irreversible ecological consequences. On the other hand, there have been a large number of people, especially those staying in Gujarat, who support the project. This support has been so strong that any view expressed against the project evoked sub-national feelings in the state.

By 2009, nearly 2.5 million persons had already been displaced in Gujarat which amounts to around five percent of the state's population (Lancy and Kumar 2009). The government, despite the controversies around the project since the beginning, not only continued to go ahead with the project by promising cheaper electricity, irrigation and potable water for the people of desert-prone areas but also made all the efforts to suppress the resistance to the project. This is evident in the fact that Gujarat has made the second highest number of TADA (Terrorist and Disruptive Activities Prevention Act, 1985) arrests, in order to suppress 'anti-development project' agitations (Judge 2000). The proclaimed promises of the state and counter arguments of the civil society organizations as well as pro-dam people have led to a series of judicial pronouncements on the issue of rehabilitation of the displaced as well as on the ecological consequences of the project.

Historical and Geographical Background

The Sardar Sarovar Project is part of a gigantic scheme on the river Narmada, a 1312 km long river with an average annual flow of 36.5 million Acre Feet (MAF), flowing westwards from Amarkantak (Madhya Pradesh), touching Maharashtra and ending its course in Gujarat. The Sardar Sarovar Project is a multipurpose dam project and canal system whose primary rationale is to provide irrigation, drinking water and power generation. The project was first mooted in the year 1946 by the then Provincial government and by the Central Water Commission (CWC) in 1947. However, the project kept on lingering due to inter-state dispute among the affected states. An agreement known as the Bhopal Agreement was arrived at in November 1963 by the chief ministers of Gujarat and Madhya Pradesh. The agreement, however, did not get enforced due to an inter-state dispute. It was followed by the establishment of a central committee 'Narmada Water Resources Development Committee' headed by A. N. Khosla in 1964. This committee also met the same fate as the Bhopal agreement (Menon 2003).

The Narmada Water Disputes Tribunal (NWDT) was set up in 1969, which submitted its final report in 1979. Rajasthan was also made a party in the proceedings of the tribunal considering various issues. The award has been unique since apart from orders on sharing the available waters among the four states, it included directions regarding the resettlement and rehabilitation of the project affected families; a time frame for construction of the Sardar Sarovar Dam and Narmada Sagar Dam; a cost and benefit sharing; and orders for setting up organization like the Narmada Control Authority to monitor the implementation of the award, and the Sardar Sarovar Construction Advisory Committee to guide the project construction. For reviewing the various decisions of the Narmada Control Authority, directions were also given to set up a high-powered ministerial review committee (Menon 2003). As per the Plan, the project consisted of 30 major, 135 medium and 3000 minor dams on river Narmada and its 41 tributaries. The project has the potential to irrigate 1.8 million hectares of land, ensuring potable water to around 4 crore people, and an installed capacity of 1450 MW of power (Raj, 1990). One of the major dams to be constructed was Sardar Sarovar Dam in Gujarat. However, the effectiveness of Sardar Sarovar dam has been dependent upon the upstream construction of the Indira Sagar project that included three hydro dams: Narmada Sagar (1,000 MW), Omkareshwar (520 MW), and Maheshwar (320 MW) (Wood, 1993).

The foundation stone of the Sardar Sarovar Project (SSP) was laid out by the then Prime Minister Nehru in 1961. The project envisaged a 139 m high dam across the river to irrigate more than 2.5 million ha of land in Gujarat and in Rajasthan. The core purpose was to provide drinking water facilities to 8,215 villages and 135 urban centres, mostly located in the Saurashtra and Kachchh areas and to get potable water in 881 villages affected by fluoride. Other benefits included protection against floods in the downstream villages and to stop the advancement of deserts like Little Rann of Kachchh. Around 37,533 hectares of land in total was to be submerged in the three states (Menon, 2003). The estimated cost (as per the Report of CC Patel and

Associates Ltd. 1988) of the project was Rs 11,154 crore (1987-88 price level) envisaging an increased annual production of Rs 1,400 crore due to agriculture, domestic water supply and power generation.

Of the total power generated, Gujarat has to be allocated 16 percent, with the rest being split between Maharashtra (27 percent) and MP (57 percent). This higher allocation of power benefit to Maharashtra and MP was to compensate for their loss of large tracts of land and forest due to submergence and since Gujarat was to get the most of the irrigation benefits of the dam (Culler 2007: 06). The command area was 3.43 million ha in Gujarat (of which 1.869 million ha was cultivable) and 0.135 million ha (of which 0.075 million ha was cultivable) in Rajasthan. The SSP's canal network was supposed to be the largest in the world, estimated to be 90,389 km (Parasuraman et al. 2010).

The World Bank signed an agreement with the Indian government in 1985 to partially finance the Sardar Sarovar Project. However, as the construction of the dam started, the resistance against the project also flared up. The mounting criticism of the World Bank for ignoring the social and ecological impact of the dam before funding it led to the establishment of the first ever independent review by the Bank to assess the project. The report submitted was highly critical about the project. The report condemned the gaps in the social and ecological impact analysis of the project, besides other issues. It suggested that the World Bank should withdraw itself from the project (Morse and Berger 1995). The Bank officially did so in 1993. The withdrawal of the World Bank, however, could not de-motivate the government and the work on the site continued till 1995 when the Indian Supreme Court halted the work of the project until further investigation. The construction work was restored by the order of Supreme Court in the year 1999. The subsequent judgements were like a roller coaster for the civil society activists, raising hope and despair from time to time. The construction of the dam was approved in 1987 and it was inaugurated in September, 2017.

Displacement and Resettlement

The Sardar Sarovar Dam in Gujarat is arguably the most controversial dam ever built in India. A large amount of literature is available supporting the project as well as opposing it. One of the major issues of contention in all these literatures have been the rehabilitation and resettlement of those displaced due to the project. There are studies (Aiyar and Kaushal 2019; Wood 1993; Patel 1992) which supported the project and applauded the rehabilitation and resettlement policy as well as its implementation; while there are a larger number of texts enumerating the sufferings of those displaced including tribal population (Morse and Berger 1992; Daud Commission Report 2001; Report of Habitat International Coalition 2002; Oza 1997; Dharmadhikary 2006).

The project was expected to submerge 37,533 hectares of land (7,112; 9,599 and 20,822 hectares of land in Gujarat, Maharashtra and Madhya Pradesh, respectively) and displace around 152,000 persons residing in 245 villages. As per the official estimates, the project was expected to displace 4,763 families (in 19 villages) in Gujarat, 4,307 (in 33 villages) in Maharashtra and 23,614 families (in 178 villages) in Madhya Pradesh (Government of India 2017). The figures increased further since the construction of the project was delayed for many years and no new resettlement surveys were carried out. It is also to be noted that none of the estimates included the 57,000 people displaced by canals, those moved to make space for the creation of compensatory wildlife sanctuaries or those resettled to clear the way for people displaced by the dam (Everard 2013).

The resettlement and rehabilitation of displaced people at such a large scale was a big challenge. The NWDT award declared that the Gujarat government will be responsible for the resettlement and rehabilitation of the oustees of all the three states (Dash 2010). The awards announced by the NWDT report, and subsequently amended by the Gujarat government, were more advanced than provisions for any other water resources project made earlier in India. For example, as per the awards, an oustee in any one criterion, such as, a co-sharer of original joint holding; a landless agricultural laborer; an encroacher on land owned by the government or the Forest Department; and a major son of a family, would be provided two hectares (five acres) of land. Every family would be given Rs. 45,000 for the construction of a core house in addition to a plot for the house measuring 60 x 90 feet; subsistence allowance of Rs. 4,500; free of cost house electrification at the rate of 1.5 point per house; and insurance for house, death, personal accident and assets. Besides this, the resettlement sites would have all the required basic services such as an approach road, primary school, dispensary, children's park, tree plantations, drinking water, electricity, issuance of ration card, accessibility to cooperative society and arrangements for vocational training (Dash 2010).

The provision of 'land for land' was an innovative and positive step towards the restoration of livelihood given the fact that a majority of the displaced were from rural areas and were agriculturists. But the NWDTA and Gujarat government overlooked the need for the resettlement of those submerged by secondary relocations. It also did not provide for compensation or land allotment for women-headed households, unmarried daughters, deserted or divorced women and widows. Its patriarchal definition of a family saw women as a part of the family and separate provisions were not made for land ownership. Widows were the worst affected as those displaced prior to the announcement of the NWDTA were not compensated even though they had the '*khata*' (legal entitlement) to land. In cases where widows were not taken care of by their sons, without land or alternative sources of income generation, they were the most vulnerable section of development dislocates (Bhatia 1997).

Three Independent Reviews on Rehabilitation and Resettlement of the SSP: Morse-Berger independent review instituted by the World Bank (1992); the Daud Commission Report (2001), set up by the government of Maharashtra to assess the status of those affected in the state; and the Habitat International Coalition (2002), an independent NGO, for an assessment in Gujarat and Madhya Pradesh, unanimously highlighted the negative consequences of displacement on the livelihood of the oustees. While reviewing the Sardar Sarovar Project, Morse and Berger (1992:3) were dismayed to note that 'no basis for designing, implementing, and assessing rehabilitation was in place, and no one knew the scale of the displacement that would result from the dam'. Some of the observations that form the basis of this conclusion were: A distinction was made between the 'revenue villages' and 'forest villages'. The residents of the former are considered project affected persons (PAPs) and those without a formal '*khata*' are categorized as 'landless' or 'encroachers', and therefore not liable to compensation. Many villages were not included as revenue land because of incomplete land surveys. Due to shortage/non-availability of suitable and adequate cultivable land, the PAPs were shown good cultivable land but allotted poor quality rocky barren land. Families/villages were scattered over various resettlement sites due to a shortage of land, breaking up families and community networks. Women suffered further as they lost out on customary land rights and the supplementary income from the common property resources. Their access to resources post-displacement was mediated via their husbands and wider kinship networks (Modi 2004). The biggest gap in the resettlement policy has been the lack of effective participation of the displaced communities. The local people had no information about the submergence of the area which led to chaos and confusion among the displaced. It further led to spread of rumours among the community.

The majority of the oustees belonged to tribal communities who were traditionally engaged in subsistence agriculture in forests. To resettle the tribals, the Gujarat government promised to offer each male adult above the age of 18 five acres of land regardless of their earlier forest holdings which, from the Forest Department's viewpoint, were largely encroached and not legally owned lands. Additional compensation was to be given for the loss of houses and livestock. The government identified large expanses of land in the command area of the project. With the help of non-governmental organizations (NGOs), tribal groups were shown the available areas and given the right to choose compensatory land (Pathak 1991). However, it was time and time again highlighted that the tribals would not be able to cope with the shift to market-oriented farming in resettlement areas. The same was also anticipated in the Morse and Berger Report (1992) which asserted that resettlement of the tribals would lead them to get entangled in debt cycles, losing land to moneylenders or local landowners. It would also render a serious blow to their tribal customs and ways of life. Non-parity of the rehabilitation package across MP, Gujarat and Maharashtra also led to severe inequity. As all the displaced persons were to be resettled in Gujarat, oustees from MP and Maharashtra were not willing to settle in Gujarat because of different cultural and language backgrounds.

Socio-Economic Consequences

The project had many adverse socio-economic consequences on the 20 million people living in the Narmada basin, depending on the river for survival. The basin has been behind with low agricultural yields, lower literacy, lower life expectancy, and a lack of medical, educational, and banking facilities (Sharma 2009). The submergence villages have been largely dependent upon farming, fishing, forest produce, especially agriculture for meeting their own needs, while some of this was also useful for generating some cash income. Though this was not a static economy and has been changing with increasing contact with the outside world, the core still remained. In their assessment of the social and economic impact of the Sardar Sarovar Project, Jagadeesan and Kumar (2015:245) reported that 'For every acre of land cultivated in the submerged village, more than an acre was cultivated illegally in the forest land. As a result, while the average operational land holding of the household was only 4.2 acres, the land area actually operated was 9.2 acres'.

More than 60 percent of those displaced belonged to tribal communities based on subsistence, natural resource-based, less-monetized economy, with limited connections to the market. Similarly, the use of purchased inputs has been limited. Houses, agricultural implements, etc., were mostly constructed from materials obtained from the forests. Even labor, for example, for house construction, was not paid labor, but was based on the traditional concepts of shared-labor like *laaha*, where people work for each other on reciprocal basis (Dharmadhikary and Oza 2019). The economy and lifestyle of the resettled villages were vastly different. The resettled villages had a monetized economy that was much more integrated into the market, with agriculture inputs being purchased and outputs being sold. Many other necessities (like material for house construction) were also largely being purchased from the market. Post resettlement, most of these communities no longer had access to common property resources like forests, rivers, or fish. About 5000 families of the fishing community have been deprived of their means of livelihood (Dharmadhikary and Oza 2019).

The adivasis people and rural population also suffered culturally as many of the resettled people were compensated with land in far off regions. This had an adverse impact on familial and social ties that these people had established over many years. When relocated to a different region, the resettled population had to learn new languages and adjust to the new culture, which could take years. About 700 years old, 'Harsud', with 5600 families was also submerged, or rather it was 'destroyed' by the state apparatus (Sharma, 2009). With the lack of amenities, poor land, breaking up of communities, hostile hosts at several places, a tough market to compete with and thrown to face a cash economy, the process of marginalization and pauperization started (Oza 1997).

The Narmada is one of the most sacred rivers in the country; and a custom unique to the Narmada is the parikrama—circumnavigation. In this ancient practice, thousands of people walk from the source of the river to the mouth and back again. The parikrama is to be done only on foot, and one cannot cross the river except at the mouth. One is not allowed to carry any food or supplies. Villages all along the Narmada therefore collect grain to feed those undertaking the parikrama. The dams—those built and under-construction—have submerged the route of the parikrama. Villages on the banks have been submerged and the reservoir has brought new villages on the new banks. But these villages have no tradition of support for the parikrama. Thus, this old custom is now threatened (Dharmadhikary 2006).

The economic feasibility of the project has also been debatable. The total cost of the Sardar Sarovar Project is still a much-debated issue. Doubts are raised about the project's financial viability. In 1981, the Tata Engineering Consultants had estimated the project cost to be Rs 4,877 crore. In 1985 it was revised to Rs 6,500 crore. In 1991, Babubhai Patel (then Chief Minister of Gujarat) had told the Gujarat assembly that the cost stood at Rs 9,000 crore, while in the state budget for 1992-93 it was put at Rs 9,400 crore. All these cost estimates referred to the base cost and not the total project cost (the total cost of any project is its base cost plus physical and price contingencies). The Narmada minister therefore later put the revised cost at Rs 22,000 crore. Here again, the reference has been to the base cost. The total cost therefore could not be less than Rs 50,000 crore. This indicates a blatant disregard for facts and underlines the overall attitude of secrecy and misinformation adopted by the state government (Oza 1996). There are many activists who assert that the irrigation benefits of the project have also been mis-calculated. For example, Baba Amte has given the details of the extent of irrigation the project is likely to provide to the drought-stricken areas of Gujarat. 'Apparently, in Saurashtra, more than 80 percent of the taluks are not likely to get water from the SSP; in Kutch 5 out of 9 taluks will not get any water; about two-thirds of the 62 taluks getting water from the SSP are neither drought prone not arid; and two-thirds of the 52 drought-prone or arid taluks of Gujarat would get little or no water from the project' (Ghosh 1990:58).

Environmental Consequences

Besides the resettlement of the displaced, the second major issue of contention in the case of SSP, as in other mega projects, has been the ecological consequences of the project. The Sardar Sarovar Project was conceptualized without any comprehensive environmental impact assessment (EIA). The project was initially declined by the Government of India in 1983 due to serious gaps in the facts presented about ecological impacts of the project. It was in 1987 that the Ministry of Environment and Forests provided approval to the project with a precondition that the concerned state governments will carry out a comprehensive ecological impact assessment of the project by 1989. 'The studies were tied to the construction schedule, so the compromise became known as the pari passu principle: environmental impacts were to be determined and mitigation measures put in place in concert with construction' (Kapur 1997: 694). However, in reality, the majority of these conditions were not complied by the project authorities.

The construction of the dam has major environmental implications on the surrounding areas because it required large amounts of land to be cleared for the space for building. The dam submerged 13,386 ha of forest land (165.91 ha in Gujarat, 2,731 in MP and 6,488.54 ha in Maharashtra); 11,318 ha. cultivable land and 14,072 ha. land designated for other uses. Over

53,000 hectares of forest area was decimated including deciduous forests that were valuable for fire word and forest bio products. The habitat of endangered species such as the tiger and wolf were destroyed, bringing them closer to extinction. The number of trees felled in just nine out of 33 submergence villages in Maharashtra was 5,72,000 (information obtained under the Right to Information by Parasuraman et al. 2010). 'The estimate of the Union Department of Environment in regard to the environmental cost of loss of forest was placed at Rupees 30,293 crore for the Narmada Sagar Project and Rs 8,190 crore for the Sardar Sarovar Project' (Ghosh 1990: 58).

The ecologists assert that the worst environmental impact of the project will be visible in Gujarat in the coming decades, as the majority of the area to be irrigated is either moderately or severely prone to water logging and salinity. Hence, approximately one million hectares of fertile land would be lost. The initial plan stated that submerged forest area would be compensated by afforestation of an equivalent amount of non-forest land. This does not seem to be a satisfactory solution of submergence as reforestation cannot replace a natural forest. 'There is no feasible way to completely recover the loss of these forests, or of saving much of the biological diversity that they contain. This was heightened by the fact that compensatory afforestation in the case of SSP is being done in Kutch, an ecological zone completely different from the Narmada Valley. There will therefore be an inevitable loss' (Gelder et al 2002: 81). The experts designated by the Narmada Control Authority to gauge the plantation stated that it would not be possible to recreate the tropical deciduous forests submerged due to Sardar Sarovar Project, in the arid district of Kutch and any such effort will be 'mitigatory' and not 'compensatory' (Ojha 1989; Kushalappa 1992). The changes to the existing ecosystem will lead to the extinction of rich flora and fauna of the area. The compensatory afforestation site also lacks biodiversity and does not provide forest corridors enabling wildlife to cross over.

Another important issue has been the annual rate of siltation per 100 km of catchment area of the dams, which is quite high. A study by the Bengaluru based Indian Institute of Science revealed that at least 100,000 hectares of irrigated land will be affected by severe water logging as well as salinization of the soil (Gokhale 1991). The data from several large reservoirs in India shows that the actual rate of siltation is on the average 200-400 percent higher than the siltation rate assumed while planning the project (Irrigation Committee Report 1972; Public Accounts Committee Report 1993).

For the prevention of water logging; optimization of water utilization; and preservation of the quality of water resources, a command area with adequate drainage system must have been established, which has not been done in the case of SSP. The impacts of the project on ecology and local economy of people staying downstream have been overlooked; environment gaps are ignored and an adequate environmental impact analysis has been found to be missing.

Many critics including Claude Alavares have called the Narmada Valley Project the 'world's greatest planned disaster' (Claude and Billorey 1988). While the resettlement and rehabilitation under the SSP has been more unlike other dam-building projects in India in which 'oustees' have been given, at most, cash for their loss of land. In the Narmada case, though the people were stated to be better compensated, it failed to take care of the socio-psychological concerns of those displaced (Dash 2010). Besides this, the ecological consequences of the project will be an issue of debate for many decades to come. This has to be understood that 'If rejuvenation of rivers is to receive a central place in water resources development and the Narmada is to remain alive, these issues need to be brought into discussion and resolved as soon as possible' (EPW 2014:10).

CHAPTER 8

SOCIAL RESISTANCE AGAINST DAMS AND DISPLACEMENT IN INDIA AND ROLE OF CIVIL SOCIETY ORGANIZATIONS

Civil society organizations come to the fore to resist the hegemonic power play of the state and become a 'secondary power' when the public in general is unable to control and challenge the state monopoly (Oommen 1975). These organizations enable people in organizing and acting as a pressure group to keep the state machinery on track. The last two decades have witnessed a strong presence of these civil society organizations at the global as well as the national level, cutting across issues. While Beteille (2001:300) termed the last decade of the twentieth century as 'decade of the NGOs', Dhanagare (1988:39) considers the rise and growth of action groups and their efforts in uplifting the vulnerable sections as the 'striking feature of contemporary social reality in India' (Pattnaik and Panda 2005).

Conflicts over water and dams can be traced throughout the last century. For instance, in the 1910s, the conservationist John Muir lobbied public opinion against the building of the O'Shaughnessy Dam in Yosemite National Park in California. Most of these protests, however, were more local in nature with limited attention and intervention from outsiders. The opposition to dams became more vivid in the late 1950s as the pace of dam building accelerated. More recent examples of campaigns hae occurred alongside the bulding of the Three Gorges in China, Pak Mun in Thailand, Ilisu in Turkey, Ralco in Chile, Epupa in Namibia, and Lesotho Highlands Water in Lesotho (WCD 2000). There was a shift in the approach of the protests by the civil society organizations and individual activists in the last few decades. By the late 1980s, environmentalists and sociologists began to play a more important role in the planning process, and by the mid-1990s the involvement of affected peoples and NGOs in the process became more significant.

In the initial era of agitations, the focus was more on proper resettlement of displaced persons rather than questioning the need of displacement per se.

This may be due to the prevalent traditional infrastructure-oriented model of development being in the minds of people in the forefront of research and social action (Saxena 2008a). However, the late 1980s witnessed a heightened interest in resettlement of displaced persons triggered by people's resistance to land acquisition; inaccessibility to common property resources and failed rehabilitation policies in the past (Saxena 2008b) paving a way for an alternative paradigm of development.

Resistance against injustice is not new in India. The pre-independence era witnessed many movements to challenge the colonial intentions to control natural resources for economic gains. There were many such protests carried out by the tribal communities against state intervention in forest resources (Kothari 1996). This conflict was termed as a conflict between the political economy of profit and the moral economy of provision (Gadgil and Guha 1992). One of the earliest resistances against dams in India can be registered in the 1920s and 1930s when an organized movement was launched against the construction of the Mulshi Dam and Bhatgar Dam project in the 1930s in Maharashtra. Independent India followed the western model of development, which led to an unequal distribution of wealth as well as inequity in the development of various regions. With the prevalent development model in mind, large scale projects were carried out with focus on providing the benefits of these projects primarily to the urban elite and industrialized masses. This further led to the understanding that displacement and henceforth sacrifice of the few is justified for the larger interest of the nation. However, since the 1970s, the social activists as well as human rights organizations in India started raising their voice against the injustice faced by marginalized communities, including tribal people. This led to the emergence of several movements to oppose mainstream notion of development and displacement (Sahu 2019). Some of the key issues have been: victimization of marginalized communities in the pretext of development; unsustainable and indiscriminate use of natural resources; inadequate resettlement and rehabilitation and consequent impoverishment of the of the displaced communities. It was highlighted that though millions of people have been displaced due to these development projects, only a small section of them were able to restore their sources of sustenance. As the majority were left out, forced displacement has brought them untold miseries by shattering their lives (Sharma 2010).

Besides the macro social movements in India which gathered limelight at the national and global forums (such as the Sardar Sarovar Project), various micro-social movements showcased an exceptional strength of collective action and resistance to protect common interests. Deviating from the process and ideology of the classical social movements, these New Social Movements converged diverse themes of protests bringing people from different backgrounds under one roof. It focused its energy on issues such as sustainable use of natural resources, unequal access to common property resources, exploitative power relations, centralisation of decision-making and its consequent impact on vulnerable sections of the society (Pattnaik 2013). Some of the prominent movements have been a, protests against the hydro-power projects such as Hirakud, Rengali, Nathpa Jhakri, Karcham Wangtoo and Baspa II; against the mining operations such as Lafarge, Nabinagar, Kucheipadar; and tribal resistance movements of the Gonds and Bhils. Various tactics and strategies were adopted by the civil society organizations and individual activists such as litigation, non-violence to confrontation to uphold the rights to equality and justice for the displaced persons. These strategies and their effectiveness in upholding the rights of the subaltern groups have been discussed below.

Protests and Agitations

Numerous protests were carried out on dam sites across the world to resist the displacement and to mobilize people against the dams. Many such protests were carried out against World Bank-funded big dam projects during the 1980s and 1990s (Nayak 2010). The systematic and collective resistance to the mega projects on the one hand forced international funding agencies to disassociate themselves from these projects (World Bank's withdrawal in the case of four dams along the Chico River in the Philippines in 1973-1977 and withdrawal from the Sardar Sarovar Project in India in 1993); it also led to many policy initiatives outcomes at the international level such as the World Bank's Involuntary Resettlement Policy (1996), the Asian Development Bank's Policy on Involuntary Resettlement (1996), and IFC's Performance Standard for Land Acquisition and Involuntary Resettlement (2006). This insistence on complying with human rights standards by the international aid agencies has also put the state agencies under pressure to involve affected population and civil society organizations during the conception, process and implementation of these mega projects to get a certain measure of legitimacy (Patkar September 19, 1998).

In India, the protests and agitations against growing intensity of land acquisition for various projects reached their culmination in the context of the Sardar Sarovar Project which resulted in an unprecedented displacement of 152,000 people mostly of the tribal communities (Sharma, 2010). This led to direct confrontation between the civil society groups and the government. The collective efforts against the verdict of the Narmada Water Dispute Tribunal were initiated in the form of *Narmada Dharangrastra Samiti*, which in 1989 became the Narmada Bachao Andolan (NBA). Mobilisation through hunger strikes, road rallies, *Jal Satyagrahas*, *padayatra*, village level meetings and ground surveys of the project-affected people were undertaken, in order to counter the pro-dam arguments of the government (Bisht 2011). Though in most of these campaigns, the civil society organizations showed tremendous strength by adopting non-violent strategies taking inspiration from the Gandhian satyagraha including non-cooperation, civil disobedience, refusal to cooperate with project authorities, blocking all project-related works and refusal to leave their villages (Nayak 2010); in a few instances there were direct confrontation with the state agencies leading to arrests of local communities as well as social activists. The state agencies used various tools to suppress these movements. For instance, Gujarat made the second highest number of TADA (Terrorist and Disruptive Activities Prevention Act, 1985) arrests, in order to suppress ‘anti-development project’ agitations (Judge 2000). This, rather than slowing down the movement, has provided an impetus to build stronger resistance against suppression. The justification of this response can be found in protest-repression nexus theory which asserts that when faced with government sanctions or coercion, dissidents are expected to respond with resistance (Chong 1991).

Though, it would be an overstatement to say that these mobilizations have been fully successful in achieving the goals of their campaigns; many of these mass scale mobilizations led to the withdrawal of many ongoing projects in India such as the Rathong Chu project in Sikkim (1997) and the Bedthi project in Karnataka (1998). It further led to the review of the rehabilitation package for Tehri and Koel Karo projects (Centre for Science and Environment 1999:136-41; Hemadri 1999: xxvi-xxvii).

Publications

Besides carrying out anti-dam campaigns, the social activists and social researchers published extensively about the socio-economic consequences of dam highlighting the impoverishment caused to subaltern groups due to these projects. To name a few: Edward Gold Smith and Nicholas Hildyard published *The Social and Environmental Effects of Large Dams* in 1984 and its subsequent volume in 1986 and 1992, respectively; and the California based bi-monthly International Dam Newsletter started by Philip William in 1985 was later renamed World Rivers Review. All these publications helped in accelerating the movement by expanding the transnational network (Khagram 2004: 185). Michael Cernea and Robert Goodland in their various reports explained the socio-economic impacts caused by big dams during the 1970s (Khagram 2004: 190-91; Cernea 1997, 1998, 1999, 2000, 2002, 2003, 2006). A WWF report, 'Rivers at Risk' (2007), identified 21 rivers at risk from dams being planned or under construction. Joyce, Stephanie's (1997), 'Is it worth a dam? Environmental Health Perspectives'; Mahapatra's (1991) 'Development for whom? Depriving the dispossessed tribals'; WHO's report (1999) 'Human health and dams'; and Scudder's (2005) *The Future of Large Dams: Dealing with Social, Environmental, Institutional and Political Costs* raised pertinent questions on the dams. A recent report (2021) compiled by United Nations University's Canadian-based Institute for Water, Environment and Health, in its case studies (the US, France, Canada, India, Japan, and Zambia and Zimbabwe) titled 'Ageing water infrastructure: An emerging global risk' highlighted that ageing dams in India, the US, other nations pose a growing threat (Perera et al. 2021).

In India, experts and activists wrote extensively, challenging the feasibility of large irrigation projects on technical and financial grounds; long term environmental, social and economic implications; and sharing the life experiences of those displaced under various hydro-projects. In 1983, Kalpvriksha published a report on costs imposed by dams. There is a vast amount of literature available both in favour and opposing these projects in India. An intense debate among the proponents and opponents of the dam erupted on the pages of India's premier journal Economic and Political Weekly between 1989 and 1990 (Dhawan, 1990). While Rangachari (2006) and Duggal (2001), on the Bhakra Dam project, came to the defense of the project as well as the resettlement policy; Dharmadhikary's (2005) *Unravelling Bhakra: Assessing the Temple of Resurgent India* provides a compelling alternative analysis. Similarly, in the case of the Sardar Sarovar Project, there were studies (see study of Aiyar and Kaushal 2019) which applauded the rehabilitation and resettlement policy, a larger text enumerated the sufferings of those displaced including tribal population (see report of Morse and Berger 1992; Fisher 1992; Dharmadhikary 2006; Pathak 1991). The national press was full of articles on debating the dams (such as Ravi Sharma's 'Real Cost of Big Dams' and 'Need for Frank Discussion', 1982; and Darryl D'Monte's 'High Dams at a High Cost', 1983). Arundhati Roy's closely-documented essay entitled 'The Greater Common Good' in Outlook magazine (1999), criticizing of the Narmada Valley project both in principle and in its application is a proof of rising social awareness about the issue.

Lobbying at the international and national level

Both in terms of framing and in institutional-political and operational ways, these anti-dam movements networked vertically by crossing borders and building international alliances and coalitions. The movements mobilized not only NGOs or civil society organizations but also urban intelligentsia, often described as 'rooted cosmopolitans' or 'movement brokers' who significantly influenced the struggles at the ground and at global levels (Sikor and Newell 2014; Borras 2016). The transnational network grew to become increasingly better connected and more sophisticated, especially from the mid-1980s onwards. Numerous advocacy organizations such as Probe International in Canada, The European Rivers Network in France; The Association for International Water and Forest Studies in Norway; Friends of the Earth in Japan; Both Ends in the Netherlands; Urgewald in Germany; AidWatch in Australia; Christian Aid, Oxfam, and Survival International in United Kingdom; International River Network, Cultural Survival, and the Lawyers Committee for Human Rights in the United States; the Assembly of the Poor in Thailand; and countless others allied themselves together to reform and halt big dam building around the world (Khagram 2004).

For instance, in case of NBA, international pressure was created with the help of numerous international environmental and human rights organizations such as the US' Environmental Defense Fund, Friends of the Earth, Japan Tropical Rainforest Action Network, the UK's Survival International, and Sweden's The Swallows (Payne and O'Bannon 1994). Furthermore, three of the NBA's activists testified at a special hearing of the US Congress Sub-Committee on Natural Resources, Agricultural Resources and Environment, which was followed up the hearing by urging the Bank to reconsider its funding of the project. Concerted international lobbying was done by the NBA while negotiating the dams commission along with some key organizations (Bisht 2011). The movement expanded its scope by inviting like-minded NGOs and conscious citizens from all over India to form an alliance, called the National Alliance of Peoples Movement (NAPM), which raised basic issues about whose interest's government served in implementing projects in public sector or several industrial, mining and infrastructure projects for the private sector (Sharma 2010).

Their involvement in the respective contexts broadened the scope of the movement, provided a vision and ideology, including the organizational know-how, and a powerful political voice to the cause of protest (Shah et al. 2021). The international lobbying in the case of SSP shifted the focus from fighting for the rehabilitation of families and communities to fighting against the environmental destruction and later, in 1987-1988, to the 'no-dam' position (Udall 1995). Many scholars criticized the global attention to the anti-dam projects asserting that it would shift the focus on local issues of social justice (displacement and resettlement in specific) to more general issues such as international funding of these projects and its environmental impacts (Sen 1999). However, many others asserted that the international lobbying has been effective in bringing the issue to the forefront, thereby strategically helping the local movements (e.g., Khagram 2004; Johnston 2018).

Though, the issue of environmental justice raised by the large dams is indeed global in terms of its discursive importance and the widespread socio-territorial transformations it generates, how it translates in organized protests and how the protests eventually develop depends significantly upon the specific local context and histories, more than the global alliances (Shah et al. 2021).

Mobilization at International Conferences and Workshops

With the emergence of an 'international civil society' (Fisher 1997), civil society organizations have demonstrated the ability to empower local lives and to create alternative discourses of development. The explosion of coalitions of transnational NGOs, especially in Asia has been supported by social media and international conferences. Transnational advocacy has accelerated through NGOs and other social groups engaged in efforts to develop better policies and accountability mechanisms addressing development induced displacement (Price 2009). For instance, the International River Network (IRN) organized a conference on the undelivered benefits, social problems, and environmental costs of big dams in San Francisco in 1988 attended by 63 big dam critics from 23 countries. The outcome of the conference was the San Francisco Declaration. The declaration demanded an independent assessment of big dam projects and a Moratorium on all big dam buildings not having the participation of project affected persons, free access to project information, environmental impact assessments, comprehensive resettlement plans, and full cost/benefit analysis. They also endorsed a watershed management declaration recommending numerous alternatives to big dams (see IRN 1988).

It was followed by the International Conference of People by Dams held in Curitiba, Brazil (1997) and workshop promoted by the World Bank and World Conservation Union, 'Large Dams, Learning from the Past, Looking to the Future' in Gland, Switzerland (1997). In June 1994, a coalition of 326 social movements and non-governmental organizations (NGOs) from 44 countries around the world endorsed a statement known as Manibeli Declaration calling for independent monitoring and evaluation of preparation of large dam projects and systematic monitoring and auditing of project implementation, by persons outside the Bank and with no stake in the outcome of the project. Thereafter the World Bank began negotiations with the International Union for the Conservation of Nature (IUCN), co-hosting a workshop to discuss their findings on the basis of an agreement negotiated with the World Bank, which was signed in 1994 (Bisht 2011). The International Commission on Large Dams (ICOLD), an international NGO founded in 1928 in Paris kept on organizing conferences/symposiums/ workshops with the sole purpose of sharing professional information and knowledge of the design, construction, maintenance, and impact of large dams. These conferences offered a common platform for social researchers, activists as well as state representatives to initiate an open and transparent dialogue on the future of large dams around the world. The specific issues of dams were intensively discussed in these conferences leading to the establishment of the World Commission on Dam to review all major dams built around the world (Khagram 2004: 198-205). The issue of displacement and resettlement has continued to incite more academic and policy interest in recent years too (for instance, International Conference on Development-Induced Displacement and Resettlement at the Refugee Studies Centre in Oxford 2013).

Litigations

Facing the apathy of the state despite adopting various strategies, the civil society organizations have sought salvage from the judicial organs of the state. Increasing opposition to large dams has resulted in national and international litigation. Public Interest Litigations proved to be an effective and innovative tool to safeguard and protect the human rights of the marginalized. The world's third largest hydroelectric dam, Belo Monte, faced a strong legal battle in the Federal Court of Brazil challenging laws as well as social and environmental impacts of the project. In India, a strong battle was fought in the Courts against the SSP by the NBA. The NBA took a plea in the court that the forcible displacement of tribals and other marginal farmers from their land and other sources of livelihood was not in the national or public interest and was a violation of their fundamental rights under Article 21 of the Constitution of India read with ILO Convention 107 to which India is a signatory (Shelton, and Anton 2011). The verdict of the

Supreme Court of India led to the suspension of the work in 1995 asserting that the construction work cannot be resumed unless the concerned state governments carried out adequate impact assessments. Though the construction work was later resumed and the project got completed in the year 2014, this opened a plethora of PILs in Indian courts against large hydroelectric projects, such as the Tehri Dam, Vishnu Prayag Hydro Electric Project (Uttarakhand), Teesta (Sikkim), and Chandil Dam (Jharkhand) to name a few.

Summing Up

In the last few decades, the anti-dam movement has had an impetus due to the active support from the diverse groups—the displaced, economists, social scientists, human rights activists, national media and international media. Various strategies used in anti-dam struggles have created a strong public opinion on the earlier less deliberated issues like displacement and environmental impacts and has also given confidence to the displaced or mostly the tribals to raise their voices against their human rights violations. (Centre for Science and Environment 1999:133-34). 'Nevertheless, though the messages emanating from NGOs are frequently uncomfortable, and sometimes even misinformed, the world owes a huge debt to its diverse campaigning pressure groups and other environmental and sustainability NGOs for persistently pushing back the barriers of ignorance and hegemony on the journey to a sustainable future' (Everard 2013).

As the consent of the affected communities becomes an important factor to ascertain state legitimacy to carry on these projects, the affected communities rather than taking displacement for granted, have started raising questions regarding the rationale behind the project, the prospective beneficiaries, their role in decision making as well as the propriety of the displacement and resettlement. All these aspects have radically altered the discourse regarding displacement and resettlement into an issue of development and displacement and if need be, of ideal resettlement (Patkar September 19, 1998).

'If the 1980s were a decade of displacement, then the 1990s can aptly be termed 'the decade of popular resistance to displacement'. Mounting antagonisms to development-induced displacement resulted in new forms of political activism paralleled with new agendas in research' (Baviskar 1995: 218). These anti-dam movements have highlighted the serious issues regarding the planning of development projects and the paradigm of development itself. It has exposed the violence and suppression perpetrated in the name of 'public purpose' and 'national interest' while indicating with similar movements—the alternative path of humane, just and sustainable governance rooted in a truly democratic polity (Fernandez and Thukral 1989; Thukral 1992; Kothari 1996). 'The struggle of the tribal people and their determination to make any sacrifice in order to protect their civil and political rights, their right to livelihood and habitat clearly demonstrate that people at the grass roots are not going to accept the onslaught of market forces. Hence, the emergent issue is to decide whether to accept the prevailing definition of development as provided by the market and the state or to look for alternatives emerging out of the people's struggles' (Pattnaik 2013: 76).

CHAPTER 9

HUMAN RIGHTS OF THE DISPLACED AND JUDICIAL INTERVENTION

The judicial intervention in the case of hydroelectric projects is not new. The NGOs, social activists and victims have sought respite from federal courts across the world against the state monopoly to control the natural resources and its blatant ignorance of the rights of the subaltern taking the plea of larger public good. For instance, in the case of the Bakun Dam project (*Kajing Tubek v. Ekran Bhd & Ors* 1996), the High Court of Malaysia ordered that EIA was mandatory and also identified that the plaintiffs have right to participate as destruction of the forests would uproot and immensely affect their lives (Gabungan 1999). Similarly, a lawsuit was filed in Thailand against the Xayaburi Dam's Power Purchase Agreement. The appeal asked the Supreme Court to review the order of lower court in recognition of the severe transboundary impacts of the Xayaburi Dam on communities in Thailand (Deetes 2012). More such litigations were witnessed against the big dam projects around the world in the last decade. For instance, London's Court of Appeal reopened one of the biggest lawsuits ($7 billion) filed by 200,000 claimants against Anglo-Australian mining giant BHP (Broken Hill Proprietary), over the collapse of the Fundao Dam in 2015 which killed 19 and obliterated villages, known as Brazil's worst environmental disaster. In a recent case (Ridley 2021), Buckfire & Buckfire, a Michigan-based law firm filed two class-action lawsuits on behalf of 19 victims, each of whom sustained catastrophic damage from the Edenville Dam and Sanford Dam failure that flooded Midland and surrounding areas (Buckfire & Buckfire's Blog 2022).

In India, the large hydroelectricity projects have been a subject of litigation in the High Courts in various states as well as in the Supreme Court of India for many decades. The plea varied from issues such as ecological consequences of projects, lack of people's participation in the resettlement process as well as challenging the very need of the project. A few most contentious issues have been: defining public purpose; the issue of compensation and resettlement of the displaced; ecological concerns and the rights of the tribal communities. This chapter endeavours to analyze the intervention of the judiciary in some of these human rights issues.

Issue of Public Purpose

The public purpose has been one of the most contentious issues in the judiciary in India. The reason for the same has been the colonial Land Acquisition Act (LLA) 1894. The LLA was the only law in India guiding the acquisition of land and compensation to the affected people, until 2013, when the Right to Fair Compensation and Transparency in Land Acquisition, Rehabilitation and Resettlement Act replaced the LAA. The Act did not define the term 'public purpose' and granted the executive broad discretion to interpret what constitutes a legitimate public purpose. The power of the state known as eminent domain under the Act was more or less understood in reference to the concept given by Hugo Grotius in *De Jure Belli ac Pacis* as early as in 1625 (Desai 2011:95):

> *The property of the subject is under the eminent domain of the state, so that the state or he who acts for it may use and even alienate and destroy such property, not only in cases of extreme necessity [...] but for ends of public utility*

He further adds that:

> *when this is done, the state is bound to make good the loss to those who lose their property.*

Taking the clue from the same, Indian judiciary has time and again in various judgements uphold the right of the State to define public purpose. Hoops and Tagliarin (2019), in their study titled 'The Legal Boundaries of "Public Purpose" in India and South Africa: A Comparative Assessment in Light of the Voluntary Guidelines' after reviewing more than 1269 land acquisition cases brought to the Supreme Court between 1950 and 2016, found that 'only 6.2 percent cases questioned the legitimacy of the purpose for which the land was expropriated; and, in only about 1 percent of the total dataset of 1269 cases, the Supreme Court invalidated the acquisition on grounds of violating the requirements of public purpose'. These figures can be substantiated through various case laws. For instance, in *Somavanti v. State of Punjab* (1962), the court ordered that the government's declaration of 'public purpose' would constitute 'conclusive evidence' that the land in question was needed for a public purpose. Similarly, in *Indrajit C. Parekh of Ahmedabad and Another vs. the State of Gujarat and Others* (1975), the Court decided that the public purpose requirement was satisfied even if the government had only nominally contributed to the acquisition in the amount of one rupee. Similar judgements were passed in many other cases (see *Bajirao T. Kote (Dead) By Lrs. and Another vs. State of Maharashtra and Others* 1994; *Daulat Singh Surana & Ors Vs. First Land Acquisition Collector & Ors* 2006; *Sooraram Pratap Reddy vs. District Collector* 2008). However, a change was witnessed in the attitude of the Indian judiciary after 2010. In many case laws after 2010, the Court seemed to have applied a pro-poor interpretation to the 'public purpose' phrase. For instance, in *Dev Sharan vs State of Uttar Pradesh* (2011), the court explicitly stated:

> *Any attempt by the State to acquire land by promoting a public purpose to benefit a particular group of people or to serve any particular interest at the cost of the interest of a large section of the people, especially of the common people, defeats the very concept of public purpose.*

This was well supported by many similar cases such as *Banda Development Authority vs Motilal Agarwal* (2011); *Radhy Shyam vs. The State of Uttar Pradesh* (2011); and *Kedar Nath Yadav vs. State of West Bengal & Others* (2016). The new legislation (The Right to Fair Compensation and Transparency in Land Acquisition, Rehabilitation and Resettlement Act) has tried to fill this gap and has clearly defined the term public purpose. Though it is still a contentious issue, with new legislation coming into force, it is expected that some uncertainty about the definition of public purpose and eminent domain will come to an end.

Compensation and Resettlement

The concept of resettlement emerged specifically in the 1990s across the world with the World Bank Involuntary Resettlement Policy (1996) and United Nations Guiding Principles on Internal Displacement (1998) coming into existence. In India, the colonial Land Acquisition Act, 1894 was the only law dealing with land acquisition and other related issues. The Act had a limited provision of 'adequate compensation' with no legal obligation on the state. There were no provisions for rehabilitation, protection of community rights and consent. The rates of compensation were nominal. Even in post-independent India, no specific policy measures were initiated to rehabilitate those displaced until the formation of National Policy on Resettlement and Rehabilitation for Project-Affected Families, 2003.

In the absence of any law or policy guidelines, the civil society organizations looked towards judicial intervention taking a stance that the right to adequate rehabilitation is the logical corollary of the right to life with dignity as provided under Article 21 of the Indian Constitution. The courts in its various judgements upheld the right to rehabilitate the displaced. For instance, in *B D Sharma v. Union of India* (1992), the court ruled that:

> *Rehabilitation should be so done that at least six months before an area is likely to be submerged, rehabilitation should be complete and should be in respect of homestead substitution of agricultural property and such other arrangements which are contemplated under the rehabilitation Scheme.*

The Court reiterated the same in the case of *Narmada Bachao Andolan v. Union of India* (2000) and *N.D. Jayal and Another v. Union of India* (2004). In the *Narmada Bachao Andolan v. Union of India* (2000), Court in its order stated:

> *Rehabilitation is not only about providing just food, clothes or shelter. It is also about extending support to rebuild livelihood by ensuring necessary amenities of life. Rehabilitation of the oustees is a logical corollary of Article 21. The oustees should be in a better position to lead a decent life and earn livelihood in the rehabilitated locations.*

However, despite the judicial pronouncements asserting a time frame as well as adequate resettlement of the displaced, the court in general lauded the benefits of a dam and has drawn a demarcating line between the realm of policy and the permissible areas for judicial interference. The position that the court can only ascertain whether the government applied its mind to the issue of rehabilitation on the basis of the materials placed before it has been consistently reiterated in every case that has been filed challenging developmental projects (Khaitan and Nitya Priya 2009:116). Even in Narmada's case where the construction of dam was challenged on various issues including rehabilitation, the court explicitly stated that

> *It is for the Government to decide how to do its job. When it has put a system in place for the execution of a project and such a system cannot be said to be arbitrary, then the only role which a Court may have to play is to see that the system works in the manner it was envisaged.*

In all such case laws, the inclination of the judiciary has clearly been towards the traditional infrastructure-oriented development model, in which dams are considered an indispensable condition for development, with the focus primarily being on the existence of resettlement policy rather than its actual implementation.

Ecological Concerns

The initial phase of the environmental movements across the world laid emphasis primarily on the conservationist impulse which endeavoured to prevent the destruction of flora and fauna occurring as a direct consequence of the project. Gradually, the environmentalist viewpoint seems to have matured and evolved much beyond the limits of the 'conservationist' to 'ecologically sustainable development'. Large Dam projects were opposed not only for immediate destruction they caused, but for their long-term impacts on the ecosystems (Engineer 1990).

Environmental consequences of the development projects were initially not integrated into the primary resettlement reform campaigns initially. It was not even a prominent issue of discussion within the World Bank until the early 1980s (Gupta 2021). The office of Environmental Affairs was comparatively less effective in the Bank's power structure. For example, the loan agreement of Sardar Sarovar Project only mentioned that there should be an environmental work plan in place by December 1985. What constituted an 'environmental work plan' was not discussed in detail (Wade 2011). The Narmada Water Dispute Tribunal also did not address the environmental issues specifically (Khagram 2004). However, in subsequent years, it became a much-debated issue in India with a large number of cases filed in courts on the pretext of ecological consequences of these projects and their impact on the accessibility of natural resources to those displaced. For instance, in the case of *N.D. Jayal And Anr vs Union of India and Ors* (2003), the petitioners alleged that as the concerned authorities have not correspondingly complied with the conditions attached to the environmental clearance, the project must be halted till the same is complied with. The similar plea was also taken in the case of *Tehri Bandh Virodhi Sangharsh Samiti vs. State of UP* (1992) and in *Narmada Bachao Andolan v. Union of India* (2000).

In all these cases, there seemed to be a soft-cornered approach of the judiciary towards dams as the quintessence of sustainable development. A shift in the judicial mindset, however, was witnessed in the case of *Alaknanda Hydro Power v. Anuj Joshi* (2013). In this case, the Supreme Court of India stayed construction of any new dams in the state of Uttarakhand. This order came in the background of the Uttarakhand disaster. In another case, *Srinagar Bandh Aapada Sangharsh Samiti v. Alaknanda Hydropower Co. Ltd.* (2014), the principal bench of the National Green Tribunal (NGT) in 2016 held that the Srinagar Dam is absolutely liable for the damage caused to people during the floods of June 2013 and directed the project authorities to deposit Rs 9.26 Crores as compensation for environmental damage to the victims of the flood in Srinagar (Uttarakhand). This kind of adversarial order against dams was unprecedented in the history of environmental litigation in India and can inspire a large number of such petitions in various courts in India (Sinha and Oxe 2021).

Rights of the Tribal Communities

Land as a social justice concern for Adivasis has a long historical precedent in rebellions and struggles across central India (Arnold 1984; Pati 2011; Bates and Shah 2014). The last few decades have witnessed the adverse impact of displacement and denial of access to forests on the lives of these tribal communities. On paper, strong laws exist to give formal support to these rights, but these have never been implemented more than half-heartedly, and even then, with much variation between states and even across territories within states. However, rights enshrined in laws remain as important mobilisation factors for movements working towards their actual implementation. Activists across India have adopted various strategies such as mass mobilisation, lobbying, media campaigns as well as public interest litigation to protect the rights of tribal communities (Oskarsson 2018).

The Courts have played a positive role in acknowledging the rights of tribal communities in many case laws in India. For example, in the *State of M.P vs Behru Singh & Ors* (2012), the Madhya Pradesh High Court gave relief to tribal communities by ordering the state to provide two hectares of agricultural land to adult sons of tribal families displaced by the Man Dam, one of the 30 large dams in the Narmada valley. The judgement was given on a public interest litigation demanding rehabilitation of tribal families of 17 villages submerged by the dam reservoir. The court further directed the state to provide the land within four months (Misra 2009). Though the court upheld the rights to the tribals in many such cases, the court's understanding of the rights seems to have been in contradiction to the international human rights principles. The court in most of the judgements have reiterated that the tribal should be rehabilitated properly; however, it failed to comment on the compulsory acquisition of land and participation of the affected tribal communities. In *Narmada Bachao Andolan vs State of M.P. & Anr* (2011) the court stated that:

> *The displacement of the tribals and other persons would not per se result in the violation of their fundamental or other rights. The effect is to see that on their rehabilitation at new locations they are better off than what they were. At the rehabilitation sites they will have more and better amenities than*

those they enjoyed in their tribal hamlets. The gradual assimilation in the mainstream of the society will lead to betterment and progress.

The court failed to provide a full reasoned analysis of the human rights situation focused on the various administrative procedures put in place by the state to deal with the issues arising from the Sardar Sarovar Project. Instead, the majority judgment takes the view that ‘it is not fair that tribals and the people in undeveloped villages should continue in the same condition without ever enjoying the fruits of science and technology for better health and have a higher quality of life’. The stance of the court seems to assert that the state is making tribal people a favour by displacing them. The consequence seems to be that participation is not necessary since the oustees will in any case be much better off after displacement. Given this stand, it is worth examining that the court finally arrives at the conclusion that displaced people, especially the adivasis among them, are being actually helped by the state since their displacement will provide an opportunity to uplift them from their present living conditions (Cullet 2001).

Summing Up

The judgement of the Supreme Court of India in the case of SSP has been one of the most critically analyzed orders in the recent Indian history of dams. The civil society organizations as well as social scientists criticized the judgement stating that it limited itself mainly to considerations relating to governmental efforts at complying with the legal framework provided by the relevant Indian Acts and international legal instruments and failed to address the links between environmental management and human rights protection from the perspective of fundamental rights. The crucial point is that the judges do not actually indicate what these displaced people are entitled to and until a framework is put in place, one may infer that this silence is equivalent to denying them a relief and rehabilitation package (Cullet 2001).

SECTION IV:

CONCLUSION

CHAPTER 10

IS THERE A WAY FORWARD?

This book has endeavoured to discuss the issue of dam induced displacement and resettlement from the human rights perspective. Though the issue itself opens a plethora of unending debates on various offshoots of the topic concerned, to sum up the debate, I will deliberate upon four pertinent questions raised by the German government in response to the WCD final report about dams at the symposium on the benefits and concerns about dams held in 2001 in Dresden. These pertinent questions are: What sort of development should we be aiming at? How can we ensure that this development involves the equitable distribution of benefits and burdens, opportunities and risks? How can we ensure that human rights are observed? How can we ensure that account is taken of the ecosystems' limited ability to cope?

What sort of development should we be aiming at?

Two contrast arguments exist in the debate of development and displacement. There are many who treat mainstream development as given, and displacement, though painful, is considered an indispensable cost of development. This group admits that the adverse consequences of displacement must be minimized but not at the cost of development. The majority of those who endorse this view are policy makers, managers and applied academics. The state has acted as a primary agent for advancing this agenda of development. The judicial stance in India, in most of the case laws, also endorse this view point. There is another group which is critical to the current model of development and asserts that displacement manifests a developmental crisis. In this viewpoint, displacement is seen as the ultimate ugly face of development and evidence of uneven and unfair distribution of costs and benefits. This approach, rather than talking about adequate resettlement, questions the very notion of development and raises more pertinent issues of rights, governance and negotiation (Dwivedi 2002). This viewpoint has been effectively articulated in social movements and has been well documented in academic research in India as well as across the world in order to critique development structures and the political processes that sustain such structures.

Despite these contrasting viewpoints, there is a consensus on the issue that development-induced displacement causes considerable social, economic and cultural disruption and losses to both individuals and communities (Dreze et al. 1997; Dwivedi 1999; Morse et al. 1992; Parasuram 1993; Thukral 1992; Scudder 1993; Oliver-Smith 1991; WCD 2000; Cernea 2000). While the huge infrastructural projects can be considered beneficial in the broad development paradigm, it has fostered social and economic inequalities serving the interests of narrow elite, destroying the environment, displacing and impoverishing people dependent on land (Asthana 2012). Vandana Shiva (1994) called this traditional model of development as an indicator of 'maldevelopment'.

However, these inequities of development and resettlement of persons displaced by it have acquired a degree of centrality in public and policy discourses never witnessed before. The ongoing struggle of the project affected communities across the world to protect their right to livelihood and habitat has kept challenging the prevailing definition of development supported by the market and the state. This has led to the creation of a space for ironing out social inequalities and opening up alternative voice claims to represent marginalized groups. It has also been asserted that there is a need to look for an alternative, more inclusive model of development. The underlying question raised is whether development truly means only profit for the elite or it is about protecting the rights of the subaltern. If 'public interest' is stated to be the core reason for the inception of these projects, then there is a need to redefine the term to treat the interests of the affected peoples as 'public interest'.

It is pertinent to understand that causes of development depend on the meanings of development, at least in part. Development is socially produced and reproduced as well as socially constructed and reconstructed. Moreover, in order to reform or transform development, the meanings of development may have to be contested and reconstituted (Khagram 2004:211). It is high time to question the taken for granted equivalence between big hydropower projects and development partly by critiquing the vision of development that legitimated these projects. Thus, explicating, interpreting, and understanding meanings of development are in and of themselves important scholarly tasks (Ferguson 1990). Furthermore, development should not be considered only as a contested concept for scholarly research in isolation. It is also an intensely conflict-ridden empirical phenomenon. Various case studies discussed in this book offered compelling evidence that the resistance to big dams have not been only due to unequal distribution of benefits of these projects but also challenging the very notion of development. This requires a paradigm shift by governments towards development under the neoliberal agenda of market-driven economies. In the background of this argument, participatory approach to development seems to be the only way out.

How can we ensure that this development involves the equitable distribution of benefits and burdens, opportunities and risks?

Considering displacement as an indispensable consequence of development, many principles/guidelines were framed to minimize the adverse consequences. All these policy guidelines emphasized that at first instance, efforts need to be made to avoid and minimize displacement wherever possible. Secondly, wherever it becomes unavoidable, time-bound mitigative efforts must be made to address all the social and economic losses. Despite these principles being in existence for the last three decades, the resettlement experiences in most of the dam induced displacement have been impoverishing for the displaced community. 'Forced displacement tears apart the existing social fabric; it disperses and fragments communities; dismantles patterns of social organization and interpersonal ties. The social capital lost through social disarticulation remains unperceived and uncompensated by planners, and this real loss reverberates long and detrimentally during subsequent periods' (Cernea 1997: 1575).

One of the major factors behind this is improper cost-benefit analysis of the projects. In the past, if the expected benefits of a dam exceeded the predicted costs, the project went ahead. The social cost of the project was never an issue of concern for project authorities. These projects have not even quantified the cost and benefits which could have been easily anticipated within the traditional financial and economic framework. For instance, the Public Accounts Committee of the Parliament in India stated that scrutiny of 32 major projects in independent India has shown cost overruns of 500 percent and more. Furthermore, no retrospective cost benefit analysis has been made in most of the big dams. The emergence of equity as a critical ingredient of development underlines that this 'balance sheet' approach is unacceptable as it ignores the typical mismatch between the distribution of the gains and losses of a project across different societal groups. Large dams can be seen as an extreme example of this dilemma, as public resources—both monies and rivers—are devoted to projects that all too often result in inequitable distribution of costs and benefits (WCD 2000). However, in the last few decades, the emphasis has been laid on adopting an equity-based approach, emphasizing the need to calculate social cost along with financial cost. The approach requires calculation of all costs (economic, social, environmental); systemic calculation of tradeoffs (between project benefits and displacement costs); differential weights to costs and benefits; recognition of customary rights at par with legal rights; and the need for full and proper compensation (Pearce 1994).

The end of the twentieth century saw the emergence of another trend relating to large dams—the decommissioning of large dams. Decommissioning of the ageing dams has emerged as another issue of challenge across the world. These are a large number of dams which are more than 100 years old and no longer serve a useful purpose. These are too expensive to maintain safely. The bigger the dam, the more problems decommissioning or removal are likely to face, and the more expensive they are likely to be. More studies, therefore, are needed to address the costs, benefits and impacts of decommissioning as the stock of dams ages and choices must be made between refurbishing and decommissioning.

While calculating the risks and benefits, it is also important to take care of the specific needs of certain vulnerable groups such as women, ethnic minorities, disabled, aged, infants, who may be more adversely affected by resettlement than others and who may have limited ability to claim or take benefits of resettlement assistance and related development benefits. In many ways the problems of women, indigenous peoples, encroachers and squatters, and other such groups are different and merit special attention in the planning and implementation of resettlement. Indigenous peoples constitute a disproportionately large segment of those adversely affected by development projects. Although policies of the World Bank and the Asian Development Bank exist to protect tribal peoples and their cultures against the harmful effects of development projects, there remain enormous obstacles to their social, economic and political participation in the development process (Parra 2001). Similarly, minimal attention has been paid to the impact of displacement on women. Most of the resettlement guidelines have been found to be gender blind. Even in Cernea's seminal work on 'Displacement and Resettlement, Risks and Reconstruction' (Cernea 1997), references to gender are of an add-on character (Mehta and Srinivasan 2000). The focus of resettlement planning being on the household, with men, by and large, being the heads of the household, all transactions are, therefore, conducted through them. Gender analysts also point out the way in which these development projects are endured differently by women and men. Hence, the need is to integrate gender concerns into every aspect of the policy. In place of gender-neutral policies, as advocated in many resettlement studies (March et al. 1999), emphasis must be laid on having a 'gender inclusive approach' to the displacement and resettlement.

How can we ensure that human rights are observed?

It seems that the legacies of the world's 45,000 large dams continue to cause controversies with as many as 472 billion river dependent people have had their livelihoods negatively affected by dams. The issue of social justice is at the core of this debate on development induced displacement. The concept of due process of law is intrinsically woven into the idea of natural justice. Due process involves an expectation that a state will act legitimately (Udombana 2006). Within the context of internal displacement, due process contemplates the minimum procedural requirements that must be followed to prevent arbitrary displacement (UN Guiding Principles on Internal Displacement 1998).

This can be better understood in reference to the WCD's (2000) report which laid emphasis on equity and the distribution of costs and benefits. The discourse is based on utilitarianism where 'greatest good of the greatest number' is considered to be a justification for huge infrastructural projects, even if it is at the cost of the few. Here the benefits of the projects are accrued to the groups other than those who bear the social and environmental costs. Those who bear the costs are quite often poor, vulnerable (such as indigenous peoples), or unrepresented (such as future generations). In the light of the range of opportunities that exist for making affected people beneficiaries and enabling them to contribute to the stream of project benefits, such outcomes are unacceptable on equity grounds. Human rights discourse asserts that to have more equitable outcomes of these projects. The major hurdle in achieving the same has been the lack of participation from the affected communities in the resettlement planning and implementation processes. Participation provides project authorities with the perspectives of displaced people, so critical to the planning for their complex long-term reestablishment. Moreover, as experience has shown, when people are consulted in the planning of a resettlement package for them, subsequently they do not retract, and even lend a helping hand to the management in implementing those plans. Despite the known virtues of participation, the participation seems to lack sufficient support in higher bureaucratic echelons. 'It is perhaps oxymoronic to speak of "participation" in reservoir-driven relocation, since the move is inherently involuntary. Yet, successful resettlement depends in very large part on an active participation of those forced to move' (Horowitz et al. 1993).

This obvious premise, however, does not go well with the current top-down mechanism of resettlement established by the state. In such a scenario, the role of civil society organizations becomes even more significant. It is due to the numerous campaigns successfully sustained by the civil society organizations that some changes are visible in the way the resettlement agencies now see their task as one of sharing project benefits with the affected people, and not simply returning them to their pre-project poverty level. The emergence of a large number of such organizations in the last few decades has ensured that the poor performance of the project authorities is rightly highlighted. Such pressures subsequently have been leading to affirmative action and positive change. The powerful organizations can no longer afford to ignore the rights of the weak and marginalised, or to impose resolutions without being publicly debated and agreed to by all the major stakeholders (Mathur and Marsden 1998). Besides this, social science input had a strong influence in creating a pressure as well as in determining the outcome. Baseline demographic and socio-cultural studies played an important role in informing planners about distinct social and cultural features of people living in the proposed impact areas. Despite these efforts, the battle has not been won yet and ensuring social justice to project affected communities still seems to be a daunting task for these individual activists, academicians and NGOs.

Though the people's struggles do not reject totally any sort of possibility of displacement and resettlement, all the ongoing and future displacement should be considered in the light of the displacement and experiences of resettlement hitherto. The major criterion regarding resettlement should be the public purpose of the development project and the accompanying displacement. The other criteria must be the manageability of the displacement (Patkar September 19, 1998). As the demand for electricity is spiralling across the world in response to increasing population, industrialisation and changing lifestyle; and dams being seen as an only solution, it is timely to reappraise the contribution of dams to our quest for a world in which the needs of all are met equitably and sustainably (Everard 2013:27).

How can we ensure that account is taken of the ecosystems' limited ability to cope?

It has been well substantiated by various studies that building and operating dams has serious—and largely negative impacts—on ecosystems, biodiversity and human livelihoods (WCD 2000). The large-scale alteration of natural hydrological regions continues to exert substantial and generally negative impacts on fisheries, water-based livelihoods, aquatic ecosystems and a wider set of ecosystem services. The reality of large dams is that they effectively remove one entire ecosystem and replace it with another set of biophysical conditions in which a new ecosystem will form. This occurs not only at the dam site but with major ramifications across substantial lengths of river and areas of drainage basins, all with direct and indirect consequences for the livelihood and potential of people dependent upon them. Furthermore, various scientific studies estimate that reservoirs emit large amounts of greenhouse gases, perhaps even as much as four percent of total human induced greenhouse gas emissions.

There is, however, a transition in thinking about the ecological consequences of large dams, starting from a point of substantial ignorance or denial and moving towards the kinds of principles espoused by the WCD. Efforts are now being made to mitigate the environmental impacts of the dam. In many countries, though, environmental impact assessment as well as a comprehensive plan to mitigate the possible impacts of the dams have become mandatory requirement; the greatest 'sin of omission' of our historic utilitarian view of water as a resource to be siphoned off to meet urban, irrigation and industrial needs is that it assumes that there are ready retrospective fixes for the implication of these projects on ecosystem from which it is withdrawn (Everard 2013).

One of the central conceptual limitations of all the resettlement policies and its implementation has been that it seems to see environmental management separate from human rights. It is important to understand that the environment has an irrevocable relationship with the human population living in and around. Therefore, while talking about the preservation of forests and biodiversity, it should never be used to exclude the human rights challenge that is posed by the construction of a dam set to displace thousands of people (Cullet 2001). Furthermore, by focusing on growing water and energy demands solely on a product and provide basis, we tend to overlook opportunities for a whole range of alternative technologies such as water and energy efficiency measures, water reuse, and alternative forms of renewable energy, food production and security. To assess the wisdom and consequences of that, we need a more inclusive and farsighted conceptual and decision support paradigm that accounts for the dynamics of the ecosystem and all who benefit from them.

Summing Up

Large dams have increasingly been characterised by bitter conflict and deep feelings of resentment and injustice. Correcting this situation will require not only new processes for making decisions, but building confidence in these processes and their ability to deliver genuinely better outcomes for water and energy resource development. In seeking to build this confidence we do not, in many cases, begin with a clean slate, but with a difficult legacy that needs to be recognized. This legacy can only be overcome if there is a rapid investment of confidence in the legitimacy of the processes that are put in place. 'Even the best planned programs carry with them risks for the people who must move. But adequate research, planning and resources can help relocated communities reconstruct and develop' (Cernea and Guggenheim 1993: 227). Cernea (2008:7) wrote: 'unevenness and the high frequency of failures keep forced displacement on the global agenda of the development's unsolved pathologies. Hence, the need to rethink the very foundation upon which planning and execution of involuntary resettlement is predicated'.

It has to be understood that there are no shortcuts to equitable and sustainable development. Hence, it is important to focus on reducing the negative impacts of these projects by 'increasing the efficiency of use of existing assets; avoiding and minimising ecosystem impacts; engaging in participatory, multicriteria analyses of development needs and options; ensuring that displaced and project-affected peoples livelihoods are improved; resolving past inequities and injustices, and transforming project affected people into beneficiaries; conducting regular monitoring and periodic review; and developing, applying and enforcing incentives, sanctions and recourse mechanisms' (McDonald and Webber 2010:142). The need is to adopt WCD's (2000:214) seven strategic priorities while conceptualizing such projects, to form a 'new framework for decision-making': Gaining public acceptance; Comprehensively assessing options; Addressing existing dams; Sustaining rivers and livelihoods; Recognizing entitlements and sharing benefits; Ensuring compliance and Sharing rivers for peace, development and security.

Reforming the compensation and resettlement processes and reconstructing livelihoods in the context of the 'inevitability' of development-induced displacement are clearly issues that need to be continually addressed. However, reforming these processes to ensure that affected people are adequately and justly compensated for lost stakes, can only be a short-term policy correction. In the near future, policies addressing the question of displacement will need to move beyond a focus on damage control. Institutional reform thus becomes an important policy concern. It entails having in place institutional mechanisms for informing stakeholders and seeking their approval prior to any act of displacement. Compared to policy interventions directed at balancing interests, the institutionalization of consultation, participation and negotiation is more complex and seems to be a medium-term policy goal. The long-term policy objective must be to separate development from displacement. In other words, policy actions that have displacement as an outcome cannot qualify as development. This implies an imagination and practice of development that respects people's existing life-worlds, values and rights. In policy terms, this means affirming people's rights to planning, management and development of their own resources (Dwivedi 2002). Therefore, a new framework for public discourse is required to provide a starting point for discussions, debates and reassessments by state agencies, civil society organizations, private sector, funding agencies, academics and various stakeholders. Collective learning and decision making are necessary to enable diverse stakeholders to work together to address issues at the earliest stages of planning and to find common ground without compromising individual values for losing a sense of purpose.

REFERENCES

Abraham, Itty. 1997. "Science and Secrecy in the Making of the Postcolonial State." *Economic & Political Weekly* 32: 33–34.

Leedom-Ackerman, Joanne Leedom. 2009. "Portal to Antiquity: Hasankeyf, Turkey." *World Literature Today* 83, no. 4: 58–60. https://doi.org/10.1353/wlt.2009.0063.

ADB. 1995. *Policy on Involuntary Resettlement*. Manila: Asian Development Bank.

—. 1998. *Handbook on Resettlement: A Guide to Good Practice*. Manila: Asian Development Bank.

—. 2002. *ADB's Planned Responses to the World Commission on Dams: Strategic Priorities, Good Practices, and Institutional Responses*. Manila: Asian Development Bank.

—. 2003. *Gender Checklist: Resettlement*. Manila: Asian Development Bank.

—. 2009. *Safeguard Policy Statement*. Manila: Asian Development Bank.

Adeola, Romola, and Frans Viljoen. 2018. "Climate Change, Development Projects and Internal Displacement in Africa." *Journal of African Law* 62, no. 3: 335–50. https://doi.org/10.1017/S0021855318000219.

Agarwal, B. 1994. *A Field of One's Own: Gender and Land Rights in South Asia*. Cambridge: Cambridge University Press.

Aiyar, Swaminathan, S. Anklesaria, and Neeraj Kaushal. 2019. "Are Resettled Oustees from the Sardar Sarovar Dam Project 'Better Off' Today?." *Economic & Political Weekly* 54, no. 12.

"Alaknanda Hydro Power *v.* Anuj Joshi." 2013. *Manu/SC*/0795/2013. August 13.

Altinbilek, D. 2004. "Development and Management of the Euphrates-Tigris Basin." *International Journal of Water Resources Development* 20, no. 1: 15–33. https://doi.org/10.1080/07900620310001635584.

"Amazon Watch." 2011. *International Rivers, Regional Judge Overturns Ban on Construction of Controversial Belo Monte Dam in the Brazilian Amazon*. Oakland: Amazon Watch, March 5, 2011.

"Amazon Watch." 2012. *After 21 Days, Indigenous Occupation of Belo Monte Dam Ends in Discord*. Oakland: Amazon Watch, July 12, 2012.

"Amazon Watch. 2012a." *Amazonian Indigenous Peoples Occupy Belo Monte Dam Site*. Oakland: Amazon Watch. Aug. 1, 2012.

Anaya, James. 2010. "Cases Examined by the Special *Rapporteur*." *United Nations Documents à/HRC*/15/37/Add 1: 32.

Anand, R. L. 1956. "Punjab Agriculture Facts and Figures." *Economic & Statistical Organization*. Government of Punjab.

Arnold, D. 1984. "Rebellious Hillmen: The Gudem-Rampa Rebellions (1829–1914)." In *Subaltern Studies I: Writings on South Asian History and Society*, edited by R. Guha. New Delhi: Oxford University Press: 89–141.

ASCOM. 2012. "MPF." *MPF Pede suspensa˜o Das Obras de Belo Monte*. NoTapajos.com, Accessed July 24, 2012, Accessed July 27, 2021. http://notapajos.globo.com/lernoticias.asp?t=MPF-pede-suspensao-obras-Belo-Monte&id=50604.

Ashley, C., and K. Hussein. 2000. *Developing Methodologies for Livelihood Impact Assessment: Experience of the African Wildlife Foundation in East Africa*. Working Paper 129. London: Overseas Development Institute.

Asthana, Vandana. 2012. "Forced Displacement: A Gendered Analysis of the Tehri Dam Project." *Economic & Political Weekly* 47, no. 47/48: 96–102.

Atkins, E., ed. 2018. "Dams, Political Framing and Sustainability as an Empty Signifier: The Case of Belo Monte.". *Area*. Area Royal Geographical Society *(with IBG)* 50, no. 2: 232–9. https://doi.org/10.1111/area.12364.

Kote, Bajirao T. *(Dead)*. 1994. *By Lrs. and Another vs. State of Maharashtra and Others* vol. 2. State (Corporation) Commission: 442.

Balat, Mustafa. 2003. "Southeastern Anatolia Project (GAP) of Turkey and Regional Development Applications." *Energy Exploration & Exploitation* 21, no. 5: 391–404. https://doi.org/10.1260/014459803322986231.

Banda Development Authority v. Agarwal. 2011. *CWP* vol. 3604.

Basgelen, N. 2006. "A Unique Global Heritage Starting to Count Its Remaining Days: Hasankeyf and Tigris Valley." *Archaeology/Monument-Environment* 17: 114–9.

Bates, C., and A. Shah, eds. 2014. *Savage Attack: Tribal Insurgency in India*. New Delhi: Social Science Press.

Barber, Margaret, and Gráinne Ryder. 1993. *Damming the Three Gorges. What Dam Builders Don't Want You to Know*. Toronto: Earthscan Publications.

Bartolome, L. J., C. de Wet, H. Mander, and V. K. Nagraj. 2000. "Displacement, Resettlement, Rehabilitation, Reparation, and Development." *WCD Thematic Review*: 1.3. Cape Town: World Commission on Dams.

Barry, and Woods. 2013. "The Environment." In *Human Rights: Politics and Practice*, edited by U. K. Michael Goodhart. Oxford University Press.

Baviskar, A. 1995. "In the Belly of the River: Tribal Conflicts over Development in the Narmada Valley." *Dellhi*. Oxford University Press.

Baxi, Upendra. 1989. "Notes on Constitutional and Legal Aspects of Rehabilitation and Displacement." In *Development, Displacement and Rehabilitation*, edited by Walter Fernandes and Thukral, Enakshi Ganguly. New Delhi: Indian Social Institute.

BBMB. 2002b. *Status Note on Bhakra Dam Oustees*. Chandigarh: Bhakra Beas Management Board.

Sharma v. Union of India. 1992 [Suppl.] vol. 3 SCC 93.

Beddis, R. A. 1963. "The Aswan High Dam and the Resettlement of the Nubian People." In *Geography* 48, no. 1: 77–80.

Berchin, I. I., J. Garcia, M. L. Heerdt, A.Q. Moreira, A. C. M. da Silveira, and J. B. S. O. de Andrade Guerra. 2015. "Energy Production and Sustainability: A Study of Belo Monte Hydroelectric Power Plant." *Natural Resources Forum* 39, no. 3–4: 224–37. https://doi.org/10.1111/1477-8947.12085.

Berreman, G. D. 1963. *Hindus of the Himalayas*. Berkeley: University of California Press.

Bermann, C. 2007. "Impasses e Controvérsias Da Hidroeletricidade." *Estudos Avançados* 21, no. 59: 139–53. https://doi.org/10.1590/S0103-40142007000100011.

Béteille, Andre. 2001. "Civil Society and the Good Society." *Sociological Bulletin* 50, no. 2: 245–58. https://doi.org/10.1177/0038022920010208.

Bhatia, Bela. 1997. "Forced Evictions in the Narmada Valley." In *The Dam and the Nation*, Edited by Derez et al. New Delhi: Tata Institute of Social Studies. Oxford University Press.

Bhatia, Ramesh, R. P. S. Malik, and Meera Bhatia. 2007. "Direct and Indirect Economic Impacts of the Bhakra Multipurpose Dam, India." *Irrigation & Drainage* 56, no. 2–3: 195–206. https://doi.org/10.1002/ird.315.

Bidwai, Praful. 2012. "The Politics of Climate Change and the Global Crisis: Mortgaging Our Future." *Black*. New Delhi: Orient. Swan.

Biricik, Murat, and Recep Karakas. 2012. "Birds of Hasankeyf (South-Eastern Anatolia, Turkey) Under the Threat of a Big Dam Project." *Natural Areas Journal* 32, no. 1: 96–105. https://doi.org/10.3375/043.032.0111.

Bisht, Tulsi Charan. 2009. "Development-Induced Displacement and Women: The Case of the Tehri Dam, India." *Asia Pacific Journal of Anthropology* 10, no. 4: 301–17. https://doi.org/10.1080/14442210903271312.

Bisht, Medha. 2011. "Conceptualising Movements Against Large Dams: Case Study Analysis of NBA Strategies, Linkages and State Response." *Social Change* 41, no. 3: 397–411. https://doi.org/10.1177/004908571104100304.

Biswal, Tapan. 2015. *Human Rights, Gender and Environment*. New Delhi: Viva.

Borras, S. M. 2016. *Land Politics, Agrarian Movements and Scholar Activism*. The Hague: International Institute of Social Studies.

Bratman, E. Z. 2014. "Contradictions of Green Development: Human Rights and Environmental Norms in Light of Belo Monte Dam Activism." *Journal of Latin American Studies* 46, no. 2: 261–89. https://doi.org/10.1017/S0022216X14000042.

"Brasil." 2007. *Plano Nacional de Energia* 2030. Brasília: MME/EPE.

Bratman, Eve. 2015. "Passive Revolution in the Green Economy: Activism and the Belo Monte Dam." *International Environmental Agreements: Politics, Law & Economics* 15, no. 1: 61–77. https://doi.org/10.1007/s10784-014-9268-z.

Bremer, Nicolas C. 2016. "Transboundary Environmental Impact Assessment of Large Dams in the Euphrates–Tigris Region: An Analysis of International Law Binding Iran, Iraq, Syria and Turkey." *Review of European Community & International Environmental Law* 25: 1.

Brown, J. C., and M. Purcell. 2005. "There's Nothing Inherent About Scale: Political Ecology, the Local Trap, and the Politics of Development in the Brazilian Amazon." *Geoforum* 36, no. 5: 607–24. https://doi.org/10.1016/j.geoforum.2004.09.001.

Bro, A. S., E. F. Moran, and M. F. Calvi. 2018. "Market Participation in the Age of Big Dams: The Belo Monte Hydroelectric Dam and Its Impact on Rural Agrarian Households." *Sustainability* 10, no. 5: 1592. https://doi.org/10.3390/su10051592.

Brubaker, Andrew, and Linda Adams. 2018. *Evaluation Approach Paper Corporate Evaluation of the Safeguard Policy Statement*. Manila: Asian Development Bank.

Brüntrup, M., W. Scheumann, A. Berger, L. Christmann, and C. Brandi. 2014. "What CanBe Expectedfrom International Frameworks to Regulate Large-Scale Land and Water Acquisitions in Sub-Saharan Africa?." *Law & Development Review* 7, no. 2: 433–71.

"Buckfire and Buckfire's Blog." 2021. *Buckfire Law Files Two Class-Action Lawsuits Against Dam Owners*, Accessed December 23, 2021. https://buckfirelaw.com/blog/class-action-lawsuits-dam-owners-state-of-michigan/. MI.

C^andido, Fleury, L. C., and J. Almeida. 2013. "The Construction of the Belo Monte Hydroelectric Power Plant: Environmental Conflict and the Development Dilemma." *Ambiente and e Sociedade* 16, no. 4: 141–56. https://doi.org/10.1590/S1414-753X2013000400009.

Calvi, M. F., Emilio F. Moran, R. F. Bd Silva, and Mateus Batistella. 2020. "The Construction of the Belo Monte Dam in the Brazilian Amazon and Its Consequences on Regional Rural Labor." *Land Use Policy* 90: 104327. https://doi.org/10.1016/j.landusepol.2019.104327.

Castro, N. J., A. L. S. Leite, and G. A. Dantas. 2011. "Análise Comparativa Entre Belo Monte e Empreendimentos Alternativos: Impactos Ambientais e Competitividade Econômica." *Grupos de Estudos do Setor Elétrico*. Rio de Janeiro: 1–13.

Centre for Science and Environment. 1999. *The Citizens' Fifth Report*. New Delhi: National Overview.

Cernea, M. M., and S. E. Guggenheim. 1993. *Anthropological Approaches to Involuntary Resettlement: Policy, Practice and Theory*. Boulder, CO: Westview Press.

Cernea, M. M. 1996. *Impoverishment Risks and Livelihood Reconstruction: A Model for Resettling Displaced Populations*. Washington, DC: World Bank Environment Department.

Cernea, Michael. M. 1996. "Understanding and Preventing Impoverishment from Displacement: Reflections on the State of Knowledge." In *Understanding Impoverishment: The Consequences of Development Induced Displacement*, edited by Christopher McDowell. Oxford: Berghahn Books.

—. 1997. "The Risks and Reconstruction Model for Resettling Displaced Populations." *World Development* 25, no. 10: 1569–87. https://doi.org/10.1016/S0305-750X(97)00054-5.

—. 1998. "Impoverishment or Social Justice? A Model for Planning Resettlement." In *Development Projects and Impoverishment Risks: Resettling Project-Affected People in India*, edited by H. M. Mathur, and Marsden David. New Delhi: Oxford.

—. 1999. "Development's Painful Social Costs: Introductory Study." In *The Development Dilemma: Displacement in India*. Edited by Parasuraman. Basingstoke: Macmillan, in *Association with the Institute of Social Studies, The Hague*.

—, ed. 1999. *The Economics of Involuntary Resettlement: Questions and Challenges*. Washington, DC: World Bank.

—. 2000. "Risks, Safeguards, and Reconstruction: A Modal for Population Displacement and Resettlement." In *Risks and Reconstruction: Experiences of Resettlers and Refugees*, edited by M. Cernea, and C. McDowell. Washington: World Bank.

—. 2000. "Risks, Safeguards and Reconstruction: A Model for Population Displacement and Resettlement." *Economic & Political Weekly* 41: 3659–78.

—. 2002. "For a New Economics of Resettlement: The Sociological Critique of the Compensation Principle." *International Social Science Journal* 55, no. 175: 37–45.

—. 2005. "The Ripple Effect in Social Policy and Its Political Context: Social Standards in Public and Private Sector Development Projects." In *Privatising Development: Transnational Law, Infrastructure and Human Rights*, edited by M. B. Likosky: 65–103. Leiden: Martinus-Nijhoff.

—. 2006. "Re- Examining Displacement: A Redefinition of Concepts in Development and Conservation Policies." *Social Change* 36, no. 1: 8–35. https://doi.org/10.1177/004908570603600102.

—. 2008. "Compensation and Benefit Sharing: Why Resettlement Policies and Practices Must Be Reformed." *Water Science & Engineering* 1, no. 1: 89–120. https://doi.org/10.1016/S1674-2370(15)30021-1.

Cernea Michael, M., and J. Maldonado. 2018. *Challenging the Prevailing Paradigm of Displacement and Resettlement: Risks, Impoverishment, Legacies, Solutions*. Abingdon: Routledge.

Chakravorty, Sanjay. 2015. "Improving an Unworkable Law." *Hindu,* January 7, 2015.

Chambers, R., and G. Conway. 1992. *Sustainable Rural Livelihoods: Practical Concepts for the 21st Century*. IDS Discussion Paper 296. Brighton: IDS.

Claude, Alvares and Ramesh Billorey. 1988. *Damming the Narmada: India's Greatest Planned Environmental Disaster.* Dehra Dun: Natraj Publishers.

Daily, China. 1993. *Company Set Up to Run Giant Dam Project*.

—. 1998. *High, Dry and Ready to Thrive in Chongqing* July 22, 2018.

Chong, Dennis. 1991. *Collective Action and the Civil Rights Movement*. Chicago: Chicago University Press.

Chongqing Statistical Bureau. 1998. *Statistical Yearbook of Chongqing*. Chongqing: China Statistical Publishing House (in Chinese).

Colson, E. 1971. *The Social Consequences of Resettlement: The Impact of the Kariba Resettlement on the Gwembe Tonga*. Manchester: Manchester University Press.

—. 1999. "Engendering Those Uprooted by Development." In Engendering Forced Migration: Theory and Practice." In *Engendering Forced Migration. Theory and Practice*, edited by Doreen Indra. Oxford: Berghahn Book Company.

Connell, J. 2015. "Is 'Good' Resettlement Policy Unimplementable? Learning from Advocacy in Cambodia." *Development in Practice* 25, no. 5: 655–72. https://doi.org/10.1080/09614524.2015.1050998.

Culletf, Philippe. 2001. "Human Rights and Displacement: The Indian Supreme Court Decision on Sardar Sarovar in International Perspective." *International & Comparative Law Quarterly* 50, no. 4: 973–87. https://doi.org/10.1093/iclq/50.4.973.

Culler, Philip, ed. 2007. *The Sardar Sarovar Dam Project: Selected Documents*. Aldershot: Ashgate.

CWRC. 1993. *Survey on Inundation Losses of the Three Gorges Project*. Unpublished Survey Report. Wuhan: Changjiang Water Resources Commission.

—. 1994. *Outline on the Handling of Reservoir Inundation and Resettlement Planning for the Three Gorges Project on the Yangtze River* [Unpublished document]. Wuhan: Changjiang Water Resources Commission.

—. 2007. *A Research Report on the Overall Planning for the Sustainable Using of Water Resources in the Three Gorges Reservoir Area* [Unpublished document]. Wuhan: Changjiang Water Resources Commission.

Dafallah, H. 1975. *The Nubian Exodus*. London: C. Hurst.

Damodaran, Vinita, and Felix Padel. 2018. "Investment- Induced Displacement in Central India A Study in Extractive Capitalism." *Comparative Studies of South Asia, Africa & the Middle East* 38, no. 2: 396–411. https://doi.org/10.1215/1089201x-6982156.

Feng, D., Hong Zhu, and Yihan Wang. 2021. "Agency and Mobility in the Context of Development-Induced Migration: The Case of Three Gorges Out-Migrants." *Journal of Ethnic & Migration Studies* 47, no. 12: 2745–59. https://doi.org/10.1080/1369183X.2020.1739375.

Darryl, and D'Monte. 1983. *High Dams at a High Cost*. Bombay: Economic Scene, November 16, 1983.

Dash, Satya Prakash. 2008. "Resettlement and Rehabilitation in Orissa: A Study of the Upper Indravati Hydro-electric Project." *Social Change* 38, no. 4: 661–88. https://doi.org/10.1177/004908570803800406.

Dash, Niladri Ranjan. 2010. "Sardar Sarovar Dam: A Case Study of Oustees in Gujarat, India." In *Ethnic Minorities and Regional Development in Asia: Reality and Challenges*, edited by Huhua Cao. Amsterdam: Amsterdam University Press.

Das, Preeti Jain. 2020. *The RFCTLARR Act, 2013: Are the Outcomes Fair?* New Delhi: TERI.

Das, Samir Kumar. 2005. "India: Homeless at Home." In *Internal Displacement in South Asia*, edited by Paula Banerjee, Sabyasachi Basu Ray Choudhary, and Samir Kumar Das. New Delhi: SAGE.

Daud Commission report. 2001. Geneva: International Environmental Law Research Centre.

"Daulat *Surana & Ors vs. First* Land Acquisition Collector and Ors." 2006. *Insc* 798.

De Debasree. 2014. "Development-Induced Displacement: Impact on Adivasi Women of Odisha." *Community Development Journal* 50, no. 3: 448–62.

Deetes, Pianporn. 2012. *Thai Villagers File Lawsuit on Xayaburi Dam International Rivers*.

Demirbaş, A. 2002. "Turkey's Energy Overview Beginning in the Twenty-First Century." *Energy Conversion & Management* 43, no. 14: 1877–87. https://doi.org/10.1016/S0196-8904(01)00124-8.

Demirbas, Ayhan, Ayse Sahin-Demirbas, and A. Hilal Demirbas. 2004. "Turkey's Natural Gas, Hydropower, and Geothermal Energy Policies." *Energy Sources* 26, no. 3: 237–48. https://doi.org/10.1080/00908310490256590.

Demirsoy, A. 1996. *General Zoogeography and Zoogeography of Turkey*. Ankara, Turkey.

Derneği, Doga. 2006. *Review of the Environ- Mental Impact Assessment Report Submitted for the Ilisu Dam and Hydro-Electric Power Project*. Ankara, Turkey.

—. "Land Acquisition Law and the Proposed Changes." *Economic & Political Weekly* XLVI, nos. 26 and 27.

Desai, Mihir. 2011. "Land Acquisition Law and the Proposed Changes." *Economic & Political Weekly* 46, no. 26/27: 95–100.

Sharan v. State of Uttar Pradesh. 2011 vol. 4 SCC 769.

de Wet, Chris John. 2000. "The Experience with Dams and Resettlement in Africa". Prepared for Thematic Review 1.3. *Displacement, Resettlement, Rehabilitation, Reparation and Development*. Cape Town: World Commission on Dams.

—. 2001. "Economic Development and Population Displacement: Can Everybody Win?." *Economic & Political Weekly* 36, no. 50: 4637–46.

Dhanagare, D. N. 1988. "Action Groups and Social Transformation in India." *Lokayan Bulletin* 6 5: 37–59.

—. 2001. "Displacement, Development and Large Dams." *Social Change* 31, nos. 1–2: 104–9. https://doi.org/10.1177/004908570103100209.

Dharamadhikary, Shripad. 2001. *Unravelling Bhakra: Assessing the Temple of Resurgent India*. Madhya Pradesh: Manthan Adhyayan Kendra.

Dharmadhikary, S. 2005. *Unravelling Bhakra: Assessing the Temple of Independent India. Badwani*. Manthan Adhyayan Kendra.

—. 2006. "The Narmada—Death of a River." *India International Centre Quarterly 33, No. 1*: 65–78.

Dharmadhikary, Shripad, and Nandini Oza. 2019. "Resettled Oustees from Narmada Valley A Flawed Survey, Discussion on Are Resettled Oustees from the Sardar Sarovar Dam Project 'Better Off' Today? by Swaminathan S Anklesaria Aiyar and Neeraj Kaushal." *Economic and Political Weekly*. IIV No. 44.

Dhawan, B. D. 1990. *Big Dams: Claims and Counter Claims*. New Delhi: Commonwealth Publishers.

Diamond, Sara, and Christian Poirier. 2010. *'Brazil's Native Peoples and the Belo Monte Dam: A Case Study.' NACLA Report on the Americas: After Recognition* vol. 24.

Dixit, A. K. 1973. "Models of Dualism." In *Models of Economic Growth*, edited by J. A. Mirlees, and N. H. Stern. London: McMillion.

Dolatyar, M., and T. S. Gray. 2000. *Water Politics in the Middle East: A Context for Conflict or Co-Operation?* London: Macmillan.

Hughes, J. D. 2000. "The Dams at Aswan: Does Environmental History Inform Decisions?." *Capitalism Nature Socialism* 11, no. 4: 73–81. https://doi.org/10.1080/10455750009358941.

Downing, T. E. 2002. *Avoiding New Poverty: Mining Induced Displacement and Resettlement*. Paper prepared for London: Managing Mineral Wealth Workshop.

—. 2002a. "Creating Poverty: The Flawed Economic Logic of the World Bank's Revised Involuntary Resettlement Policy." *Forced Migration Review* 12: 13–4.

—. 2002b. *Avoiding New Poverty: Mining-Induced Displacement and Resettlement*. London: International Institute for Environment and Development.

Downing, T. E., and C. Garcia-Downing. 2009. "Routine and Dissonant Culture: A Theory About the Psychosocial Cultural Disruptions of Involuntary Displacement and the Ways to Mitigate Them Without Inflicting Even More Damage." In *Development and Dispossession: The*

Anthropology of Displacement and Resettlement, edited by A. Oliver-Smith. Santa Fe: School for Advanced Research Press.

Drydyk, Jay. 1999. "Development Induced Displacement and Rawls's 'General Conception' of Justice. Economic Policy." *Population Displacement & Development Ethics (Project Report)*. Ontario: Carleton University.

Duan, Y., and S. Steil. 2003. "China Three Gorges Project Resettlement: Policy, Planning and Implementation." *Journal of Refugee Studies* 16, no. 4: 422–43. https://doi.org/10.1093/jrs/16.4.422.

Duan, Yuefang, and B. McDonald. 2010. "Policy of Resettlement with Development in China's Three Gorges Project". Conference on Modern Hydraulic Engineering. London: London Science Publishing Limited.

Duan, Yuefang, and Brooke Wilmsen. 2012. "Addressing the Resettlement Challenges at the Three Gorges Project." *International Journal of Environmental Studies* 69, no. 3: 461–74. https://doi.org/10.1080/00207233.2012.676374.

Dubash, N. K., M. Dupar, S. Kothari, and T. Lissu. 2001. "A Watershed in Global Governance?." *An Independent Assessment of the World Commission on Dams. Lokayan: World Resources Institute and Lawyers' Environmental Action Team.*

Dubé, François. 2016. "Thirty Years of Development-Induced Displacement in China." *Forced Migration Review* 51: 88–9.

Dudgeon, D. 2005. "River Rehabilitation for Conservation of Fish Biodiversity in Monsoonal Asia." *Ecology & Society* 10, no. 2: 15. https://doi.org/10.5751/ES-01469-100215.

Duggal, S. K., J. K. Bhalla, and R. S. Dogra. 2001. *Socio-economic and Environmental Impacts of Bhakra Beas Project – An Assessment.* Chandigarh: Bhakra Beas Management Board.

Duggal, Er. 2002. "Flood and Sedimentation Status of Bhakra Reservoir - A Case Study." In *Unravelling Bhakra: Assessing the Temple of Resurgent India*. "S.K., J.K." In *Bhalla and N. K. Bhatia*, edited by Shripad Dharamadhikary. Madhya Pradesh: Manthan Adhyayan Kendra.

Dwarkadas Shrinivas vs Sholapur Spinning and Weaving Colo. Ltd. 1954. Association for Institutional Research: SC119.

—. 2002. "Models and Methods in Development-Induced Displacement (Review Article)." *Development & Change* 33, no. 4: 709–32. https://doi.org/10.1111/1467-7660.00276.

Dwivedi, Ranjit. 1999. "Displacement, Risks and Resistance: Local Perceptions and Actions in the Sardar Sarovar." *Development & Change* 30, no. 1: 43–78. https://doi.org/10.1111/1467-7660.00107.

—. 2002. *Social Review of Ilisu Dam Resettlement Action Plan*. London: Export Credit Guarantee Department.
ECGD. 1999. *Stakeholders Perception of Involuntary Resettlement*. London: Export Credit Guarantee Department.
Eletrobras. 2009. "Rima Relatorio de Impacto Ambiental Aproveitamento Hidreletrico Belo Monte." *Ministério Das Minas e Energia. Brazil: Brasilia*.
Eken, G., M. Bozdogan, S. Isfendiyaroglu, D. T. Kiliç, and Y. Lise. 2006. *Turkiyenin Önemli Doga Alanlan* [*Turkey's Key Bio- Diversity Areas*]. Ankara, Turkey.
"Empresa de Pesquisa Energética." 2015. *Balanço Energético Nacional*. [Ministério Das Minas e Energia]. Brazil: Brasilia.
Emrah, Yalcin, and Sahnaz Tigrek. 2016. "Hydropower Production Without Sacrificing Environment: A Case Study of Ilisu Dam and Hasankeyf." *International Journal of Water Resources Development* 32, no. 2: 47–266.
Engineer, Rusi. 1990. "The Sardar Sarovar Controversy: Are the Critics Right?." In *Big Dams: Claims and Counter Claims*, edited by B. D. Dhawan. New Delhi: Commonwealth Publishers.
EPW. 1974. "Priority to Power, Too Late." *Economic & Political Weekly* 9, no. 41: 1725–7.
—. 2014. "Dialogue Needed on Sardar Sarovar." *Economic & Political Weekly* 49: 37.
Everard, Mark. 2013. *The Hydropolitics of Dams: Engineering or Ecosystems*. London: Zed Books.
Fahim, H. M. 1981. *Dams, People and Development: The Aswan High Dam Case*. New York: Pergamon Press.
—. 1983. *Egyptian Nubians – Resettlement and Years of Coping*. Salt Lake City: University of Utah Press.
Fearnside, Phillip M. 2006. "Dams in the Amazon: Belo Monte and Brazil's Hydroelectric Development of the Xingu River Basin." *Environmental Management* 38, no. 1: 16–27.
https://doi.org/10.1007/s00267-005-0113-6.
Fekri, Hassan A. 2007. "The Aswan High Dam and the International Rescue Nubia Campaign." *African Archaeological Review* 24, no. 3/4: 73–94.
Ferguson, James. 1990. *The AntiPolitics Machine: Development, Depoliticization, and Bureaucratic Power in the Third World*. Cambridge: Cambridge University Press.
Fernandes, Walter, and E. Thukral, eds. 1989. *Development, Displacement and Rehabilitation*. Delhi: Indian Social Institute.

Fernandes, Walter. 2001. "Development Induced Displacement and Sustainable Development." *Social Change* 31, no. 1–2: 87–103. https://doi.org/10.1177/004908570103100208.

—. 2006. "Liberalization and Development Induced Displacement." *Social Change* 36, no. 3: 109–23.

Fernea, R. A. 1998. *Including Minorities in Development: The Nubian Case* [Unpublished report]. Washington: D.C. World Bank.

Fisher. "William and Armonk." 1992. *Toward Sustainable Development? Struggling over India's Narmada River*. New York: M.E. Sharpe.

—. 1997. "Doing Good? The Politics and Antipolitics of NGO Practices." *Annual Review of Anthropology* 26, no. 1: 439–64. https://doi.org/10.1146/annurev.anthro.26.1.439.

FPGA. 1968. "'Dicle Havzası istiks¸af raporu [The Tigris Basin reconnaissance report].' in Euphrates Planning Group Authority in 'Hydropower Production Without Sacrificing Environment: a Case Study of Ilisu Dam and Hasankeyf.' Emrah Yalcin and Sahnaz Tigrek". 2016. *International Journal of Water Resources Development* 32, no. 2: 247–66 (Euphrates Planning Group. *Authority*).

Franchetto, B. 2011. *Alto Xingu: Uma sociedade multilíngue*. Rio de Janeiro: Museu do Índio.

"Friends of River Narmada." 2008 [Introduction], Accessed August 19, 2018. http://www.narmada.org/introduction.html.

Fu, C., J. Wu, J. Chen, Q. Wu, and G. Lei. 2003. "Freshwater Fish Biodiversity in the Yangtze River Basin in China: Patterns, Threats and Conservation." *Biodiversity & Conservation* 12, no. 8: 1649–85. https://doi.org/10.1023/A:1023697714517.

Fujikura, R., and M. Nakayama. 2009. "Lessons Learned from the World Commission on Dams." *International Environmental Agreements: Politics, Law & Economics* 9, no. 2: 173–90. https://doi.org/10.1007/s10784-009-9093-y.

"Gabungan." 1999. *Resettlement of Indigenous Peoples. World Commission on Dams Final Report*. Cape Town: World Commission on Dams.

Gadgil, Madhav, and Ramchandra Guha. 1992. *This Fissured Land*. New Delhi: Oxford University Press.

Ganguly-Scrase, R., and K. Lahiri-Dutt. 2013. *Dispossession, Placelessness, Home and Belonging: An Outline of a Research Agenda*. London: Routledge.

vol. G1. 2010. "Obra Nem Começou, Mas Já Atrai Migrantes e Investimento para Altamira." *MUL1547975-9356,00-OBRA+NEM+COMECOU.* http://g1.globo.com/Noticias/Economia_Negocios/0. Accessed December 22, 2015.

van Gelder, Jan Willem, Frank van der Valk, Jan Maarten Dros, and Janette Worm. 2002. "The Impacts and Financing of Large Dams." *A Research Paper Prepared for WWF International*. Amsterdam: Living Waters Programme.

Ghatak, Maitreesh, and Parikshit Ghosh. 2011. "The Land Acquisition Bill: A Critique and a Proposal." *Economic & Political Weekly* XLVI, no. 41.

Ghosh, Arun. 1990. "A Plea for Open Government: Case of Narmada Project." In *Big Dams: Counter Claims*, edited by B. D. Dhawan. New Delhi: Commonwealth Publishers.

Gokhale, Veena. 1991. "India's Narmada Valley Hydro Project." *Eco Decision, Environment & Policy Magazine* 1.

Gonzalez-Parra, C. 2001. "Indigenous People and Mega Common Property Resources." In *Risks and Reconstruction: Experiences of Resettlers and Refugees*, edited by M. Cernea, and C. McDowell. Washington, DC: World Bank.

Goodland, K. 2007. "The Institutionalised Use of Force in Economic Development." In *Environmental and Human Health Through Global Governance*, edited by C. L. Soskolne, L. Westra, L. J. Kotze, B. Mackey, W. E. Rees, and R. Westra. Lanham: Lexington Books.

Government of India. 2013. *The Right to Fair Compensation and Transparency in Land Acquisition, Rehabilitation and Resettlement Act*. New Delhi: Ministry of Law and Justice.

—. 2014. *The Right to Fair Compensation and Transparency in Land Acquisition, Rehabilitation and Resettlement (Amendment) Ordinance. No. 9 of.* New Delhi: Ministry of Law and Justice.

—. 2017. *Rehabilitation of Families Displaced Due to Sardar Sarovar Project*. New Delhi: Ministry of Water Resources. Press Information Bureau.

Goyal, Sangeeta. 1996. "Economic Perspectives on Resettlement and Rehabilitation." *Economic & Political Weekly* 31, no. 24.

Grimm, C. D. 1991. *Turmoil and Transformation: A Study of Population Relocation at Manantali, Mali* [Unpublished PhD thesis]. Binghamton: State University of New York Press.

Gross Trevor, L. 2009. "American University: Washington College of Law." *Comment* 6, no. 2*(C) Proportionality Test Applied to The Merowe Dam Project In Sudan.*

Gu, Chaolin, and Chunxiao Huang. 1999. *Sanxia Kuqu Chengzhen Yimin Qianjian de Wenti Yu Duice* [*Study on the Resettlement and Reconstruction of Cities in the Three Gorges Reservoir Area*]." *Changjiang liuyu ziyuan yu huanjing (Resources and Environment in the Yangtze Basin)* 8: 353–9.

"Guidelines and Principles for Social Impact Assessment." 1994. *Interorganizational Committee on Guidelines and Principles for Social Impact Assessment.*

Guiding Principles on Internal Displacement. 1998. Geneva: UN High Commissioner for Refugees.

Gupta, Namita. 2021. *'Environmental Consequences of Dams: A Study of Select Hydroelectric Projects in India.' in Environment, Development and Sustainability in India: Perspectives, Issues and Alternatives*, edited by Manish K. Verma. Singapore: Springer Nature.

"Habitat International Coalition Report." 2002. *The Impact of the 2002 Submergence on Housing and Land Rights in the Narmada Valley Report of a Fact-Finding Mission to Sardar Sarovar and Man Dam Projects*. New Delhi: South Asia Regional Programme.

Hagen, Renee V., and Tessa Minter. 2020. "Displacement in the Name of Development. How Indigenous Rights Legislation Fails to Protect Philippine Hunter-Gatherers." *Society & Natural Resources* 33, no. 1: 65–82. https://doi.org/10.1080/08941920.2019.1677970.

Hall, Anthony, and Sue Branford. 2012. "Development, Dams and Dilma: The Saga of Belo Monte." *Critical Sociology* 38, no. 6: 851–62. https://doi.org/10.1177/0896920512440712.

Han, X., L. Feng, C. Hu, and X. Chen. 2018. "Wetland Changes of China's Largest Freshwater Lake and Their Linkage with the Three Gorges Dam." *Remote Sensing of Environment* 204: 799–811. https://doi.org/10.1016/j.rse.2017.09.023.

Harvey, D. 2003. *The New Imperialism*. Oxford: Oxford University Press.

—. 2007. *A Brief History of Neoliberalism*. Oxford: Oxford University Press.

Hasan, Mohammed. 2006. "Creating New Economic Opportunities for Displaced People: Approaches to Income Restoration." *Social Change* 36, no. 1: 87–108. https://doi.org/10.1177/004908570603600104.

Haynes, Jeffery. 2008. *Development Studies*. New Delhi: Rawat.

Heggelund, Gørild. 2004. *Environment and Resettlement Politics in China: The Three Gorges Dam*. Burlington, VT: Ashgate.

—. 2006. "Resettlement Programmes and Environmental Capacity in the Three Gorges Dam Project." *Development & Change* 37, no. 1: 179–99. https://doi.org/10.1111/j.0012-155X.2006.00474.x.

Hemadri, Ravi. 1999. "'Dam, Displacement, Policy and Law in India', Contributing" [Paper], prepared for Thematic Review, Social Issue 1.3." In *Displacement. Resettlement, Rehabilitation, Reparation & Development, Cape Town*. World Commission on Dams.

Hoops, Björn, and Nicholas K. Tagliarino. 2019. "The Legal Boundaries of 'Public Purpose' in India and South Africa: A Comparative Assessment in Light of the Voluntary Guidelines." *Land* 8, no. 10: 154. https://doi.org/10.3390/land8100154.

Horowitz, Michael M. 1993. "Resettlement at Manantali, Mali: short term success, long-term problems." In *Anthropological Approaches to Resettlement: Policy*. "D: Loenig, C. Grimm and Y. Konate." In *Theory, and Practice*, edited by M. M. Cernea, and S. Guggenheim. CO: Westview Press.

Huang, Z.-L. 2001. "Biodiversity Conservation for the Three Gorges Project." *Biodiversity Science* 9: 472–81.

Hvistendahl, Mara. 2008. "China's Three Gorges Dam: An Environmental Catastrophe?." *Scientific American*. America: Springer Nature.

ICCPR. 1966. *International Covenant on Civil and Political Rights*. Geneva: United Nations.

ICESCR. 1966. *International Covenant on Economic, Social and Cultural Rights*. Geneva: United Nations.

IFC. 2002. *Handbook for Preparing a Resettlement Action Plan*. Washington, (DC): International Finance Corporation.

—. 2003. *Compliance Advisor/Ombudsman Report, A Review of IFC's Safeguard Policies, Core Business: Achieving Consistent and Excellent Environmental and Social Outcomes*. Washington, (DC): International Finance Corporation.

IIPA. 2002. *Large Dams in India: Environmental, Social and Economic Impacts*. New Delhi: Indian Institute of Public Administration.

"Ilisu Hydropower Consultants." 1983. *The Cizre Dam and HEPP Project Feasibility Report*. Ilisu Hydropower Consultants: Binnie & Partners, Gizbili Consultancy Engineering, James Williamson & Partners, Kennedy & Donkin and COBA.

"Inclusive Development International." 2014. *World Bank's Draft Safeguards Fail to Protect Land Rights and Prevent Impoverishment: Major Revisions Required*." www, Accessed April 23, 2015. http://inclusivedevelopment.net/joint-statement-world-banks-draft-safeguards-fail-to-protect-land-rights-andprevent-impoverishment-major-revisions-required.

Indrajit, C. "Parekh of Ahmedabad and Another *vs.* State of Gujarat and Others." 1975. *Indlaw*: SC579.

Indra, D. 1999. *Engendering Forced Migration: Theory and Practice*. Oxford: Refugee Studies Programme.

International Rivers. 2012. "Belo Monte Massive Dam Project Strikes at the Heart of the Amazon", Accessed December 22, 2015.

http://www.internationalrivers.org/files/attached-files/Belo_Monte_FactSheet_May2012.pdf.

Inter-American Commission on Human Rights. 2011. *Indigenous Communities of the Xingu River Basin, Para, Brazil*. Costa Rica: IACHR.

IRN. 1988. *International Rivers Network, San Francisco Declaration and Watershed Management Declaration*. Berkeley: IRN.

—. 1997. "'The Three Gorges Dam Update.' in 'Global Capital, National Development and Transnational Environmental Activism: Conflict and the Three Gorges Dam.', Lee Yuen-Ching Bellette." *Journal of Contemporary Asia* 43, 2013 1: 102–26.

Irrigation Committee report. 1972. New Delhi: Government of India.

Jagadeesan, S., and D. M. Kumar. 2015. *The Sardar Sarovar Project: Assessing Economic and Social Impacts*. New Delhi: SAGE.

Jayewardene, R. 2008. "Can Displacement Be Turned into Development by Compensation Alone?." In *Can Compensation Prevent Impoverishment? Reforming Resettlement Through Investments and Benefit-Sharing*, edited by M. M. Cernea, and H. M. Mathur. New Delhi: Oxford University Press.

Jaysawal, Neelmani, and Sudeshna Saha. 2018. "Impact of Displacement on Livelihood: A Case Study of Odisha." *Community Development Journal* 53, no. 1: 136–54. https://doi.org/10.1093/cdj/bsw026.

Jean, Dreze, Meera Samson, and Satyajit Singh. 1997. *The Dam and the Nation: Displacement and Resettlement in the Narmada Valley*. New Delhi: Oxford University Press.

Jing, J. 1997. "Rural Resettlement: Past Lessons for the Three Gorges Project." *China Journal* 38: 65–92. https://doi.org/10.2307/2950335.

Jobin, W. 1999. *Dams and Diseases: Ecological Design and Health Impacts of Large Dams, Canals and Irrigation Systems*. London: E and F N Spon.

Joesten, Joachim. 1960. "Nasser's Daring Dream: The Aswan High Dam." *World Today* 16, no. 2: 55–63.

Johnston, B. R. 2018. "Large-Scale Dam Development and Counter Movements: Water Justice Struggles Around Guatemala's Chixoy Dam." In *Water Justice*, edited by R. Boelens, T. Perreault, and J. Vos. Cambridge: Cambridge University Press.

López-Pujol, J., and Ming-Xun Ren. 2009. "Biodiversity and the Three Gorges Reservoir: A Troubled Marriage." *Journal of Natural History* 43, no. 43–44: 2765–86. https://doi.org/10.1080/00222930903220010.

Jorgenson, D. W. 1961. "The Development of a Dual Economy." *Economic Journal* 71, no. 282: 309–34. https://doi.org/10.2307/2228770.

Joyce, Stephanie. 1997. "Is It Worth a Dam?." *Environmental Health Perspectives* 105, no. 10: 1050–55. https://doi.org/10.1289/ehp.971051050.

Judge, Paramjit S. 2000. "Resettlement and Rehabilitation of the Displaced." In *Environmental Management: An Indian Perspective*, edited by S. N. Chary, and Vinod Vyasulu. New Delhi: Mc Million.

Sousa, W. C., J. Reid, and N. C. S. Leitão. 2006. "Custos e Benefícios do Complexo Hidrelétrico Belo Monte: Uma Abordagem Econômico-ambiental." *Conservation Strategy Fund* 04. "Júnior" 90.

"Júnior, Sousa, W.C., and Reid, J." 2010. "Uncertainties in Amazon hydropower development: Risk scenarios and environmental issues around the Belo Monte dam.". *Water Alternatives* 3, no. 2: 249–68.

Tubek v. Ekran Bhd. & Ors. 1996. No. S5-21-60-1995.

Kapur, Devesh, John P. Lewis, and Richard C. Webb. 1997. *The World Bank: Its First Half Century* vol. I and II. Washington, DC: Brookings Institution Press.

Kasparek, M., and C. C. Bilgin. 1996. "Kuçlar." In *Türkiye Omurgahlar Tür Listesi*, edited by A. Kence, C. C. Bilgin, and Ankara Tübitak. Turkey.

Kaygusuz, K. 1999. "Energy Situation, Future Developments, Energy Saving, and Energy Efficiency in Turkey." *Energy Sources* 21, no. 5: 405–16. https://doi.org/10.1080/00908319950014722.

"Kedar Nath *Yadav vs. State of West Bengal and Others*." 2016. *Civil Appeal* 8438.

Khagram, Sanjeev. 2004. *Dams and Development*. New Delhi: Oxford University Press.

Khaitan, Bulbul, and Nitya Priya. 2009. "Rehabilitation of the Displaced Persons in India." *NUJS Law Review* 2009: 111–24.

KHRP. 1999. *The Ilisu Dam: A Human Rights Disaster in the Making*. London: Kurdish Human Rights Project.

—. 2003. *Go~-Der and Human Rights Association. Internally Displaced Persons: The Kurds in Turkey*. London: Kurdish Human Rights Project.

Kibaroglu, Aysegül, and Ramazan Caner Sayan. 2021. "Water and 'Imperfect Peace' in the Euphrates–Tigris River Basin." *International Affairs* 97, no. 1: 139–55. https://doi.org/10.1093/ia/iiaa161.

Kiliç, D. T., and G. Eken. 2004. "Türkiye 'Nin Önemli Ku§ Alanlari – 2004 Güncellemesi [Turkey's Important Bird Areas].'." *Doga Dernegi-Bird Life International*. Ankara, Turkey.

Kitchen, W. H., and M. Ronayne. 2002. "The Ilisu Dam Environmental Impact Assessment Report: Review and Critique." *Public Archaeology* 2, no. 2: 101–16. https://doi.org/10.1179/pua.2002.2.2.101.

Klein, Peter Taylor. 2015. "Engaging the Brazilian State: The Belo Monte Dam and the Struggle for Political Voice." *Journal of Peasant Studies* 42, no. 6: 1137–56. https://doi.org/10.1080/03066150.2014.991719.

Klimes, Martina. 2020. "Water Diplomacy and Sustainable Management in Mesopotamia." *ISPI Dossier*, Accessed December 20, 2021. https://www.ispionline.it/it/pubblicazione/water-diplomacy-and-sustainable-management-mesopotamia-25178.

Klingensmith, Daniel. 2007. *One Valley and a Thousand: Dams, Nationalism and Development*. New Delhi: Oxford University Press.

Koenig, D. 1995. "Women and Resettlement." In *The Women and International Development Annual*, edited by R. Gallin, and A. Ferguson, Boulder: Westview Press.

—. 2009. "Urban Relocation and Resettlement: Distinctive Problems, Distinctive Opportunities." In *Development and Dispossession: The Anthropology of Displacement and Resettlement*, edited by A. Oliver-Smith. Santa Fe: School for Advanced Research Press.

Kohli, K., and D. Gupta. 2017. *Mapping Dilutions in a Central Law: A Comparative Analyiss of Rules Made Under the Right to Fair Compensation and Transparency in the Land Acquisition, Rehabilitation and Resettlement (RFCTLARR) Act, 2013*. New Delhi: Centre for Policy Research.

Kothari, Smitu. 1996. "Whose Nation? The Displaced as Victims of Development." *Economic & Political Weekly* 31, no. 24: 1476–85.

Kushalapa, K. A. 1992. "Special Monitoring of Compensatory Afforestation in Kachh District – Gujarat: A Report" *Annexed to the Agenda for the 15th Meeting of the Environment Sub-Group of the Narmada Control Authority*.

Lambert Lazarus, S. 2015. "The Equator Principles: Retaining the Gold Standard – A Strategic Vision at 10 Years." In *Responsible Investment Banking: Risk Management Frameworks Sustainable Financial Innovation and Soft Law Standards*, edited by K. Wendt: 123–41. Heidelberg: Springer. https://doi.org/10.1007/978-3-319-10311-2_7.

Land Acquisition Act. 1894. New Delhi: Government of India. Ministry of Law and Justice.

"Lancy, Lobo and Shashikant Kumar." 2009. *Land Acquisition, Displacement & Resettlement in Gujarat*: 1947–2004. New Delhi: SAGE.

Lavoyer, Jean-Philippe. 1998. "Guiding Principles on Internal Displacement: A Few Comments on the Contribution of International Humanitarian Law." *International Review of the Red Cross* 38, no. 324: 467–80. https://doi.org/10.1017/S0020860400091270.

Lee, Christopher. 2014. "Globality and Aesthetics." *Third Text* 28, no. 1: 32–45. https://doi.org/10.1080/09528822.2014.869985.
—. 2013. "Global Capital, National Development and Transnational Environmental Activism: Conflict and the Three Gorges Dam." *Journal of Contemporary Asia* 43, no. 1: 102–26. https://doi.org/10.1080/00472336.2012.739933.
Leite, M., D. Amora, M. Kachani, L. de Almeida, and R. Machado. 2013. "A Batalha de Belo Monte." *Folha de S. Paulo*. http://arte.folha.uol.c, Accessed March 14, 2021. http://om.br/especiais/2013/12/16/belo-monte/capitulo-3-sociedade.html.
Lei, X. 1998. "Going Against the Flow in China." *Science* 280, no. 5360: 24–6. https://doi.org/10.1126/science.280.5360.24.
Lewis, Arthur. 1954. "Economic Development with Unlimited Supplies of Labour." *Manchester School of Economic & Social Studies* 22: 132–91.
Li, D., Y. Song, and Z. Ouyang. 2003. *Research on the National Forestry Nature Reserve System Plan*. Beijing, China: China Land Press.
Likosky, Michael B. 2005. *Privatising Development: Transnational Law, Infrastructure and Human Rights*. Leiden/Boston: Martinus-Nijhoff Publishers.
Lily, Kuo. 2020. "Anxiety Grows as China's Three Gorges Dam Hits Highest Level." *The Guardian*, Accessed March 14, 2021. https://www.theguardian.com/world/2020/aug/20/china-three-gorges-dam-highest-level-hydro-electric-floods.
Lucas, Henry. 2000. "What Do You Mean, 'Social Policy Analysis'? Reflections on Concepts and Methodology." *IDS Bulletin* 31, no. 4: 98–108. https://doi.org/10.1111/j.1759-5436.2000.mp31004010.x.
Mahapatra, L. K. 1991. "Development for Whom? Depriving the Dispossessed Tribals." *Social Action* 41, no. 3: 271–87.
—. 1999. *Resettlement, Impoverishment and Reconstruction in India*. New Delhi: Vikas.
Mahaprashasta, A. A. 2016. "Singur Verdict Will Help Mamata Consolidate Her Position in Bengal." *Wire*, Accessed October 10 2021. https://staging.thewire.in/politics/will-singur-verdict-consilidate-mamata.
Mallakh, R. E. 1959. "Some Economic Aspects of the Aswan High Dam Project in Egypt." *Land Economics* 35, no. 1: 15–23. https://doi.org/10.2307/3144704.
March, C., I. Smyth, and M. Mukhopadhyay. 1999. *A Guide to Gender-Analysis Frameworks*. Oxford: Oxfam.
Marsh, N. n.d. "Wars Downstream". http://www.ukdf.org.uk/ts5. , Accessed December 20, 2021. UK Defence Forum.

Martellaro, J. A. 1991. "Water Resources in the People's Republic of China: Control and Management." *China Economic Review* 2, no. 2: 145–56. https://doi.org/10.1016/1043-951X(91)90001-O.
Mathew, Areeparampil. 1996. "Displacement Due to Mining in Jharkhand." *Economic & Political Weekly* 31, no. 24: 1524–28.
Mathur, H. M., and Marsden David. 1998. "Development Projects and Impoverishment Risks: Resettling Project-Affected People in India." *New Delhi: Oxford.*
Mathur, Hari Mohan. 2001. "Livelihood Issues in Projects That Involve Resettlement: Experiences of a Coal Mining Project in Eastern India". Paper presented at ISEDKDS Social Development Research Capacity Building Workshop "Livelihoods and Poverty Reduction: Lessons from Eastern India." Bhubaneswar: Orissa.
—. 2006. "Resettling People Displaced by Development Projects: Some Critical Management Issues." *Social Change* 36, no. 1: 36–86. https://doi.org/10.1177/004908570603600103.
—. 2006b. "Mining Coal, Undermining People: Compensation Policy and Practice of Coal India." In *Reforming Resettlement*, edited by Michael M. Cernea, and Hari Mohan Mathur. New Delhi: Oxford University Press.
—. 2013. *Displacement and Resettlement in India: The Human Cost of Development*. London: Routledge.
—. 2015. "Climate Change and Displacement: Learning from Resettlement in the Development Context." *Social Change* 45, no. 1: 118–30. https://doi.org/10.1177/0049085714561939.
McCully. 2001. "Silenced Rivers: The Ecology and Politics of Large Dams. London." In *The Future of Large Dams: Dealing with Social, Environmental, Institutional and Political Costs*, edited by Thayer Scudder. London: Earthscan Publications.
McDonald-Wilmsen, B., and M. Webber. 2010. "Dams and Displacement: Raising the Standards and Broadening the Research Agenda." *Water Alternatives* 3, no. 2: 142–61.
McDonald, B., M. Webber, and D. Yuefang. 2008. "Involuntary Resettlement as an Opportunity for Development: The Case of Urban Resettlers of the Three Gorges Project, China." *Journal of Refugee Studies* 21, no. 1: 82–102. https://doi.org/10.1093/jrs/fem052.
McDowell, C., and G. Morell. 2007. "Development and Displacement: Institutionalizing Responsibility." *Development* 50, no. 4: 33–8. https://doi.org/10.1057/palgrave.development.1100428.

Mehta, Lyla, and Bina Srinivasan. 1999. "Balancing Gains and Pains: A Perspective Paper on Gender and Large Dams." *Cape Town*: Working paper prepared for the World Commission on Dams.

—. 2000. "Balancing Pains and Gains: A Perspective Paper on Gender and Large Dams." *Cape Town*: Final paper prepared for the World Commission on Dams.

Mehta, L. 2009a. "The Double Bind: A Gender Analysis of Forced Displacement and Resettlement." In *Development: Confronting Marginalisation and Gender Injustice*, edited by L. Mehta. New Delhi: SAGE.

Mejia, Maria Clara. 1999. "Economic Dimensions of Urban Involuntary Resettlement: Experiences from Latin America." In *The Economics of Involuntary Resettlement: Questions and Challenges*, edited by M. Cernea. Washington, DC: World Bank.

Menon, M. S. 2003. "Sardar Sarovar Project: Another Perspective." *Economic & Political Weekly* 38, no. 39: 4095–6.

Mikiyasu, Nakayama, and Ryo Fujikura. 2001. "Political Bias and Methodological Failure in Assessing Environmental Impacts of Development Projects: Comparative Analysis of the High Aswan Dam and Calaca Thermal Power Plant Development Projects." *Journal of Comparative Policy Analysis: Research & Practice* 3: 291–310.

"Ministerio de Minas e Energia." 2012. *Piano Decenal de Expansao de Energia*, Brazil: Brasilia.

"Ministereo Publico Federal." 2016. *MPF Pede Paralisac¸~ao de Belo Monte por Risco de Colapso Sanitario— Procuradoria da Republica no Para [MPF asks for Belo Monte shutdown due to risk of sanitary collapse]*, Accessed April 12, 2021. http://www.mpf.mp.br/pa/salade-imprensa/noticias-pa/mpf-pede-paralisacao-de-belomonte-por-risco-de-colapso-sanitario.

"Ministereo Publico Federal." 2017. *TRF1 Suspende Licenc¸a de Operac¸~ao Da Usina de Belo Monte—Procuradoria Regional Da Republica Da 1a Regi~Ao [TRF1 Suspends the Operating License for the Belo Monte Plant]*, Accessed April 11, 2021. http://www.mpf.mp.br/regiao1/sala-de-imprensa/noticias-r1/trf1-suspende-licenca-de-operacao-de-belo-monte.

Mishra, D. K. 2011. "Behind Dispossession: State, Land Grabbing and Agrarian Change in Rural Orissa". Paper presented at International Conference on Global Land Grabbing, Institute of Development Studies. University of Sussex.

Mishra, Ratnakar. 2014. "Displacement: A Socio-economic Rights Perspective." *Vikalpa: The Journal for Decision Makers* 39, no. 4: 11–22. https://doi.org/10.1177/0256090920140402.

Misra, Savvy Soumya. 2009. "Court Rules in Favour of Tribals." *Down to Earthed*, Accessed April 11, 2021. https://www.downtoearth.org.in/news/court-rules-in-favour-of-tribals-3827.

El Moattassem, M. 1994. "Field Studies and Analysis of the High Aswan Dam Reservoir." *International Water Power & Dam Construction* 46.

Modi, Renu. 2004. "Sardar Sarovar Oustees: Coping with Displacement." *Economic & Political Weekly* 39, no. 11: 1123–6.

MoEA. 2001. *Address to the Nation by the President of India Shri K. R. Narayanan on the Eve of Republic Day. January 25, 2001*. New Delhi: Government of India.

Morvaridi, Behrooz. 2004. "Resettlement, Rights to Development and the Ilisu Dam, Turkey." *Development & Change* 35, no. 4: 719–41. https://doi.org/10.1111/j.0012-155X.2004.00377.x.

—. 1995. "Finding and Recommendations of the Independent Review." In *Toward Sustainable Development: Struggling over India's Narmada River*, edited by William F. Fisher. NY: M.E. Sharpe.

Morse, Bradford, and Thomas Berger. 1992. *Sardar Sarovar: Report of the Independent Review*. Ottawa: Resource Futures International Inc.

MoRD. 2013. *Ministry of Rural Development the Right to Fair Compensation and Transparency in Land Acquisition, Rehabilitation and Resettlement Act 2013*. New Delhi: Government of India.

Müller, Beat, Michael Berg, Zhi Ping Yao, Xian Feng Zhang, Ding Wang, and August Pfluger. 2008. "How Polluted Is the Yangtze River? Water Quality Downstream from the Three Gorges Dam." *Science of the Total Environment* 402, no. 2–3: 232–47. https://doi.org/10.1016/j.scitotenv.2008.04.049.

"Murdock, Salem, M." 1989. *Arabs and Nubians in New Halfa – A Study of Settlement and Irrigation*. Salt Lake City: University of Utah Press.

Andolan v. Union of India and Others. 2000. *Writ Petition (Civil)* vol. 319 of vol. 1994, Judgment of 18 Oct. 2000, reprinted in 2000 (7) SCALE 16-22 Oct. 2000.

Andolan v. The State of Madhya Pradesh. 2008. AIR 2008 MP 142, 2008 (2) MPHT 490.

Andolan v. State of M.P. & Anr. 2011. *Civil Appeal* vol. 2082 of vol. 2011.

Nayak, Arun Kumar. 2010. "Big Dams and Protests in India: A Study of Hirakud Dam." *Economic & Political Weekly* 45, no. 2: 69–73.

—. 2013. "Development, Displacement and Justice in India: Study of Hirakud Dam." *Social Change* 43, no. 3: 397–419. https://doi.org/10.1177/0049085713494299.

NBSAP. 2001. "National Biodiversity Strategy and Action Plan." In *Unravelling Bhakra: Assessing the Temple of Resurgent India,* Authored by Dharamadhikary Shripad. Madhya Pradesh: Manthan Adhyayan Kendra.

Jayal and Another v. Union of India. 2004 vol. 9 SCC 362.

Neef, A., and J. Singer. 2015. "Development-Induced Displacement in Asia: Conflicts, Risks and Resilience." *Development in Practice* 25, no. 5: 601–11. https://doi.org/10.1080/09614524.2015.1052374.

Negi, N. S., and S. Ganguly. 2011. *Development Projects vs. Internally Displaced Populations in India: A Literature Based Appraisal*. Working Paper No. 103. Bielefeld: Center on Migration, Citizenship and Development.

Nielsen, Kenneth. 2011. "Land, Law and Resistance." *Economic & Political Weekly* 46, no. 11.

"Norte Energia, S.A.." 2010. *Projeto Basico Ambiental da Usina Hidreletrica Belo Monte*, Accessed January 20, 2021. https://docplayer.com.br/11584494-Pba-belo-monte-aproveitamento-hidreletrico-projeto-basico-ambiental-da-usina-hidreletrica-belo-monte-norte-energia-s-a-planos-programas-e-projetos.html.

OECD. "DAC." 1992. *Guidelines for Aid Agencies on Involuntary Displacement and Resettlement in Development Projects*. OECD Development Assistance Committee Guidelines on Aid and Environment No. 3. Paris: Organization for Economic Cooperation and Development.

—. 2011. *OECD Guidelines for Multinational Enterprises*. Paris: Organization for Economic Cooperation and Development.

OED. 1996. *The World Bank's Experience with Large Dams: A Preliminary Review of Impacts*. Washington, DC: World Bank.

—. 1998. *Recent Experiences with Involuntary Resettlement*. India: Upper Krishna Project *(Karantaka and Maharashtra)*. Washington, DC: World Bank.

Ojha, R. K. 1989. "Letter to the Chief Conservator of Forests (Central) Regarding Inspection of Compensatory Afforestation Sites in Gujarat." *Bhopal: Ministry of Environment and Forests*.

Oliver-Smith, Antony. 1991. "Displacement Resistance and the Critique of Development: From the Grass- Roots to the Global." *Final Report for ESCOR Refugee Studies Centre*. London: University of Oxford.

—. 2009. "Development-Forced Displacement and Resettlement: A Global Human Rights Crisis." In *Development and Dispossession: The Crisis*

of Forced Displacement and Resettlement, edited by A. Oliver-Smith: 3–23. Santa Fe, NM: School for Advanced Research Press.
Ong, L. H. 2014. "State-Led Urbanization in China: Skyscrapers, Land Revenue and Concentrated Villages." *China Quarterly* 217: 162–79. https://doi.org/10.1017/S0305741014000010.
Oommen, T. K. 1975. "Agrarian Legislations and Movements as Sources of Change: The Case of Kerala." *Economic & Political Weekly* 10, no. 40: 1571–84.
Oskarsson, Patrik. 2018. *Landlock: Paralysing Dispute over Minerals on Adivasi Land in India*. Australia: Australian National University Press.
Oza, K. K. 1996. "Is Sardar Sarovar Financially Viable?." *Economic & Political Weekly* 31, no. 29: 1921.
Oza, Nandini. 1997. "Marginalisation, Protests and Political Action: Tribals and Sardar Sarovar Project." *Economic & Political Weekly* 32, no. 29: 1790–3.
"PACa." 2013. *Geração de Energia Elétrica. Ministereo do Planejamento*, Accessed November 21, 2021. http://www.pac.gov.br/sobreo-pac.
Padel, Felix, and Samarendra Das. 2010. "Out of This Earth: East India Adivasis and the Aluminium Cartel." *Black*. Delhi: Orient. Swan.
Padel, Felix. 2012. "How Best to Ensure Adivasis' Land, Forest and Mineral Rights?." *IDS Bulletin* 43, no. 15: 49: 49–57. https://doi.org/10.1111/j.1759-5436.2012.00346.x.
Pandey, Balaji. 1998. *Displaced Development: Impact of Opencast Mining*. New Delhi: Friedrich Ebert Stifung.
Parasuraman, S. 1993. *Impact or Displacement by Development Projects on Women in India*. ISS Working Paper Series No. 159. The Hague: Institute of Social Studies.
—. 1996. "Development Projects, Displacement and Outcomes for Displaced Two Case Studies." *Economic & Political Weekly* 31, no. 24.
—. 1999. "The Development Dilemma: Displacement in India." Basingstoke: Macmillan, in *Association with the Institute of Social Studies, The Hague*.
Parasuraman, S., Himanshu Upadhyaya, and Gomathy Balasubramanian. 2010. "Sardar Sarovar Project: The War of Attrition." *Economic & Political Weekly* 45, no. 5: 39–48.
Partridge, William L. 1993. "Successful Involuntary Resettlement: Lessons from the Costa Rican Arenal Hydroelectric Project." In *Anthropological Approaches to Resettlement: Policy, Practice, and Theory* vol. 1993, edited by Michael M. Cernea, and Scott E. Guggenheim. Boulder/ San Franciscoi Oxford: Westview Press.

Patel, C. C. 1992. "Surging Ahead: The Sardar Sarovar Project Hope of Millions." *Harvard International Review* 15, no. 1: 24–7.

Patel, Sonal. 2010. "Brazil: Latin America's Beacon'. "Power." *Don't Mention the B-Word. The Economist* 154, no. 1: 48.

Pathak, Mahesh T. 1991. *Sardar Sarovar Project: A Promise for Plenty.* New Delhi: Oxford & IBH Publishing Co.

Patkar, Medha. 1998. "The People's Policy on Development, Displacement and Resettlement Need to Link Displacement and Development." *Economic & Political Weekly* 33, no. 38.

Pati, B. 2011. "Adivasis in Colonial India: Survival, Resistance and Negotiation." *Black*. Delhi: Orient. Swan.

Pattnaik, Binay Kumar, and Biswambhar Panda. 2005. "Perceiving the Role of Grassroots NGOs: From the New Social Movement Perspective." *Social Change* 35, no. 3: 1–24. https://doi.org/10.1177/004908570503500301.

Pattnaik, Binay Kumar. 2013. "Tribal Resistance Movements and the Politics of Development Induced Displacement in Contemporary Orissa." *Social Change* 43, no. 1: 53–78. https://doi.org/10.1177/0049085713475727.

Paulo, Folha de S. 2011. "Altamira Pede Suspensão de Belo Monte", Accessed December 22 2021. http://www1.folha.uol.com.br/fsp/mercado/10075-altamira-pede-suspensao-de-belo-monte.shtml.

Payne, Rodger, and Brett O'Bannon. 1994. *Environmental TSMOs and the Narmada River Dam: Rethinking Complex Interdependence*. Columbus, OH: Paper Publications for the North Central Sociological Association Annual Meetings.

Pearce, Fred. 1994. "High and Dry in Aswan." *New Scientist* 142: 30.

Perera, D., V. Smakhtin, S. Williams, T. North, and A. Curry. 2021. "Ageing Water Storage Infrastructure: An Emerging Global Risk.". UNU-INWEH Report Series. *Issue 11*. Canada: United Nations University Press Institute for Water, Environment and Health.

Pessoa, H. R. 2016. *Inquerito Civil Publico [Public Civil Inquiry]*. PA: AltaMira: Procurador da Republica.

"Picciotto, R. van Wicklin, W. and Rice, E." 2001. *Involuntary Resettlement*. New Brunswick: Transaction Publishing.

van der Ploeg, L., and F. Vanclay. 2017a. "A Human Rights-Based Approach to Project-Induced Displacement and Resettlement." *Impact Assessment & Project Appraisal* 35, no. 1: 34–52. https://doi.org/10.1080/14615517.2016.1271538.

Pred, D. 2014. "The World Bank, Can't Sacrifice the Poor to Stay in the Game". www, Accessed April 16, 2015. http://huffingtonpost.com/david-pred/the-world-bank-cant-sacri_b_5649540.html?utm_hp_ref=tw.

Price, S. 2008. "Compensation, Restoration and Development Opportunities: National Standards on Involuntary Resettlement." In *Can Compensation Prevent Impoverishment? Reforming Resettlement through Investments and Benefit-Sharing*, edited by M. M. Cernea, and H. M. Mathur. New Delhi: Oxford University Press.

—. 2009. "Prologue: Victims of Partners? The Social Perspectives of Development-Induced Displacement and Resettlement." *Asia Pacific Journal of Anthropology* 10, no. 4: 266–82. https://doi.org/10.1080/14442210903305821.

Public Accounts Committee report. 1993. "Planning Process and Monitoring Mechanism with Reference to Irrigation Projects": 141st [Report] (1992–93). *Seventh Lok Sabha*. New Delhi: Ministry of Planning. Planning Commission. Lok Sabha Secretariat.

Purohit, Makarand. 2016. "Damn the Dams, Say the Displaced." *India Water Portal*. https://www.indiawaterportal.org/articles/damn-dams-say-displaced#:~:text=%22If%20you%20are%20to%20suffer,the%20Hirakud%20Dam%20in%201948, Accessed June 14, 2021.

Shyam, Radhy*(D) Thr. Lrs & Others vs. State of U.P. & Others*. 2011 5 SCC 553: 60.

Rai, S. 2005. "Gender and Development." In *Advances in Development Studies*, edited by J. Haynes. Basingstoke: Palgrave Macmillion.

Rajagopal, Balakrishnan. 2000. "Human Rights and Development" *Thematic. Review* vol. 4 [Working paper]. Cape Town: World Commission on Dams.

Raj, P. A. 1990. *Facts*. Gandhinagar: Sardar Sarovar Project. Sardar Sarovar Narmada Nigam Ltd.

Ramesh, J., and M. Khan. 2016. "Land Acquisition Law: Winking at the States." *Hindu*, Accessed November 2, 2016, Accessed October 10, 2021. http://www.thehindu.com/opinion/lead/Winking-at-the-States/article16086906.ece.

Randell, Heather. 2016. "Structure and Agency in Development-Induced Forced Migration: The Case of Brazil's Belo Monte Dam." *Population & Environment* 37, no. 3: 265–87. https://doi.org/10.1007/s11111-015-0245-4.

Rangachari, R. 2006. *The Bhakra-Nangal Project: Socio-economic and Environmental Impacts*. Delhi: Oxford University Press.
Rawls, John. 1971. *A Theory of Justice*. Cambridge: Harvard University Press.
Reddy, G., E. Smyth, and M. Steyn. 2015. *Land Access and Resettlement: A Guide to Best Practice*. Sheffield: Greenleaf Publishing.
Hagen, R. V., and T. Minter. 2020. "Displacement in the Name of Development. How Indigenous Rights Legislation Fails to Protect Philippine Hunter-Gatherers." *Society & Natural Resources* 33, no. 1: 65–82. https://doi.org/10.1080/08941920.2019.1677970.
Ridley, Kirstin. 2021. "London Judges Reverse Course to Reopen $7 Bln Brazil Dam Lawsuit Against BHP.", Accessed July 28, 2021 https://www.reuters.com/business/energy/london-judges-re-open-69-bln-brazil-dam-lawsuit-against-bhp-2021-07-27/. Reuters.
RIMA. 2009. "The Dam Will Displace Approximately 16,000 People from the Altamira Area and Another 2,000 from Rural Locations." *Aproveitamento Hidrelétrico Belo Monte* 85: 93.
Robinson, Scott. 1999. "The Experience with Dams and Rcscttlement in Mexico." Contributing Paper, prepared for Thematic Review. *Social Issue*: 1.3: Displacement, Resettlement, Rehabilitation, Reparation and Development. Cape Town: World Commission on Dams.
—. 2003. "Rights and Risks: The Causes, Consequences and Challenges of Development-Induced Displacement." *An Occasional Paper, Brookings Institution-SAIS Project on Internal Displacement*. Washington, DC: Brookings Institution Press.
Romer, P. M. 1986. "Increasing Returns and Long Run Growth." *Journal of Political Economy* 94, no. 5: 1002–37. https://doi.org/10.1086/261420.
—. 1990. "Endogenous Technological Change." *Journal of Political Economy* 98, no. 5, Part 2: S71–S102. https://doi.org/10.1086/261725.
Ronayne, M. 2002. *The Illsu Dam: Displacement of Communities and Destruction of Culture*. London: KHRP. National University of Ireland.
—. 2005. *The Cultural and Environmental Impact of Large Dams in Southeast Turkey*. London: KHRP and National University of Ireland.
—. 2006. "Archaeology Against Cultural Destruction: The Case of the Ilisu Dam in the Kurdish Region of Turkey." *Public Archaeology* 5, no. 4: 223–36. https://doi.org/10.1179/pua.2006.5.4.223.
Roy, A. 1999. "The Greater Common Good." In *The Cost of Living*, edited by A. Roy: 7–90. New York: Modern Library.
Sahu, Skylab. 2019. "The Rhetoric of Development and Resistance by Tribal Women in Kashipur." *Social Change* 49, no. 1: 61–77. https://doi.org/10.1177/0049085718821503.

Sairinen, R. 2004. "Assessing Social Impacts of Urban Land-Use Plans: From Theory to Practice." *Boreal Environment Research* 9: 509–17.

Sakthivadivel, R., S. Thiruvengadachari, U. Amerasinghe, W. G. M. Bastiaanssen, and D. Molden. 1999. "Performance EPrice Susanna (2009) Prologue: Victims or Partners? The Social Perspective in Development-Induced Displacement and Resettlement." *Asia-Pacific Journal of Anthropology* 10, no. 4: 266–82.

Sarkar, Abhirup. 2007. "Development and Displacement Land Acquisition in West Bengal." *Economic & Political Weekly* 42, no. 6.

Säve-Söderberg, T. 1987. *Temples and Tombs of Ancient Nubia*. London: Thames & Hudson.

Saxena, K. B. 2008. "Development, Displacement, and Resistance: The Law and the Policy on Land Acquisition." *Social Change* 38, no. 3: 351–410. https://doi.org/10.1177/004908570803800301.

—. 2008. "Swelling Displacement and Elusive Rehabilitation: Deficits in Policy Interventions." *Social Change* 38, no. 4: 705–32. https://doi.org/10.1177/004908570803800408.

—. 2015. " The Ordinance Amending the Land Acquisition Law (2013): Farmers Lose Out in the Unequal Contest of Power." *Social Change* 45, no. 2: 324–36. https://doi.org/10.1177/0049085715574307.

Scoones, Ian. 1998. "Sustainable Rural Livelihoods: A Framework for Analysis." *IDS Working Papers* 72. England: Institute of Development Studies.

Scudder, Thayer, and E. Colson. 1982. "From Welfare to Development: A Conceptual Framework for Analysis of Dislocated People." In *Involuntary Migration and Resettlement*, edited by A. Hansen, and A. Ohver-Smith. Boulder: West View Press.

Scudder, Thayer. 1993. "Development-Induced Relocation and Refugee Studies: 37 Years of Change and Continuity Among Zambia's Gwembe Tonga." *Journal of Refugee Studies* 6, no. 2: 123–52. https://doi.org/10.1093/jrs/6.2.123.

—. 1997. "Resettlement." In *Water Resources: Environmental Planning, Management and Development*, edited by Asit K. Biswas. New York: McGraw-Hill.

—. 2005. *The Future of Large Dams: Dealing with Social, Environmental, and Political Costs*. London: Earthscan Publications.

Sen, Amartya. 1999. *Development as Freedom*. New York: Knopf Publishing Group.

Sen, Jai. 1999. "A World to Win – But Whose World Is It, Anyway?." In *Journal of Civil Society*, edited by John Foster, and Anita Anand. The

United Nations, *and the Multilateral Future*. Ottawa: United Nations Association in Canada.
Shah, Esha, Jeroen Vos, Gert Jan Veldwisch, Rutgerd Boelens, and Bibiana Duarte-Abadía. 2021. "Environmental Justice Movements in Globalising Networks: A Critical Discussion on Social Resistance Against Large Dams." *Journal of Peasant Studies* 48, no. 5: 1008–32. https://doi.org/10.1080/03066150.2019.1669566.
Sharma, Ravi. 1982. "'Real Cost of Big Dams' and 'Need for Frank Discussion'." *Times of India*, July 28 1982. In.
Sharma, R. N. 2010. "Mega-transformation of Mumbai: Deepening Enclave Urbanism." *Sociological Bulletin* 59, no. 1: 69–91. https://doi.org/10.1177/0038022920100104.
Sharma, Subhash. 2009. "Why the Marginalised Protest: Environmental Movements as a Critique of Dominant Development Discourse." *Social Change* 39, no. 2: 171–94. https://doi.org/10.1177/004908570903900201.
Shelton, Dinah L., and Donald K. Anton. 2011. "Problems in Human Rights and Large Dams." *Washington DC: GW Law Faculty Publications and Other Works*.
Shibl, Y. A. 1971. "The Aswan High Dam." *Beirut: Arab Institute for Research and Publishing*.
Shi, G., J. Zhou, and Q. Yu. 2012. "Resettlement in China." In *Impacts of Large Dams: A Global Assessment*, edited by Cecilia Tortajada, Dogan Altinbilek, and Altinbilek Biswas: 219–41. Dordrecht: Springer. https://doi.org/10.1007/978-3-642-23571-9_10.
Shihata, Ibrahim F. I. 1993. "Legal Aspects of Involuntary Population Resettlement." In *Anthropological Approaches to Resettlement: Policy, Practice. and Theory*, edited by Michael M. Cernea, and Scott E. Guggenheim. Boulder. San Francisco. Oxford: Westview Press.
Shiva, Vandana. 1994. *Staying Alive: Women, Ecology and Development*. London: Zed Books.
Sikor, T., and P. Newell. 2014. "Globalizing Environmental Justice?." *Geoforum* 54: 151–7. https://doi.org/10.1016/j.geoforum.2014.04.009.
Singh, Chhatrapati. 1989. "Rehabilitation and Rights to Property." In *Development, Displacement and Rehabilitation*, edited by Walter Fernandes, and Enakshi Ganguly Thukral. New Delhi: Indian Social Institute.
Sinha, D., and Y. Oxe. 2021. *Supreme Court on Sustainable Development Hydro Power Projects in Uttarakhand*. New Delhi: Vidhi Centre for Legal Policy.

Pirta, R. S., N. Chandel, and C. Pirta. 2014. "Attachment and Displacement: The Resettlers of Bhakra Dam Are Hurt." *Psychological Studies* 59, no. 1: 1–10. https://doi.org/10.1007/s12646-013-0211-0.

Singh, Sekhar, Raman Mehta, Vishaish Uppal, Asmita Kabra, Bansuri Taneja, and Prabhakar Rao. 2000. "Environmental and Social Impacts of Large Dams – The Indian Experience." *New Delhi: Indian Institute of Public Administration*.

—. 1997. *Taming the Waters: The Political Ecology of Large Dams*. Delhi: Oxford University Press.

Soltis, K. 2011. *Brazil Disregards Charges from the Inter-American Commission on Human Rights* [Report]." *Council on Hemispheric Affairs*, Accessed July 3, 2021. http://www.coha.org/brazil-disregards-charges-fromthe-inter-american-commission-on-human-rights/.

Somavanti and others v. The State of Punjab and others. 1963. AIR 151, 1963 SCR (3) 774.

"Sooraram Pratap Reddy *vs.* District Collector." 2008 9 S.C.C: 552.

Sorbo, G. M. 1985. *Tenants and Nomads in Eastern Sudan – A Study of Economic Adaptions in the New Halfa Scheme*. Uppsala: Scandinavian Institute of African Studies.

Sorensen, Brigitte Refuslund. 1996. *Relocated Lives: Displacement and Resettlement Within the Mahweli Project, Sri Lanka*. Amsterdam: VU University Press.

South China Morning Post. 1999a. *Dam Cadres Steal $217Mn*.

von Sperling, E. 2012. "Hydropower in Brazil: Overview of Positive and Negative Environmental Aspects." *Energy Procedia* 18: 110–8. https://doi.org/10.1016/j.egypro.2012.05.023.

v Sangharsh Samiti, Srinagar Bandh Aapada. "Alaknanda Hydropower Colo.." *Ltd.* 2014. Original Application No. 03 of, Principal Bench, NGT.

Stanley, Daniel Jean, and Jonathan G. Wingerath. 1996. "Nile Sediment Dispersal Altered by the Aswan High Dam: The Kaolinite Trace." *Marine Geology* 133, no. 1–2: 1–9. https://doi.org/10.1016/0025-3227(96)00019-9.

"State of M. *P vs Behru Singh & Ors*." 2012. Civil Appeal No.1211 OF 2012.

Steil, Shawn, and Yuefang Duan. 2002. "Policies and Practice of Three Gorges Resettlement: A Field Account." *Forced Migration Review* 12: 10–3.

Sterling, C. 1971a. "Super-Dams Pile Up Myriad Problems." *Washington Post*.

—. 1971b. "Aswan Dam—Predictions Came True with a Vengeance." *Washington Post*.
—. 1971c. "Health Menace Created by High Dam at Aswan." *Washington Post*.
—. 1971d. "Aswan Dam Is Losing Water It Was Designed to Save." *Washington Post*.
—. 1971e. "The Lake at Aswan Is Not Filling Up." *Washington Post*.
—. 1971f. "The Aswan Disaster." *National Parks & Conservation Magazine*.
—. 1972. "Superdams—The Perils of Progress." *Atlantic Monthly* 229: 35–41.
Stone, Richard. 2008. "Chapters 3 Gorges Dam: Into the Unknown." *Science* 321, no. 5889: 628–32. https://doi.org/10.1126/science.321.5889.628.
Sukhan, Jackson, and Adrian C. Sleigh. 2001. "The Political Economy and Socio-economic Impact of China's Three Gorges Dam." *Asian Studies Review* 25, no. 1: 57–72.
Taçkavak, E., and M. K. Atatür. 1995. "Threats to Survival of Euphrates Soft-Shelled Turtle in Southeastern Anatolia." International Congress of Chelonian Conservation, edited by S. S. Smith, and S. S. Smith. France: Proceeding Book.
Tan, Yan, Graeme Hugo, and Lesley Potter. 2003. "Government-Organized Distant Resettlement and the Three Gorges Project, China." *Asia-Pacific Population Journal* 18, no. 3: 5–26. https://doi.org/10.18356/fd7a0b3a-en.
Tan, Y. 2008. *Resettlement in the Three Gorges Project*. Hong Kong: Hong Kong University Press.
Virodhi Sangarsh, Tehri Bandh. 1992. *Samiti vs. State of UP* vol. 44 Suppl. 1 SCC.
Terminski, Bogumil. 2015. *Development-Induced Displacement and Resettlement: Causes, Consequences, and Socio-legal Context*. Germany: Ibidem Verlag. Stuttgart.
TGPCC. 2009. "Statistical Yearbook on the Implementation of the TPG Resettlement Plan" [Unpublished document]. Beijing: Three Gorges Project Construction Commission. *Economic Weekly*: 1954 [Editorial], "Bhakra-Nangal." VI vol. 28, no. Jul. 10, 1954.
The World Bank. 2015, Accessed July 15, 2021. https://data.worldbank.org/indicator/EG.ELC.HYRO.ZS.
Thukral, E. 1992. *Big Dams, Displaced People: Rivers of Sorrow, Rivers of Change*, edited by Ganguly. New Delhi: SAGE Publications.

Tvedt, Terje. 2021. *The Nile: History's Greatest River*. London: Bloomsbury Publishing.

Udall, Lori. 1995. "The International Narmada Campain: A Case of Sustained Advocacy." In *Towards Sustainable Development: Struggling over India's Narmada River*, edited by William Fisher. New York: M.E. Sharpe.

Udombana, Nsongurua J. 2006. "The African Commission on Human and Peoples' Right and the Development of Fair Trial Norms in Africa." *African Human Rights Law Journal* 6, no. 2: 298–332.

UN General Assembly. 1986. "Declaration on the Right to Development: Resolution / Adopted by the General Assembly", 4 December 1986. *A/RES/41/128*.

UN High Commissioner for Refugees (UNHCR). 1998. "Guiding Principles on Internal Displacement", 22 July 1998, available at: https://www.refworld.org/docid/3c3da07f7.html [accessed 26 March 2023]

USEPA. 1978. *Research Project Schistosomiasis in Rural Egypt: A Report of U.S. Egyptian River Nile and Lake Nasser*. Athens: United States Environmental Protection Agency.

Vanclay, F. 2003. "International Principles for Social Impact Assessment." *Impact Assessment & Project Appraisal* 21, no. 1: 5–12. https://doi.org/10.3152/147154603781766491.

—. 2017b. "A Tool for Improving the Management of Social and Human Rights Risks at Project Sites: The Human Rights Sphere." *Journal of Cleaner Production* 142, no. 4: 4072–84.

Verghese, B. G. 1994. *Winning the Future: From Bhakra to Narmada, Tehri, Rajasthan Canal*. New Delhi: Konark Publishers.

WCD. 2000. "Dams and Development: A New Framework for Decision-Making." *The Report of the World Commission on Dams*. London: Earthscan Publications.

Wade, Robert H. 2011. "Muddy Waters: Inside the World Bank as It Struggled with the Narmada Projects." *Economic & Political Weekly* 46: 40.

Walton, Susan. 1981. "Egypt After the Aswan Dam." *Environment: Science & Policy for Sustainable Development* 23, no. 4: 30–6. https://doi.org/10.1080/00139157.1981.9933135.

Wang, P., S. A. Wolf, J. P. Lassoie, and S. Dong. 2013. "Compensation Policy for Displacement Caused by Dam Construction in China: An Institutional Analysis." *Geoforum* 48: 1–9. https://doi.org/10.1016/j.geoforum.2013.04.009.

Warren, A. 1999. "Sharing project benefits to improve resettlers' livelihoods." In *The economics of involuntary resettlement: Questions and challenges*. "Van Wicklin," edited by M. Cernea vol. III. Washington, DC: World Bank.

Waterbury, John. 1979. *Hydropolitics of the Nile Valley*. Syracuse, NY: Syracuse University Press.

Weist, K. M. 1995. "Development Refugees: Africans, Indians and the Big Dams." *Journal of Refugee Studies* 8, no. 2: 163–84. https://doi.org/10.1093/jrs/8.2.163.

Welch, H. J., ed. 2004. "GAP Biodiversity Research Project 2001–2003 / Final Report" *Dogal Hayati Koruma Dernegi, Turkey: Istanbul*.

Wilmsen, B., and Andrew van Hulten. 2017. "Following Resettled People over Time: The Value of Longitudinal Data Collection for Understanding the Livelihood Impacts of the Three Gorges Dam, China." *Impact Assessment & Project Appraisal* 35, no. 1: 94–105. https://doi.org/10.1080/14615517.2016.1271542.

Wood, John R. 1993. "India's Narmada River Dams: Sardar Sarovar Under Siege." *Asian Survey* 33, no. 10: 968–84. https://doi.org/10.2307/2645096.

World, Bank. 1993. "1993: Investing in Health." *World Development Report*. New York: Oxford University Press.

—. 1996. "1996: From Plan to Market." *World Development Report*. New York: Oxford University Press.

—. 1996. *Resettlement and Development: The Bank Wide Review of Projects Involving Resettlement 1986–1993*. Washington, DC: World Bank/Environment Department: paper No. 032. Environment Department Papers.

—. 1999. "1999/2000: Entering the 21st Century." *World Development Report*. New York: Oxford University Press.

—. 2001. *Operational Policy 4.12 – Involuntary Resettlement*. Washington, DC: World Bank.

—. 2004. *Involuntary Resettlement Sourcebook: Planning and Implementation of Development Projects*. Washington, DC: World Bank.

—. 2012. *World Development Indicators*. Washington, DC: World Bank 2012.

—. 2015. *Resettlement Fact Sheet*. Washington, DC: World Bank Group.

"World's Business." 1958. "Building the World's Toughest Dam.". *Ekistics* 6, no. 37: 234–6.

World Health Organization. 1999. *Human Health and Dams*. Geneva: World Health Organization to the World Commission on Dams.

Wu, M. 1998. *Resettlement Problems of the Three Gorges Dam: A Field Report*. International Rivers Network and Human Rights in China.

Wu, N. Z., and Q. L. Liao. 1999. "The Necessity to Relocate the Resettlers Outside for the Consideration of Land Bearing Capacity – Take Yunyang County as a Case Study." *Resources & Environment in the Yangtze Basin* 8, no. 3: 20–2.

WWF report. 2007. *Rivers at Risk*. Switzerland: WWF Verlagsgesellschaft International. Gland.

Xu, X., Y. Tan, and G. Yang. 2013. "Environmental Impact Assessments of the Three Gorges Project in China: Issues and Interventions." *Earth-Science Reviews* 124: 115–25. https://doi.org/10.1016/j.earscirev.2013.05.007.

Yadav, Yogendra. 2015. "State Power sans Public Reason." *Hindu*.

Yalcin, Emrah, and Sahnaz Tigrek. 2016. "Hydropower Production Without Sacrificing Environment: A Case Study of Ilisu Dam and Hasankeyf." *International Journal of Water Resources Development* 32, no. 2: 247–66. https://doi.org/10.1080/07900627.2015.1031210.

Yang, G. S., C. D. Ma, and S. Y. Chang. 2009. *Yangtze Conservation and Development Report*. Wuhan: Yangtze Press.

Yang, Y. 1992. "Lunzheng shimo [The Complete Story of the Feasibility Study]." *Beijing: Shuili Dianli Chubanshe*.

Yi, M. 2003. *An Investigation of Resettlement and Human Rights Problems in the Three Gorges Dam Project*, Accessed January 25, 2021. http://www.internationalrivers.org.

Ying, T. S., Y. L. Zhang, and D. E. Boufford. 1993. *The Endemic Genera of Seed Plants of China*. Beijing, China: Science Press.

Yin, H. F., G. R. Liu, J. G. Pi, G. J. Chen, and C. A. Li. 2007. "On the River-Lake Relationship of the Middle Yangtze Reaches." *Geomorphology* 85, no. 3–4: 197–207. https://doi.org/10.1016/j.geomorph.2006.03.017.

Abu-Zeid, M. A., and F. Z. El-Shibini. 1997. "Egypt's High Aswan Dam." *International Journal of Water Resources Development* 13, no. 2: 209–18. https://doi.org/10.1080/07900629749836.

Sun, Z., Qun Huang, Christian Opp, Thomas Hennig, and Ulf Marold. 2012. "Impacts and Implications of Major Changes Caused by the Three Gorges Dam in the Middle Reaches of the Yangtze River, China." *Water Resources Management* 26, no. 12: 3367–78. https://doi.org/10.1007/s11269-012-0076-3.

Zhu, H., and J. Qian. 2021. "New Theoretical Dialogues on Migration in China: Introduction to the Special Issue." *Journal of Ethnic & Migration Studies* 47, no. 12: 2685–705. https://doi.org/10.1080/1369183X.2020.1739372.

Zhu, N. et al. 1996. *Sanxia Gongcheng Yiming Yu Cangqu Fazhan Yanjiu (Research on the Three Gorges Project. Resettlement and Development of Reservoir Area)*. Wuhan: University of Wuhan Press.